CW00339670

WITH ROMMEL IN THE DESERT

"AND YET IT DOES NOT SEEM TO BE DOING YOU ANY HARM!"

Rommel with the fat Italian major of a road-construction battalion who had complained of the food and wine. The author is standing on the left with Rommel's map-case.

[*See p.* 83]

Fr.

HEINZ WERNER SCHMIDT

WITH ROMMEL IN THE DESERT

CONSTABLE · LONDON

This edition published in Great Britain 1997
by Constable and Company Ltd
3 The Lanchesters, 162 Fulham Palace Road
London W6 9ER
First published in Great Britain by
George Harrap & Co Ltd 1951

Paperback edition 1998
Reprinted 1998
Printed in Great Britain by
St Edmundsbury Press Ltd
Bury St Edmunds, Suffolk

A CIP catalogue record for this book
is available from the British Library

CONTENTS

ILLUSTRATIONS

Maps

CHAPTER ONE

I JOIN ROMMEL'S STAFF

DETACHMENTS of a German expeditionary force under an obscure general, Rommel, have landed in North Africa."

The announcement was perfunctory but rather interesting. It had been issued in an Intelligence summary by the British High Command early in March 1941, and I read it in a document captured at Keren, on the Eritrean front, where I was in command of a scratch detachment of German troops—seamen from ships blockaded by the Royal Navy in the Italian Red Sea port of Massawa. I had no reason to suppose, when I idly noted this scrap of information, that I should be face to face with this particular General only eight days later, or that for months in the Western Desert I should be at his side so often when we were intensively attacked.

Rommel was an unknown figure, and no hero then. Afterwards . . .

2

Still a university student and completing my spell of military training, I was kept with the colours and led an infantry platoon through the invasion of Poland in 1939. Afterwards I served in the Siegfried Line during months of the 'phoney war' until recalled to Berlin. There I received a special assignment to the Eritrean front. I assumed that I had been honoured with this appointment because my papers showed that I had been born in South Africa. I saw no urgent reason why I should protest that my parents had left South Africâ when I was four, and I tacitly accepted the implication that I was an acknowledged expert on African affairs. This way, at least, lay adventure.

In mid-March Wavell's British and Indian troops[1] captured positions covering Keren, and it was obvious that this seemingly

[1] The 4th and 5th Indian Divisions.

impregnable gateway into Eritrea must soon be battered open. General Cunningham's force, including Brigadier Dan Pienaar's 1st South African Brigade, were also advancing rapidly through Somalia and would soon strike up through Abyssinia. Orders came from Berlin that my group of Merchant Navy volunteers were to be disbanded and returned to their ships, which were to attempt to run the blockade and get home. I was to fly to North Africa and report to the German expeditionary force that had landed at Tripoli.

I evaded capture in Asmara[1] by getting a passage aboard a Savoia, the last Italian aircraft, as far as I know, to leave there, and flew through the night (with three slightly drunken Italian pilots) to an aerodrome near Marble Arch, on the Gulf of Sirte. From there a smaller Italian Ghibli aircraft took me on to Tripoli.

During the flight westward the Savoia was unpleasantly hunted by British anti-aircraft guns, and I found it a useful distraction to think of other things—among them, to puzzle where and what I had previously heard of this man Rommel, who, presumably, was now in Tripoli. It was irritating that the name should remain elusively on the tip of my memory. Curiously enough, illumination came simultaneously with the vertical and uncomfortably close flashes of a series of flak projectiles. A bit weird, a bit eerie, I mused. Like long, ghostly fingers. And then I remembered—the 'Ghost Division' in France.

This was the nickname given to the 7th German Armoured Division because of its reputation for making unexpected appearances not only in front of but behind the French lines during the brief but spectacular Blitzkrieg. Yes, I was sure now. The commander of this division had been a Major-General Rommel. I wondered whether I should see him in North Africa.

3

A few hours later I reported, as instructed by wireless from Berlin, to the Headquarters of the German troops in Tripoli, the luxurious Hotel Uaddan. The Chief of Staff, Lieutenant-Colonel von dem Borne, ordered me to report personally to Lieutenant-General Rommel.

[1] The capital of Eritrea.

I waited in a public room. Most of the officers in the Uaddan seemed to be taking a siesta, for the Libyan sun beat down hotly that March afternoon. Oberleutnant Aldinger, whom I was soon to know as Rommel's personal aide, passed me and entered an inner lounge on the door of which a sign said simply: 'General.' He reappeared and said in undertones that the General wished to see me. I took a deep breath and straightened my uniform, which after some months in Eritrea did not look entirely as though it had come straight from the Potsdam tailor. I knocked, and in response to a deep and forceful 'Come in!' entered a spacious room.

I throw as smart a salute as I can and try to speak with military precision. 'Lieutenant Schmidt, of the German Volunteer Motorized Company in Eritrea, in accordance with instructions from the O.K.H.[1] [Army High Command], reports from duty in Eritrea, and places himself at the General's disposal.'

The General stands before me. His figure is compact and short. I gain a measure of confidence as I note that, although I am only of middle height, the General is shorter. He gives me a brief, powerful shake of the hand. Blue-grey eyes look steadily into mine. I notice that he has unusual humour-wrinkles slanting downward from above the corners of his eyes to the outer edges of his cheekbones. His mouth and chin are well-formed and strong, and reinforce my first impression of an energetic, vital personality.

'You come from Eritrea, Lieutenant?'

'Yes, sir, I landed three hours ago.'

With his right forefinger he points to the north-eastern corner of the map of Africa. 'What is the situation there?'

Expecting the question, I answer without hesitation: 'Bad, sir.' I feel I should qualify this statement, so after a short pause add: 'I do not think anything can now be done to save the situation there.'

Is it my poor military bearing, or is it my pessimistic appreciation of the Eritrean situation that causes the flashing change in the expression of Rommel's eyes? His glare and an upward tilt of his chin make me feel uncomfortable.

'What do you know about it, anyway, Herr Leutnant?' the General snaps icily. 'We shall reach the Nile, make a right-turn, and win back everything.'

I can find nothing to say, and omit even the obvious escape-

[1] Oberkommando des Heeres.

formula of '*Jawohl, Herr General.*' Rommel turns away abruptly. But he throws over his shoulder in calm tones: 'Report to the Chief of Staff, Colonel von dem Borne, who will decide what you are to do. Prepare a report of your activities in Eritrea.'

He nods. I am dismissed.

4

I had, as you know, already met the Chief of Staff. Von dem Borne was a powerfully built, slightly corpulent man with a full face. Intelligent eyes betrayed his sense of humour. This was also revealed by his words when I presented myself: 'Stay with us a while. You have probably done your fair share of running backwards in Abyssinia. I am not sure how we can employ you, but as you have some form of "African experience," though perhaps not what one might term the happiest, you may eventually be of some use.'

After a pause he added: 'Report to Major Schräpler, the II a, and tell him that as an officer F.U.P.[1] you should be placed at the disposal of Intelligence I c.'

Outside I met Oberleutnant von Hosslin, who as Ordnance Staff Officer took it upon himself to explain to me, with condescension and confusing detail, the definition and functions of the branches of the Staff.

I summarize:

I a—General Staff Officer, Operations (for own tactical decisions).

I b—General Staff Officer, Supplies. (British 'Q.')

I c—General Staff Officer, Intelligence, Enemy Order of Battle.

II a—General Staff Officer, Personnel. (British 'A.')

Von Hosslin further informed me that at 1500 hours—that was within half an hour—General Rommel was to address the officers of the 5th Light Division, who had just arrived in Tripoli, and that all Staff Officers, including myself, were to attend. Though still idle, I now thought of myself for the first time as a member of Rommel's Staff.

[1] 'F.U.P.,' 'For Useful Purposes,' corresponds with the British 'General List.'—H.W.S.

About thirty officers were assembled in one of the larger public rooms of the Uaddan. Some were chattering boisterously, others were engaged in quiet conversation. A medley of voices met my ears as I walked in and saluted. As an insignificant young lieutenant I attracted no attention. But I spotted one or two acquaintances standing with a group of Staff Officers who were unknown to me. The great majority of the gathering, however, consisted of young officers who were wearing cherished decorations for valour on the tunics of their black Panzer Group uniforms.

Before von dem Borne, the Chief of Staff, had an opportunity of checking the number of officers present, Rommel entered unexpectedly. The officers snapped to attention. Von dem Borne announced resonantly: 'Staff Officers and Panzer Regiment officers ready for the conference!' I was surprised at what seemed rather an informal way of 'reporting.' (Normally in the German Army the General would be advised briefly how many officers, and from which units, were present, how many were absent, and so on). But without further ceremony Rommel launched himself into his address:

'Gentlemen,' he said, 'I am pleased to know that after strenuous days the gentlemen of the 5th Panzer Regiment are now in Tripoli almost up to full strength. With the arrival of your Panzers the situation in North Africa will be stabilized. The enemy's thrust towards Tripolitania has been brought to a standstill. Our reconnaissance units [a battalion of armoured cars] under Lieutenant-Colonel von Wegmar have reached the Italians' advanced positions on the Gulf of Sirte at El Agheila, and have morally and materially strengthened the front. It is our task to restore the confidence of the Italian people in their arms, and to bolster up the fighting spirit of our allies.'

Rommel paused between sentences, clenching his fists with elbows bent and thrust slightly forward. That powerful chest, those energetic facial gestures, and his abrupt, precise, military manner of expressing himself clearly indicated a resolute will. The officers, all standing, listened intently to his review of the situation.

Rommel raised his voice. He shook his fist lightly.

'We *must* save Tripolitania from the attack of the British Army. We *will* hold them.' He paused.

'It comes to this: we must mislead the enemy about our own strength—*or weakness*—until the 5th Light Division has been landed in full strength. A further division will follow. The moment every Panzer is unloaded, the German 5th Panzer Regiment and the tanks of the Italian Ariete Division will parade in a fashion that will not escape the attention of, first, the Italian civil population, and, second, the enemy's spies. Details have been discussed with the commander of the Panzer Regiment. On completion of the parade, the Regiment will immediately proceed to the front, where it will remain in reserve. . . . As an example to the Italian troops I expect, from officers and men alike, exemplary discipline. Thank you, gentlemen. Heil Hitler.'

Rommel stalked out of the conference room at once, followed by his Chief of Staff and the I a, Staff Major Ehlert, a tall, dark-haired officer of whom I was to see much.

Rommel's personal aide turned hurriedly towards me. Aldinger was a small slender man aged about forty-five, with a lean face and a little toothbrush moustache. He had the General's map-board under his arm.

His free hand groped for the top button of my tunic. 'Mr Schmidt,' he said, 'you will take a room in the II a quarters, and also contact Oberleutnant Himmler. You will find him with the I c. We shall no doubt be able to place you suitably later.' He spoke in a friendly manner and with a heavy Swabian accent. I was drawn to him at once, particularly because I still felt myself a lone hand, a stray from a distant and defeated front.

I carried out Aldinger's instructions. During the evening (it would be about March 14, I think), while I was preparing my report for Rommel, I met Oberleutnant Behrendt. This was a spirited lad with a lively mind. He chattered away of his years in Egypt, and of how he had been at school in Cairo with Rudolf Hess, who, had we but known it, was within the next month or so, on May 10, to make his extraordinary flight to Scotland. Behrendt spoke excellent English and listened every night to the B.B.C. news, which he translated for Rommel.

I was still writing away at my report, half listening to the English news broadcast which Behrendt was now noting, when I caught a word that made me sit up and drop my pen—'Coburg.' The announcer went on to say that the German cargo vessel *Coburg*, of 9000 tons, which had left Massawa in an attempt to reach

A CONFERENCE BESIDE THE MAMMOTH

Rommel, wearing a peaked cap, is in the centre. Leaning over the table is the Italian General Calvi. The author is standing on the left, next to Aldinger.

ROMMEL SEATED ON A CAR

Imperial War Museum

European waters by way of the Red Sea and the Cape of Good Hope, had been sunk. She had been intercepted off Mauritius and scuttled by her crew, who, with her passengers, had been captured and taken to South Africa.

A tinge of melancholy mixed with relief overcame me. Only a few weeks ago I had been living in the *Coburg*, fully expecting to be aboard her when the attempt to break through the blockade was made. But fate and a direct order from Berlin had returned me to duties on land. A large proportion of those passengers had been members of my company of volunteers. Now they were captured and held as prisoners in the land of my birth, a country which by the accident of war was now my enemy. I now remembered that my sweetheart at home in Germany knew nothing of my whereabouts, and so, I thought, I must send a wireless message in the morning if I can.

CHAPTER TWO

BLUFF IN TRIPOLI

ROMMEL'S Panzer parade took place in the main streets of Tripoli next day. It was a bright sunny day, but the Italian population did not seem to show a great deal of interest in this display of might. The only dense group of civilian spectators was round the platform, where Rommel, who was accompanied by several Italian generals, took the salute. I stood close to my new chief.

Singly and at regular intervals the Panzers clattered and rattled by. They made a devil of a noise on the macadamized streets. Not far past the saluting base the column turned into a side-street with mighty squeaks and creaks. I began to wonder at the extraordinary number of Panzers passing, and to regret that I had not counted them from the beginning. After a quarter of an hour I noticed a fault in one of the chains of a heavy Mark IV Panzer, which somehow looked familiar to me although I had not previously seen its driver. Only then did the penny drop, as the Tommies say, and I could not help grinning. Still more Panzers passed, squeaking and creaking round that bend. The road surface was beginning to show serious signs of damage from the caterpillar tracks. The Italians stared with wide-open eyes, but otherwise were dumb. Where, I wondered, was their proverbial animation and enthusiasm? But I soon understood.

After the Panzers had passed—really passed—the saluting base there was a gap in the column. Then followed, not quite so fast, not quite so noisily, a long line of Italian tanks. The tank commanders showed themselves as conspicuously as they could. Their expressions were bold, daring, audacious. There was an immediate cheer from all sides. The crowd waved and chattered wildly. There were cries of 'Viva Italia!'

With my Staff comrades I pondered over the cool reception of the German troops who had come, after all, as allies to assist in the defence of the city. It seemed that we were tolerated rather than popular. But their own dashing blades—they were heroes to the populace.

After the last Italian tank had passed, Rommel made his first public speech in North Africa. In crisp, clear German sentences he expressed his confidence that the combined efforts of Italians and Germans would succeed in halting the advance of the British forces. Oberstleutnant Heggenreiner, the liaison officer with the Italian troops, who had been the only German officer to take part in the disastrous Italian retreat from Sidi Barrani when Wavell made his thrust in mid-December, interpreted the speech into Italian sentence by sentence. His voice was clear and carried well. There was applause only when the crowd heard Rommel's references to the achievements of the Italian troops.

Two hours after Rommel had finished speaking, the 5th Panzer Regiment (not as numerous as one might have hoped) trundled out into the desert from the eastern outskirts of Tripoli, heading for El Agheila and the front, where Wavell's forces lay. For the first time German tanks were moving on African soil with offensive purpose.

Though the Italian population had apparently been little impressed by the Panzer parade, the British spies obviously had. Broadcasts made it clear that G.H.Q. Middle East were astonished at the strength of the German expeditionary force in Tripolitania.

Next day I reported to the I a, Major Ehlert. I found him abrupt and evidently a man with a good conceit of himself. Though a report to Rommel was in course of preparation at the time, he called me into his room and swiftly gave me both an appreciation and orders. Rommel planned to mislead the enemy—and in particular the de Gaullist French, who were a potential nuisance under Leclerc away to the south among the oases. He planned a dummy attack towards the south with a motorized column, which was to be led by Lieutenant-Colonel von Schwerin. Its objective was Mursuk. As an 'experienced desert specialist,' I was to accompany the column as an adviser. It was clear that life in Tripoli would soon become monotonous: on being questioned, I had no hesitation in conceding that I was the right man for the job.

The R.A.F. bombed Tripoli that night. The wall of my room was shattered into rubble and dust, and it was this dust, I suppose, that caused sepsis in a slight splinter-wound which I received in the cheek. I was ordered briefly to hospital, and learned that I was to be replaced on the Mursuk expedition by Oberleutnant Hohmeyer, who was, at any rate, a genuine 'desert specialist' and had lived for a long time in Egypt as a civilian. He had been a great man for oasis exploration. Not unnaturally, I was disappointed at missing the experience, even though I was a tyro pretending to be an expert. But, after I had been a few days in hospital, Aldinger said: 'You will soon get a decent job on Rommel's staff, and that will dispel your sense of boredom.' His words were rather truer than I bargained for.

I gradually got to know the other staff officers, and found Oberstleutnant Heggenreiner, despite the difference in our ranks, particularly friendly. We had this in common, that he alone had taken part in the Italian retreat from Egypt, and I had been with the defeated Italians in Eritrea. I remember Heggenreiner in a chat at this time asserting that the Italian national hero, Marshal Balbo, had been shot down by his own anti-aircraft defences when flying out of Tobruk. Heggenreiner was now living in Tripoli with the Italian generals in the luxurious villa of the dead Marshal.

The General Staff were beginning to demand more comfortable quarters and more amenities. They swiftly evolved a suave and civilized routine, which required iced lemonade through the heat of the day and smart white uniform tunics for the informal hours of the evening.

But Rommel was a Spartan with no regard for such fal-lals. He issued sudden orders. The Staff were to move to Eastern Tripolitania, in order, first, to be closer to the mobile reserves behind the El Agheila defile, where we now stood against the enemy, and, second, to accustom themselves to the same climatic and living conditions as the field division. A third reason was the real danger to the Command Staff of heavy enemy air attacks, which were facilitated by the enemy's intensive espionage system in the city.

2

For several days now I had been detailed to escort the General. He was in regular consultation with his I b, Major Otto, who was responsible for all supply arrangements. Rommel checked every report on the arrival of troops and *matériel*. This did not always please him. The British were sending numerous ships with important cargoes to the bottom of the Mediterranean. A large ship loaded with munitions made Tripoli harbour, but it could not be unloaded fast enough: it was bombed, blew up, wrecked a complete block of buildings with H.E. and blast, and was itself gutted. Rommel was frequently perturbed, but he would not allow himself to be depressed. 'Thank heaven at least that both the battalions of the Panzer Regiment have arrived almost intact,' he consoled himself.

Panzers—yes, from the day of his arrival in Africa, Panzers were the all-important word; Panzers were the butter for his bread.

An order came through from the O.K.H. in Berlin appointing Rommel G.O.C. of the German Afrika Korps. But it was, I remember, weeks later before confirmation of his recent promotion from Major-General to Lieutenant-General came through. Of a Corps there was still little to see. Not even the 5th Light Division had yet landed in full strength.

Major Ehlert (I a) summed up the situation in a report: 'Enemy activity is confined to reconnaissance. Our air reconnaissance reports that the enemy is apparently reinforcing his formations and reconditioning his armour. On our side, Italian infantry units are still holding the front. The Santa Maria Battalion has especially distinguished itself in outpost positions. There are, further, the Italian Ariete Panzer Division and the Brescia Division. German reconnaissance units (armoured car battalion) have contacted the enemy. The Panzer Regiment has reached its positions as a mobile reserve. In the meantime there have also arrived barely two battalions of the Divisional Machine-Gun Battalion (motorized), two to three battalions of field artillery, one half of the Pioneer Battalion (combat engineers), supply companies, and advance elements of the 15th Panzer Division.

'The air situation,' his report went on, 'has improved in our favour, following reinforcements to our fighters and anti-aircraft artillery. The staff of the 5th Light Division under command of Lieutenant-General Streich has taken up positions at Marble Arch.

'The G.O.C. has ordered the General Staff of the Afrika Korps to take up a position in the Sirte area, with effect from to-night.'

3

The march began that evening. Rommel led the column in a car, which besides the driver also contained Aldinger and the General's batman, an N.C.O. named Gunther, a small, straw-blond little fellow who carried himself at all times with an almost irritating imperturbability. Immediately following the General were three dispatch-riders on motor-cycles. Then came the blacked-out van of the I a, in which Ehlert and Oberleutnant Hosslin checked routes and enemy positions even while we travelled. The next vehicle was my staff car. With me was an Oberleutnant in command of Signals, who at every halt made contact with his Signals truck further down the long column.

Two days later we were installed in the new G.H.Q. at Sirte. There was little on the spot save a few bare houses, a sandy landing-ground, and swarms of flies. No more iced drinks in the Uaddan, I reflected. Sirte did not please me. But I had little time to rouse about discomforts. An immediate order reached me: 'Lieutenant Schmidt to report to I a in his command truck.'

I found Rommel sitting under an awning outside Ehlert's truck, talking to Lieutenant-General Fröhlich, the Luftwaffe commander. I threw a smart salute, but neither of them noticed me. My twenty-five-year-old dignity was affronted. But no slight was intended; from a snatch of conversation I gathered they were concerned with matters of greater importance.

'The Führer has instructed me to make a snap reconnaissance with the 5th Light,' Rommel was saying. 'Now, I shall need your help in the air un . . .' The phone in the truck drowned the end of the sentence and Fröhlich's reply. He was raising objections or pointing out difficulties.

'Fröhlich . . .' Rommel interjected, with some heat; but Fröhlich went on, 'I will do what is in my power, Herr General, but . . .'

At this moment I heard the angry tones of Ehlert: 'Schmidt, come in here at once.'

CHAPTER THREE

OASIS ADVENTURE

EHLERT was seated in front of a chaotic mass of operational maps.

'Schmidt, get prepared at once for a special duty assigned to you by the General. You are to go at once to the H.Q. of the 5th Light Division and report to the I a there.'

He beckoned me closer. 'You see this map. Directly in front of El Agheila a German battalion is in position. Down here to the south is Marada oasis, apparently not occupied by the enemy. You are to take over a motorized detachment with a few armoured cars and occupy the oasis. From there you are to investigate and report whether it is possible for a strong fighting detachment operating from Marada to make a successful attack on Jalo oasis, which is held by the enemy.'

Ehlert added that the task was important and if successfully carried out might have far-reaching results. He went on thoughtfully: 'If Marada is occupied, you will take it. And if Marada is afterwards attacked, you will defend it at all costs. You will obtain further information and particulars from the divisional staff at Marble Arch. Is everything clear?'

I repeated briefly the orders received. I hadn't the courage to ask any questions, for I knew already how unsympathetically Ehlert reacted to them. As I turned to leave the truck, Ehlert handed me a Desert operational map. 'Take good care of this,' he said. 'We have only three copies. And report to the Commander before you go.'

There was a prickling sensation in my heart. I felt mixed emotions of pride and joyous anticipation of adventure, plus a trace of fear. While my kit and other requirements were being packed, I had my driver fill up with petrol, and within ten minutes was ready to leave. I reported my departure to the Commander: Rommel merely nodded.

The drive to Marble Arch was strenuous, for we were on

the look-out continually for low-flying aircraft. In the evening I sighted the great arch in the Desert, and south of it a wall of light stone, dug-in vehicles, tents, and shelters—the H.Q. of the 5th Light. I reported immediately to the Divisional I a, Major Hauser, who was later to become a General and Chief of Staff of the 14th Army in Italy. No sooner had I done so than the Divisional Commander, Lieutenant-General Streich, entered Hauser's tent.

I liked them both. They were informal and friendly, and offered me a glass of beer, a luxury not available at Rommel's Desert H.Q. They knew all about my mission and had laid on the arrangements. We discussed details, and then the I c was called in. He was also friendly but a little condescending. He was Captain von Kluge, son of the famous General, nicknamed 'The Clever Hans.'[1] I did not think the son would earn a similar name.

The Divisional mess was far more comfortable and luxurious than Rommel's. I found one could buy drinks, cigarettes, and even sweets, which appealed to me particularly as a non-smoker.

Conversation in the mess that evening turned to politics. Perhaps incautiously, I condemned as a misstatement of fact Goebbels's defence of the victimization of the Jews in 1938 as 'a spontaneous demonstration of the German Nation.' Though no friend of the Jews, I said that the anti-Semitic policy was disgraceful. A middle-aged Reservist officer, a land-owner from Mecklenburg, seemed pleased at my forthright utterance and said: 'I am glad to hear that from a young officer, but turn to your neighbour—he thinks differently.'

My neighbour was also a lieutenant, close on forty, a robust and indeed almost aggressive figure, with a massive brow, which he always kept bowed slightly as though it were too heavy for him or as if he were perpetually engaged in deep thought. I noticed no reaction in him, but introduced myself. In the somewhat strained conversation that followed I learned that he was Lieutenant Berndt, who in civil life had been an adviser in Goebbels's Ministry of Propaganda and the author of a war book, *Panzer-Hunters Break Through.* He made no comments on my attack on Goebbels, and as the evening wore on we grew quite friendly. Neither of us then foresaw that we were later to live together for many months.

[1] The German word *klug* means 'clever.'

That night the Tommies dropped flares (which we called 'Christmas trees') and anti-personnel bombs. A splinter ripped open my tent roof and opened up a fine view of the African stars.

Long before sunrise I took up my position at the head of the Marada column. We set out with about thirty vehicles, which included four armoured cars, a wireless truck, half a dozen Volkswagen, two trucks mounted with light ack-ack weapons, and two with anti-tank guns. The rest were open cars and trucks carrying riflemen, munitions, and rations. Three young officers accompanied my column—a company commander, a lieutenant also called Schmidt, who shared my armoured car in the van, and a lieutenant in charge of the wireless detachment.

We drove east until, a few miles short of El Agheila, salvoes from British artillery told us that it was time to swing south off the coastal road. We headed for the Marada tracks and kept a lookout for German armoured cars which we knew to be ranging the area. We linked up with the reconnaissance detachment after two hours of Desert travelling. The commander of a huge eight-wheeled armoured car gave us a new bearing and offered to accompany us to the Marada track. Our march continued.

Signals passed a message forward suggesting a halt. They had intercepted a message in English: 'An enemy column is moving towards us.' We searched the horizon and assumed that the observer must be hidden behind a rise quite close to what could now be clearly recognized as the road to Marada. I called for six cars and ordered them to fan out over the uneven surface of the desert towards the south. Shortly afterwards, our wireless truck reported hearing another English sentence: 'Six enemy light reconnaissance cars of unknown make moving south.'

The commander of the eight-wheeler offered to charge the suspected rise. I was worried about mines and ordered him to advance only a hundred yards and then stop. He did this. Then we intercepted another message: 'A super armoured car is advancing towards me. If enemy advances nearer, will be forced to close down observation.'

I took two light armoured cars forward to join the eight-wheeler. After a brief exchange of information with its commander, we made a full-out charge at the rise. But before we had covered a mile, we saw clouds of dust and the accelerated retreat of three small British armoured cars.

The field seemed clear. But still we were careful, and wisely. Before we reached the track leading south, one of the trucks struck a mine, fortunately with only one casualty. The commander of the eight-wheeler was beginning to lose interest in our expedition now that we had found the road. He gave us a few tips and then drove off to rejoin his comrades, while my sappers started to clear a gap through the minefield—a task that took them only half an hour.

Darkness overtook us more rapidly than was welcome. As low-flying enemy aircraft were as much of a menace as mines, we decided to take advantage of the moonlight and drive on through the night. In the earliest streaks of dawn we reached Marada oasis, found it clear of the enemy, and occupied it without firing a shot. Arabs at the oasis reported through our interpreter that a weak motorized detachment of British troops had pulled out towards the north two days before.

To our joy we found a spring from which gushed a stream of sweet water. We spent the day preparing defensive positions against possible attack. In the evening we listened to the B.B.C. news service; as usual, the war news dealt with events of the previous day. We heard it reported: 'German armoured cars moved southward from El Agheila.' We were certain that this referred to our own detachment, and felt irrationally flattered.

Our real mission began early next morning. We planned to reconnoitre the road to the oasis of Jalo, about 150 miles to the east. I left the company commander in charge of Marada. I chose two cars, each with a crew of three, for the Jalo job. Each car was armed with a light ack-ack machine-gun and four cases of ammunition. The fourth seat was packed with our petrol containers—of the type the British called 'Jerry-cans.' Two fresh-water containers were carried forward. The cars were of the ordinary rear-wheel-drive type with ordinary air-cooled radiators. They carried fascines on either side in case we got stuck in soft sand. Lieutenant Schmidt was to accompany me, and I left it to him to select two volunteer motor-cyclists and two machine-gunners.

During the first hour of our journey, as we travelled southward, I began to think we should never reach our destination. We sank into deep sand every few minutes. But gradually the colour of the sand changed to a lighter yellow and we found it firmer. Progress was easier provided we took the sand at an even and fairly fast pace. After three hours the silhouette of a flat-topped hill appeared on the southern horizon. It was time, I knew, to change direction east, but formidable and unnegotiable sand-dunes—spurs of the Kalansho sand-sea—barred the way. The lie of the land rose steeply towards the eastern plateau. I realized that we could not approach as we had planned.

When we reached the flat-topped hill, my driver remarked on the high poles he saw staked in the ground at intervals of about a mile, parallel with the high ground to the east. Thinking that they indicated a route to the south, we decided to follow them in an effort to reach the foot of the high ground and an approach to the plateau. A whole day passed in failure. I climbed on foot to the top of the plateau and found fresh spoors of wide-tracked British vehicles.

Day gave way to a starry night. We had a light meal of hard tack washed down with lime juice, posted pickets, and rested in turn. During my own hours on the alert I thought out the problem and became convinced that we were actually on the marked route to Kufra. The problem now was first to find a way through the sand-dunes, and then to by-pass the formidable rise leading to the plateau.

We continued the march at dawn. We travelled with the cars side by side, not in each other's tracks. If one was halted, the other rushed on if it could. We were able to make steady progress because the Volkswagen were so light that we man-handled them out of the ruts every time we stuck in the sand. The driver would stay at the wheel, the two passengers lift first one side to thrust a fascine under the wheel, then do the same on the other side.

I reckoned that we had reached a point nearer Kufra than Jalo. The terrain grew more impossible than ever. We had only a limited view in any direction, with dunes rising all round. Both cars simultaneously slid over a crest and into the valley of a great dune. It took us all several hours of hard work before we had them on fairly level going again. Half our petrol had been consumed. There was nothing for it but to turn back to Marada. We got there at noon the following day.

Next day I made a second attempt, with fresh men and other vehicles, to find a way through the seemingly impassable sand-dunes north-east of the flat-topped hill. We found the route to

Jalo—and discovered that the oasis was occupied by the enemy. But I could report that the route was suitable only for specially adapted transport; it was quite out of the question for heavy armour. I drove back to Marada, feeling fairly satisfied in spite of the limited success of the expedition.

A surprise awaited me at the oasis.

CHAPTER FOUR

MISSION IN THE GENERAL'S STORCH

'CONCLUDE task Marada. Report immediately to General Rommel,' said a wireless message. Though I had not slept more than an hour or two for nights on end, I set out from Marada that same evening with two of the light cars whose performance I had learned to value so highly. My objective was Advanced Headquarters, now located, according to the coded message received by the wireless truck, east of El Agheila. A week before we had encountered shell-fire in that area. I wondered how the situation had changed.

This is what had happened. The Tommies had held a useful artillery observation post on high ground north of the coast road. Its possession enabled them to harass our movements in the forward area, and was a thorough nuisance. Two companies of combat engineers were ordered to seize the O.P. Their attack succeeded. Rommel watched them go in from his Fieseler Storch[1] and saw British troops withdrawing to the east. He landed and ordered the armoured car reconnaissance group in co-operation with the tanks of the Italian Ariete Division to harry the enemy's southern flank. Frohlich, the Luftwaffe commander, was ordered to observe the effect of this action. The air report was startling: 'Rearward movement of enemy on large scale in direction of Agedabia and Benghazi . . .'

Rommel at once asked Fröhlich for further information on the areas round Mechili and east of Benghazi. The air report now seemed even more improbable: 'General movement of enemy troops eastward throughout Cyrenaica.'

'Has my hour arrived?' Rommel wondered. Was it possible that his dummy panzers, knocked together out of wood and canvas, had actually bluffed the enemy's air reconnaissance into believing that we intended to launch a major offensive? Had the enemy taken our limited action against the O.P. and the specu-

[1] Rommel's private reconnaissance plane.

lative exploitation by our armour on the southern flank as the first of vigorous, concerted moves?

Rommel was no man to waste time on fruitless speculation. He was in his element. He exploited the situation to the utmost. He improvised two attacks—one along the coast towards Benghazi by Italian troops, the other a German thrust towards Mechili. Wavell's force, it seemed clear to Rommel, had over-estimated the strength of the Axis formations. That Tripoli parade had not been a waste of time. Now it was imperative that the truth should not be discovered. Rommel's order was: 'Panzers to the head of all formations. Rear vehicles to raise dust, nothing but dust!' Who in the Desert could distinguish more than the leading vehicles of a column, if in the rear the dust clouds rose thick and turbulent?

Rommel was possessed by restlessness. He wanted to be in a dozen places at once. He used his Storch constantly, and was sometimes here, sometimes there, usually where least expected.

2

I neared the coast just east of El Agheila and found a few staff cars. Exhausted after the night drive from Marada, I dropped down to sleep for an hour or two, and at dawn woke refreshed, though my eyelids were glued together with sand. By seven in the morning I had found the Advanced H.Q. flag near the Agedabia landing-ground.

My Marada–Jalo reconnaissance report was now superfluous. Nobody was interested in the chances of an advance on Jalo. Ehlert received me with an impatient 'Where on earth have you been hiding?' He did not expect a reply. He bent over his maps and ignored me for a while. The truck was alive with the tension that develops when operations are on. Oberleutnant Hosslin, the orderly officer, also in the truck, was obviously at pains to avoid interrupting Ehlert. I followed suit and said no word. The wireless duty-officer dashed in and out with messages. Ehlert made red and blue marks on the talc of his operations map. Outside, I noticed thick dust-clouds rising away to the north-east over Msus.

The head of Lieutenant Himmler appeared at the door: 'Is the I a here?'

'Go to the devil!' barked Ehlert, without looking up. I wished I were out in the Desert.

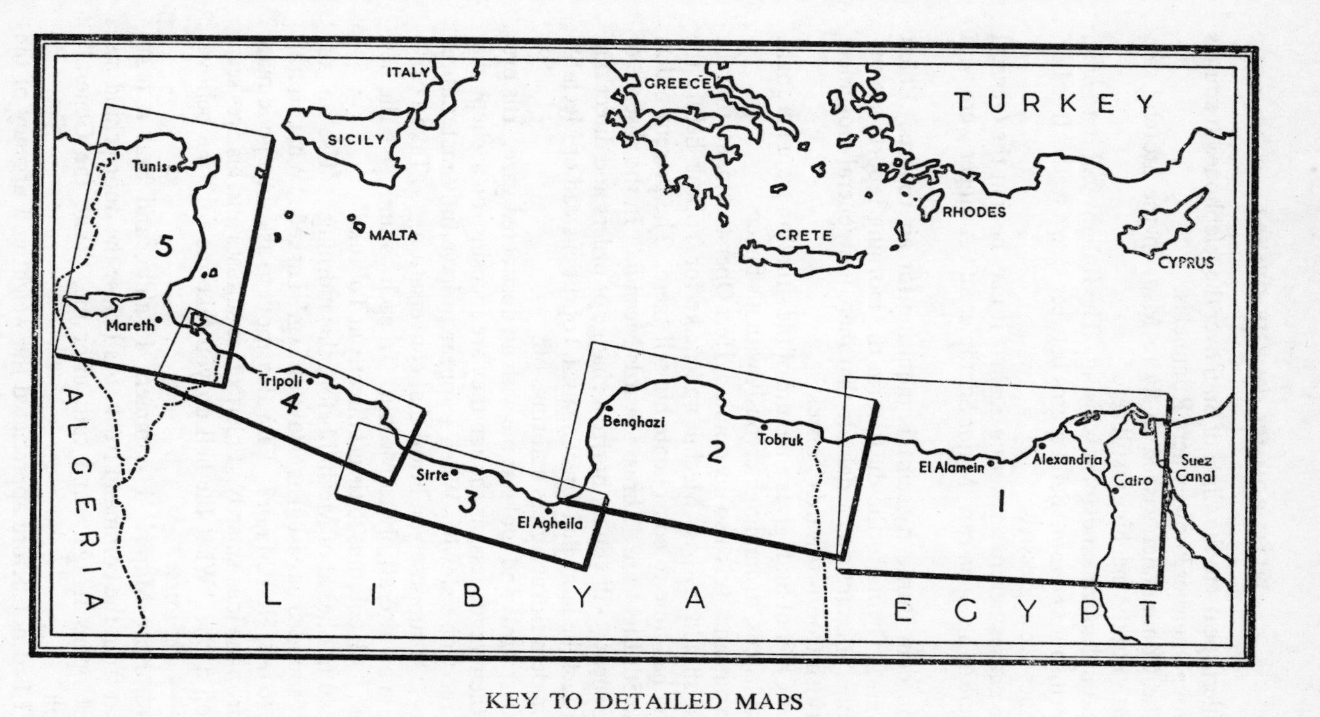

KEY TO DETAILED MAPS

Map 1, *page* 57. Map 2, *page* 113. Map 3, *page* 181. Map 4, *page* 181. Map 5, *page* 217.

Ehlert speaks to the Chief of Staff over the telephone. It sounds as though neither knows where Rommel is.

'The Commander wished to fly to Msus in the Storch,' says Ehlert, 'but the machine is still here.'

An unpleasant sandstorm is rising. The Italians call it a *ghibli*, the British a *khamsin*. Sand grates between one's teeth. It is hot. The flies are aggressive.

He pauses before answering again: 'It may be that the General has left in his open car. Major Schräpler and Aldinger were with him....'

Von dem Borne, it seems, is inquiring for air reports. Ehlert answers: 'Owing to the dust storm the morning reports are unreliable. It seems pretty definite that there is a general movement of British troops towards Tobruk.'

The Chief of Staff gives a picture of the situation from his angle. Ehlert listens, drumming nervously with his fingers.

He puts in: 'It is also my opinion, Herr Oberstleutnant, that the thrust should by-pass Mechili and make for Tobruk before the enemy has time to consolidate himself there. The present orders to the 5th Light are "Thrust towards Mechili." In the absence of the General, will you authorize a change of orders and direct that the attack be launched direct against Tobruk instead of Mechili?'

Von dem Borne agrees and rings off.

Ehlert turns and looks at me with an abstracted gaze. His eyes lose their vagueness, as though they are focusing on a shape that they recognize slowly. When I appear to have fully materialized he says: 'I suppose you heard that conversation.... Take a car—no, use an aircraft, fly to Mechili. To each column give the new order: "All columns to thrust directly at Tobruk."'

I had not heard of Mechili before this morning. 'Use an aircraft' sounded as casual as 'Have an egg.' I asked: 'What aircraft am I to use, Herr Major?' I am also about to ask for a good map, but drop the idea smartly. Ehlert's face suffuses and his eyes seem to pop a bit. 'What the hell do you take me for?' he bellows. 'A —— wet-nurse?'

'No, Herr Major!' I stammer. I salute, and beat a hasty retreat from the command truck. As I close the door behind me, Ehlert opens it again and calls after me, 'Take the General's Storch.'

If I had not before appreciated the weight and urgency of the orders given me, I did so now when told to use the General's personal and most important means of transport.

I found Rommel's N.C.O. pilot. He was at first reluctant to believe that I, an insignificant lieutenant, had authority to use the General's plane. And then, when he had been convinced that I was not mad on that score, he declared it would be lunacy to attempt flying in the sandstorm. Perhaps he was right. But at that moment our conversation was interrupted. Through the dust clouds we could see and hear enemy bombs exploding near by; we had not detected the R.A.F. machines approaching because of the howl of the storm.

This seemed to convince the N.C.O. that flying was possible, or perhaps safer than staying close to headquarters. He produced a small map, on which we located Mechili with some difficulty, and climbed into the cockpit. I was in my shirtsleeves because of the heat. Without even a razor or a toothbrush in my pocket, I set off for the front in the General's plane.

Rommel's pilot seems to have some difficulty in gaining height. After we have made several circuits, I note with relief that we are gradually lifting. Occasionally there are gaps between the clouds of dust, and I catch momentary glimpses of moving columns. The order 'By-pass Mechili—straight for Tobruk' reverberates in my head. I marvel at the Chief of Staff's display of initiative in ordering a change of plan of such magnitude without Rommel's knowledge.

I keep hoping the storm will die down, but we have been flying for three-quarters of an hour and the gale seems to be growing steadily worse. The N.C.O. has little control over the tiny plane. It swings and sways madly, like a kite on a string in a high wind.

I shout at the pilot: 'We must reach our destination—you realize how important it is!'

'Quite, Herr Leutnant,' he acknowledges, 'but what is impossible is impossible.'

As if to emphasize the pilot's reply, we are thrown vertically upwards; then down, down we drop, to what seems a certain death. But we straighten out.

The pilot, with the air of having reached a decision, calls out: 'I am responsible for the operation of this machine. I am going to land.'

I make no reply, but wonder how he is going to manage it: we cannot make out the ground. But somehow, through the murk, he eases the plane down and our wheels rumble along the rough desert for a few yards. Those Storch aircraft could land on a tennis court.

I jumped out rather dazed, one thought uppermost in my mind—the importance of my message. I dare not fail! The pilot was trying to stake and rope his machine to the ground in the teeth of the wind. I shouted an order to him that he stay where he was until the storm subsided, while I sought other transport.

Blindly I ran off into the sandstorm, conscious of the passing of each precious minute. Would it be hours, perhaps? A sense of loneliness and futility overwhelmed me at times. I felt far from anywhere as I stumbled on. Then in the red haze ahead I made out the vague outline of a Volkswagen approaching. A swirl of thicker dust obscured it, but I raced on and shouted with all the power of my lungs. The driver sighted me and slowed down. He stared at me in astonishment as I leaped at the car and sank into a seat. The driver's warning, 'Please mind the tomatoes,' was too late. I breathlessly introduced myself and my predicament.

The driver was a noted German war-correspondent, Baron von Esebeck. He too had lost his bearings, and said there seemed no sign of life for miles round. It was difficult to determine the position of the sun through the swirling sand. At this time of day we reckoned, the sun should be about south, so we bore left. It was impossible to guess whether the enemy was ahead of us or in rear; but it was clear that we must drive eastward.

Shortly before sunset we ran into a large-calibre artillery-piece being hauled by a tractor. We had met a party of eight German gunners who were also lost in the Desert with their 88 mm. anti-aircraft gun, a huge caterpillar limber truck, and a supply truck. We could do no more than doss down for the night with them.

One of the soldiers let slip the welcome information that the supply truck was filled with fresh eggs. I boiled three eggs each for von Esebeck, his driver, and myself, while the war correspondent brewed coffee. The storm was subsiding, and though one's teeth still grated on sand, the food tasted excellent and the coffee was nectar.

The air at dawn was crystal clear. For miles around, as far as we could see, there was no trace of man or vehicle. We made out a dry salt-pan away to the south-east. I tried vainly to locate it on von Esebeck's map. The Desert here was strewn with boulders. The war correspondent and I decided to head for the salt-pan and make speed across its smooth surface. A sound idea, marred only by an alarming swoop at us by a low-flying Hurricane.

We had motored for several hours before we sighted a column in the distance moving north-east. Von Esebeck was fretting that we would reach Mechili too late for him to be able to report its fall as an eyewitness. We had left the salt-pan and were nearing a slight rise when we saw in the air, to the north-west and a little abaft us, a low-flying aircraft sustain a direct hit and hurtle in flames to the ground. We did not know whether it was friend or foe, and raced towards the wreck to investigate. On the way we ran pell-mell upon a defended post. To our relief, it was German—a light ack-ack gun position. We shouted to the N.C.O. in command, 'Which way to Mechili?' He answered: 'You are coming from Mechili way.'

And he added that the attack on Mechili was just about to begin.

With relief and, indeed, joy I located the Divisional Staff of the 5th Light a few minutes later. I hurriedly said good-bye to von Esebeck, with thanks for his help, and reported to Major Hauser. He heard me calmly. 'Just like Ehlert,' he said, 'to think out something like that.' He discussed the new order with General Streich. But the Divisional Commander had received his orders from Rommel in person only a few hours previously, and so was about to attack Mechili.

We went for the little fort in the Desert, and the British positions round it, from three directions. The engagement was sharp but lasted only a couple of hours. We took the British commander, Major-General Gambier-Parry, in his tent. The haul of prisoners numbered almost 3000. We had a further spectacular success. A mobile force of motor-cyclists caught up with a British column moving eastward across the Desert below the Jebel Akhdar near by, and to their astonishment held up the two heroes of the British advance to Benghazi: Lieutenant-General Sir Richard O'Connor, who had just been knighted for his successes against the Italians, and Lieutenant-General Sir Philip Neame, V.C. So we had three generals in the bag.

Mechili landing-ground was littered with destroyed planes. British machines swooped down to attack it afresh at short intervals. At the height of one assault, 'my' Fiesler Storch dropped in out of the sky. Out stepped Rommel, smiling buoyantly, fresh from a personal reconnaissance of the Desert scene.

The command trucks of the captured British generals stood on a slight rise. They were large, angular vehicles on caterpillar tracks, equipped inside with wireless and facilities for 'paper' work. We christened them 'Mammoths' then, but I did not realize that these useful trucks would be used by Rommel and his staff and commanders right through the long struggle that was now beginning in the Desert.

Rommel inspected the vehicles with absorbed interest after a brief interview with the captured British generals. He watched them emptied of their British gear. Among the stuff turned out he spotted a pair of large sun-and-sand goggles. He took a fancy to them. He grinned, and said, 'Booty—permissible, I take it, even for a General.' He adjusted the goggles over the gold-braided rim of his cap peak.

Those goggles for ever after were to be the distinguishing insignia of the 'Desert Fox.'

CHAPTER FIVE

AT THE GATES OF TOBRUK

ROMMEL led the onward march against Tobruk before daybreak. The night before the German Afrika Korps staff had come up to Mechili. I avoided any meeting with Major Ehlert. Rommel allocated one of the Mammoths to General Streich of the 5th Light, and kept two for himself and his personal staff. He had the German cross painted on them all. We had taken a fair number of enemy vehicles, and I was allotted an open staff car similar to the one that Rommel generally used.

Aldinger, who was about to leave in the leading car with Rommel, gave me instructions. 'Herr Schmidt, from now on you will always travel immediately behind the General's car. You are to be entirely at his disposal.'

2

These were dramatic days. On March 27 King Peter had taken over control of Yugoslavia after the 'Palace Revolution' at two in the morning. On the 28th our Italian allies had been trounced by the Royal Navy in the battle of Cape Matapan. The following day, with the arrival of the 1st South African Brigade in Diredawa, in Abyssinia, it became clear that the fate of Addis Ababa was sealed. Asmara was to fall two days later.[1] Rommel's move at El Agheila began hesitantly on the 30th. By April 2 we had forced the British out of Mersa Brega on the coast and also out of Agedabia, and the next day they evacuated Benghazi, always a difficult city to hold. Simultaneously a pro-Axis *coup d'état* was achieved in Iraq by Rashid Ali, and Wavell had another problem to think about. Foreign Minister Eden and General Sir John Dill, the British Chief of the Imperial General Staff, had both just

[1] Entered by the 5th Indian Division (Major-General L. M. Heath) on April 1.

been in Athens in answer to an appeal by the Greeks for military aid. Wavell had to undertake to send troops from the Middle East to Greece, which Germany invaded on the morning of April 6, at the same time entering Yugoslavia.

By April 7 we had taken Derna. Addis Ababa had fallen, and my old haunt, Massawa,[1] was on the eve of surrender; but in the Desert Rommel was on top.

3

During a brief halt Rommel received a wireless signal from Behrendt: 'Derna reached.' Oberleutnant Behrendt, assistant to the I c, had been placed by Rommel in command of a mixed group of troops with a few anti-tank guns, temporarily formed into a combat group, and had been ordered to make for Derna. He had outpaced the Italian forces moving along the coast road and had taken a number of prisoners.

The Luftwaffe for some days past had been flying companies of reinforcements for the 15th Panzer Division across the Mediterranean. The Divisional Commander, General von Prittwitz, was the first of the new men to set foot in Africa. Rommel had the briefest of interviews with him, and then von Prittwitz led the advance on Tobruk. He ran straight into the forward defences and was killed—the first German general to fall at the head of his troops in Africa.

At nightfall Rommel and the rest of us on his staff reached a whitewashed home—in peace-time a road engineer's residence—west of Tobruk. An Australian had artistically employed the outer walls of the square building to extol the qualities of his favourite beverage, and had decorated them also with lively horse-racing scenes. Telegraph poles were spaced across the Desert between this building and the fort at Acroma. Close to this building we buried von Prittwitz and the other Germans who had fallen with him.

Staff headquarters was set up in a wadi south-west of the White House. Ehlert appropriated one of the Mammoth A.C.V.'s (Armoured Command Vehicles) as Operations Office. The other was reserved for Rommel himself.

[1] Captured by the 7th and 10th Indian Brigades and the Free French Brigade d'Orient on April 7, 1941.

Next morning Rommel set out for Acroma. His car was escorted only by my own and a light armoured vehicle. We ploughed along the dusty Acroma track, which was to be a familiar and trying line of communications for a long time until the Axis by-pass road was built, to the primitive Desert fort. From Acroma Rommel headed south-east in the direction of El Adem. Artillery fire from Tobruk was suddenly laid down around us, and startled gazelles plunged among our three vehicles. The shells followed us, well registered, for some distance.

When we had driven for half an hour we came across companies of German infantry who were taking up positions on the high ground short of El Adem. Rommel stopped for a brief talk with their officers who had been there just a few hours. Among them I met Lieutenant Schmidt, my comrade of the Marada–Jalo expedition. While the General talked, a salvo of enemy shells fell among us. A young lieutenant was killed, and my friend Schmidt lost an arm.

Two miles farther east we found General Streich with a Mammoth and his staff lying in isolation in a wide wadi. The Tobruk batteries had ceased firing now, and Rommel remarked to Streich with a twinkle: 'It is perhaps better for the English to spare their ammunition. They may yet need all they have.'

As if to belie this, we heard the howling shriek of a fresh salvo, which burst near by and was obviously meant for us. But we were quick to note that these shells had come not from Tobruk but from the south. We gazed through glasses at a ridge of high ground surmounted by a long, low building and a row of telegraph poles. 'El Adem,' says Rommel softly, glancing swiftly at his map, surveying the area again through his binoculars.

He spotted a lone armoured car, which must, we concluded, contain the enemy artillery observation officer. We were still trying to arrange counter-measures when, after a quarter of an hour, the car went away, and with it the shell-fire.

Meanwhile the Generals discussed the tactical situation. Before we drove away, Rommel reiterated to the Divisional Commander: 'We must attack Tobruk with everything we have, immediately your Panzers have taken up their positions, and before Tommy has time to dig in.'

At sunrise we left the bivouac west of the White House and again drove through the thick dust to Acroma. Columns from the opposite direction and vehicles ahead all churned up such dense clouds that we could only establish the approximate direction of the track by means of the telegraph poles along it. Again there were just the three vehicles—Rommel's, mine, and the light armoured car.

At Acroma Oberleutnant Wahl with four Panzers snapped to attention as the General arrived. I had a chat with Wahl, an engaging fellow full of fun and high spirits, while Rommel intently scanned the Tobruk strong-points in the east through his field-glasses. He was silent, as though fascinated. His compact torso was erect above his straddled legs, his elbows crooked as he held the Zeiss glasses to his eyes. His chin was thrust out. The Mechili goggles were there on his cap peak.

'Herr Leutnant, we're off!' Rommel snaps suddenly. 'Tell that officer to follow with his Panzers.' He leaps into his car and drives ahead. I pass on his orders. The Panzer officer calls up his tanks with a signal—several upward thrusts of the arm. Wahl climbs aboard his own Panzer and grins: 'Off to Tobruk!'

We drive east for some miles. Now and again bursts of shell-fire erupt about us. In a wadi we pass an Italian battery which is feverishly replying to fire from King's Cross in Tobruk.

Rommel halts and studies his map. I turn round and notice that the Panzers have been unable to keep up our pace. Away back, their dust clouds are flurrying forward. The General beckons, and I run to his side. An energetic finger thrusts at a section of the map: I recognize the western flank of the line.

'The battery is positioned correctly, but where is the Bersaglieri battalion? It should be in position on the high ground immediately ahead.'

He glances at the map again, then adds angrily: 'The Italian Command evidently indicated the wrong position.' Then: 'The Italian commander is apparently not yet with his men.'

At that moment the Panzers come up behind us. The whole wadi is suddenly plastered with shell-bursts. A salvo explodes almost on top of us. 'Drive back and order the Panzers to stay where they are until they get further instructions,' Rommel barks at me. 'I am going forward to the rise.'

It is no pleasure to drive back through the wadi towards the Panzers, where the fire is hottest. I am relieved when I have passed on the order and can instruct my driver to turn and make rapidly for the front again. I leave the car at the bottom of the rise and trot up the slope. I find Rommel lying on the ground with shells exploding right and left. He is all alone, for he has even left Aldinger behind to-day—to attend to arrears of correspondence.

I watch Rommel as he lies on his belly, intently studying the ground ahead through his glasses. His firm mouth is tight-lipped now; his prominent cheek-bones stand out white. His cap is perched on the back of his head.

'Fort Pilastrino!' he mutters. I glance quickly at his map before I crouch down behind a heap of stones and also survey the terrain ahead. The ground slopes down ahead of us, and then slopes upward again equally gradually. On the crest is a triangular-shaped ruin of stones surmounted by a close network of barbed-wire. Considerably farther back is a higher mound of stones. I surmise that this is Pilastrino and an enemy O.P.

Rommel is looking for the first time at the actual defences of Tobruk, but we have no means of gauging their strength. Now we both see a few forms moving along the perimeter of the ruins. The huntsman's urge seems to take possession of Rommel. 'Leutnant!' he commands. 'Orders to the Panzers! Attack the stone ruins ahead—two Panzers through the northern wadi, two through the southern wadi close to the ruins.'

'*Jawohl, Herr General.*' I repeat the order. I have earlier observed that there is a deeper wadi not far from the southern wadi, and rashly venture to suggest, 'Shouldn't the Panzers advance along the deeper wadi, Herr General?'

Rommel's eyes flash, and his face reddens. 'Herr Leutnant, I am not nearly as stupid as you think!'

I salute, and hurry off to carry out my instructions, mortified at my brashness. For a while the bursting of shells around me seem of little consequence.

Reaching the Panzers, I explain the orders to the lieutenant and briefly describe the ground ahead. He relays the orders to the other tank commanders through the microphone of his radio-telephone. He smiles calmly and waves to me before he closes the hatch and roars off with the other Panzers at his heels.

We watch the charge of the Panzers. They obey orders and get close to their objective—the ruins. Then an unexpected and murderous fire falls round them. A few moments later the fire of several batteries is directed at our own observation post. We race for shelter along the slope. But the shell-fire grows still fiercer. Shells drop among the battery of Italian artillery. One gun and its crew are wiped out by a direct hit. All hell is let loose until sundown, when the shell-fire ceases. We drive back to Advanced Headquarters near the White House. The Panzers do not return.

Weeks later a group of combat engineers attacking at Ras Medawwa came on the torn body of the Panzer lieutenant hanging across the barbed-wire defences in front of the ruins.

CHAPTER SIX

A GENERAL ON HIS CAMEL

THAT day the Afrika Korps laid hands on maps of the Tobruk defences for the first time. As the maps had been prepared by our allies, the Italians, you might have expected that we should have had unlimited supplies. But no, we could get only two. Rommel had one, and the other went to Streich of the 5th Light.

Rommel was impressed by the skilled siting of the defensive positions and the unexpected depth of the defences generally. The maps indeed bore out the accuracy of air reconnaissance reports, which had been somewhat doubted. Streich showed little enthusiasm for the tough task that Tobruk obviously set.

It was nightfall before we got back to our quarters.

2

In the April days that followed, Rommel's cry was 'Every man forward to Tobruk!' The rest of the 5th Light had arrived meanwhile. The 15th Panzer was being feverishly transported across the Mediterranean. Detachments of the Division's infantry support group were being landed by air at Derna. Italian formations were also arriving. Day by day the ring round Tobruk closed.

Rommel was with the troops in the front line from morning until late at night. The fire of the British and Australian artillery seemed to follow him more frequently than anybody else. Within a few days no other soldier in the Afrika Korps was as well acquainted with the Desert tracks and the range of the Tobruk guns as was Rommel—not even we of his immediate staff.

One of the staff now was Lieutenant Berndt, Goebbels's man, whom I had met at Marble Arch. Lieutenant-Colonel Graf Schwerin had been recalled from his expedition to Mursuk—the trip I had missed—and was put in command of a position astride the coast road at the eastern approaches to Tobruk. An attack by combat engineers was planned in this sector.

For some days Rommel used his Mammoth for visiting the line. It afforded admirable protection against dive-bombers, aerial strafing, and shrapnel, and we had plenty of this during our daily tours. But Rommel usually sat high up on the roof of his Mammoth, dangling his legs through the open doorway. Aldinger, who had been with him in the First World War too, was almost always with him.

The General inspired all ranks with enthusiasm and energy wherever he appeared. He could not tolerate subordinates who were not as enthusiastic and active as himself, and he was merciless in his treatment of anybody who displayed lack of initiative. *Out!* Back to Germany they went at once.

Our front-line tours began early in the morning and frequently lasted until after nightfall. Rommel often took over the wheel from his tired driver. His sense of direction was remarkable, and he had an almost uncanny ability to orient himself by the stars at night.

As often as not, when we reached Advanced Headquarters west of the White House, Ehlert would send me back at once with written orders for the divisional commanders, murmuring that after all I was familiar with the road. Every evening Rommel had discussions with von dem Borne and Ehlert. His batman, Gunther, would cook him a simple meal and then, almost without fail, Rommel would sit down to write his one daily joint letter to his wife and son Manfred.

Rommel in these days was always present in person when any attack went in against a point on the Tobruk perimeter—not with the staff of the attacking formation, but with the front-line troops. Often, to the annoyance of the tactical staff, he would give orders in person on the spot, changing plans to meet the situation. His subordinate commanders found this a real thorn in the flesh, and resented it bitterly.

3

Graf Schwerin's attack against the eastern defences of Tobruk failed after a sharp engagement. Rommel, strangely, did not seem at this time to be interested in the eastern sector. His constant aim now was to go for the fortress from the El Adem–Acroma sector. Personally, I favoured the sector between the coast road east of

Tobruk and the road south to El Adem, and regretted that it seemed to be neglected in our battle-planning. But I had learned to be discreet since I had gratuitously offered the General advice at Pilastrino, and I kept my counsel to myself.

General Streich had now disposed the 5th Panzer Regiment, under Colonel Olbricht, south of Tobruk. The last tank had barely arrived before Rommel announced that he wanted an attack on the fortress from the south. It seemed as though he could not rest while Tobruk held out as a sort of abscess on the side of his line of communication to the Egyptian frontier.

'We are expecting a further twelve mobile guns, Herr General,' reported Major Hauser, I a of the 5th Light. 'I would recommend that we await their arrival before making the attack.'

Rommel seemed to have more confidence in Major Hauser than in his chief, General Streich. 'All right, Hauser,' he nodded, 'do that.'

The plan embodied a combined attack with Panzers and infantry consisting of grenadiers and combat engineers, who had already proved their fighting qualities. The wedge made was to be widened immediately by units of the machine-gun battalions. The Panzers were not to advance to the full depth of the wedge, but to fan out on both sides and, exploiting, to attempt to roll up the enemy's front-line positions from their rear.

Though there was considerable confidence in this plan, the attack failed. The Panzers were able to break into the forward defended localities and the combat engineers reached the trenches, but the British and Australian troops fought back with great determination. They were able through flanking fire to throw back the Panzers with some losses, and to bar farther advance by the 'storm pioneers.' Enemy counter-attack tanks from Tobruk then sallied out and captured a considerable number of our combat engineers and riflemen before they had time to consolidate the positions they had reached.

Rommel was furious over this failure. He blamed General Streich. 'Your Panzers did not give of their best and left the infantry in the lurch!'

General Streich defended the conduct of his armour. 'Herr General, the Panzers would have reached their objectives despite strong anti-tank fire, if the whole sector had not been protected by deep and well-camouflaged tank-traps.'

Certainly the defences had been stronger than we expected. Later we learned that close to the scene of the attack there was a sector almost entirely bare of tank-traps. The Italians had been building them, but abandoned them when Wavell had taken Tobruk four months before. But Rommel was impatient and unsympathetic to any explanations. He considered that General Streich and Colonel Olbricht had 'lacked resolution.' He gave vent to his anger openly and used blunt words, such as presumably only one general may use to another.

One day at dusk, some while later on the eve of another assault with Panzers, Rommel visited the 5th Light H.Q. again. Aldinger and I accompanied him. At the end of the conference Rommel said to Streich, with meaningful emphasis: 'I expect this attack to be made with the utmost resolution under your personal leadership. At your disposal I will leave my aide, Lieutenant Schmidt.'

I reflect for a moment that this may mean either that I am to be useful or that I am to stick by the side of, and (if still alive) to report on, a general who has been told that he had better come back with his shield or on it. . . . I like the friendly and considerate Streich, whom I regard as an extremely brave man, and Hauser, too, and feel sorry that they are being treated so remorselessly.

I was made at home in the 5th Light H.Q. mess. On an inside bulkhead of Streich's Mammoth I noticed a large Knight's Cross made of cardboard. But instead of the usual central swastika, it carried a sketch of a large black fly. Hauser explained to me that the Knight's Cross was awarded ceremoniously every evening to the inmate of the Mammoth who had 'shot down' the largest number of the pestilential Desert flies during the day. I could understand their preoccupation with this pleasant diversion, but I also began to appreciate Rommel's more single-minded insistence that his subordinates should display initiative, aggressiveness, and 'hardness' in the face of the enemy. He had no time for frivolity.

I drove off with General Streich before dawn next morning. The Panzer attack was to go in at first light. Streich was to lead the attack himself in one of the Panzers, which now followed immediately behind our open car. Streich had with him the only operational map available in the entire Division, and now orientated himself by its aid. He instructed me meanwhile to maintain contact with the Panzer behind us.

To save time Streich chose to use the El Adem–Tobruk road as far north as he could, before swinging westward to join the Panzers in readiness. He said little and was preoccupied—probably, I thought, because of the reprimand Rommel had given him.

We went on silently for some distance. I felt the time had come to say: 'Herr General, I think we should now turn off.'

'*Ja, Ja, Schmidtchen*,' said the Divisional Commander ab-abstractedly, 'make use of the road as far as possible.' With a lowered glimmer of his torch and a glance at his map, he added, 'we can still use the road a little way.'

But his orientation did not seem to match Rommel's. Before we realized what was happening we found ourselves in a real hubbub. Shell-bursts, anti-tank missiles whizzing by, and the rat-tat-tat of machine-guns left us in no doubt that we had made a sudden appearance under the noses of the enemy. With lightning speed we leapt from the car and dived for protection behind the Panzer. We clutched at it, hauling our legs up to avoid the bursts of machine-gun bullets which were splashing knee-high against the caterpillars of the tank. Inconsiderately, I remember thinking at the time, the driver of the tank started to turn sharply and was on the point of exposing our behinds to the enemy when a rear-track snapped.

In these circumstances there was only one course to adopt. On the heels of the driver, who had already left his turret and was taking flying leaps towards the side of the road, we plunged into a group of deep shell-holes.

It was still dark, but light would come soon. We dared not remain where we were. We had just decided to make a bolt for it towards the south-west and were getting ready to leave the shell-holes when a new salvo burst round us, and we heard a cry from the driver. The General called out: 'What's the matter? Are you wounded?'

In spite of our uncomfortable situation, the General laughed aloud when the reply came: 'No, Herr General, not yet.'

Leaping and ducking, we made our way across the Desert to where our Panzers lay. By the time we reached them it was already full daylight—too late for the attack! Shells were falling round the tanks, and casualties had been suffered. Colonel Olbricht asked the General's permission to withdraw the Panzers to prepared positions.

We called up a car by wireless and it took us back to Divisional Headquarters.

Some hours later I reported to Rommel, feeling apprehensive about his reactions to the failure at dawn. I was surprised and relieved when Rommel remarked calmly: 'Schmidt, drive back to Olbricht and instruct him to bring his Panzers to Point 112.'[1] I drove back with a light heart, feeling that I bore better news than would be expected.

I sighted the Panzers on the horizon, hull-down, immobile, shutters closed. The shells from Tobruk were discharging their daily benison. 'Where on earth do the English get all their ammunition from?' I asked the driver. He made no answer—I expected none—but accelerated furiously as we ran the gauntlet of the shells into the depression. We reached the first of the Panzers, and its shutters opened. Olbricht looked out. I shouted Rommel's orders to him. 'Thank heavens,' he said, relief in his voice. 'A sensible order at last!'

A week or two later, both General Streich and Colonel Olbricht were on their way home—'bowler-hatted,' to use the English phrase, or 'on their camels,' as we said. I did not see them again after they left the Desert. But I noted that one of the officers concerned in the anti-Hitler *putsch* on July 20, 1944, was a General Olbricht. Could it have been the same man?

[1] South-west of Tobruk, west of the El Adem road.—H.W.S.

CHAPTER SEVEN

ATTACK AT PILASTRINO

ONE evening about the middle of April Rommel's favourite Panzer Reconnaissance Group arrived in the H.Q. area west of the White House. The commander, Lieutenant-Colonel von Wegmar, reported to the General. I was just about to share a precious tin of canned fruit which Berndt had got as a privilege from the Mess Officer, when Gunther, the batman, called me to Rommel.

Now few except Rommel and I, since I was always with him these days, knew the tracks leading round Tobruk to Lieutenant-Colonel Graf Schwerin's sector east of the fortress. This was the reason for my summons. Rommel introduced me to von Wegmar and said: 'You are to accompany the Reconnaissance Group along the shortest route around Tobruk to the Via Balbia,' as the Italians called the coastal road.

I used the North Star to find my bearings, by midnight had set the Reconnaissance Group on the coast road, shook hands with von Wegmar, and turned for home. My driver and I were almost exhausted when we reached H.Q. in the morning. Berndt received me with good news: 'Von Wegmar has entered Bardia.' The village on the cliff just short of the Egyptian border had not been in Axis hands since Wavell had so unceremoniously sent the Italian General Berganzoli, whom the Australians called 'Electric Whiskers,' scurrying away west from it.

A few days later the Reconnaissance Group, reinforced by a few Panzers, advanced and took Fort Capuzzo on the frontier, and also marched into Sollum. By April 27 we held Halfaya Pass and looked out from the escarpment along the coast of Egypt. Von Wegmar was recommended for the award of the Ritterkreuz (Knight's Cross) of the Iron Cross.

2

'Whoever is in possession of Pilastrino is in a position to read the other's cards. This is the key point of the Tobruk defences.' So said Rommel during a staff conference. Again and again Rommel looked at Acroma and from there to the east, to Pilastrino, a high point in the south-west sector of the fortress.

Now Rommel planned another attack. Remembering what had happened to the four Panzers, he directed that the Italian Bersaglieri battalion was to occupy the positions as originally ordered in front of the high ground facing Pilastrino, and from here he would throw in an infantry attack. He reconnoitred the ground personally and decided himself on the most suitable 'position in readiness' for the Italians.

We left the Mammoth at Advanced H.Q. and drove off in the usual little battle party—the two open cars and the armoured car, Aldinger, Berndt, and I with the General.

A report had come in that the Australians in the sector facing the Italians had been feverishly active during the night. Rommel wanted a precise picture of the situation now, and so went to see in person. As we approached the sector, we thought it completely calm and were ready to conclude that the reports of enemy activity overnight had been, as so often before, exaggerated by our Allies. Even the enemy artillery in Tobruk seemed quiet.

But the puzzle was soon solved: we found not a single Italian in the whole sector, barring a few isolated artillery batteries in the rear, entirely unprotected by infantry. We peered cautiously over a rise and were met by the sight of hundreds of discarded sun-helmets gaily decorated with multi-coloured cocks' feathers—Bersaglieri helmets. Otherwise, not a thing. It dawned on us that the Australians must have 'collected' the entire battalion of our Allies during the night.

Rommel hurriedly ordered up a scratch assortment of troops from Acroma to act as a stop-gap in the denuded sector. Then he issued a sharp order, afterwards much discussed and disputed in high Italian circles, to the effect that he would, in future, expect the immediate execution of officers who showed cowardice in the face of the enemy.

Back at his H.Q. he had a frank talk with the Italian liaison

FIELD-MARSHAL ERWIN ROMMEL
Imperial War Museum

GERMAN PANZERS ATTACKING IN CYRENAICA

Imperial War Museum

officer, His Excellency General Calvi, son-in-law of King Victor Emmanuel, a tall, thin officer with the long, narrow face and prominent nose typical of the Tuscan. He spoke German fluently, and Rommel had a fair regard for his character. But after their conversation Calvi was subdued and reserved in manner for quite a while.

The Afrika Korps Staff concluded now that the Italian soldier was, as an individual, eager to co-operate and be helpful, sometimes more so than the German; and when he was like this, he would fight bravely if well equipped and efficiently led. But the equipment and the leadership were seldom there.

3

April 30 was the date chosen for the attack on Tobruk through Pilastrino.

Rommel characteristically selected for the undertaking troops with whom he himself had been in close contact. He had men from various units formed into a combat group, roughly the strength of one regiment, under command of Major Schräpler. Thorough preparations were made for the attack with the resources available.

We went forward in the Mammoth. Rommel, Aldinger, and I watched the opening of the attack from an observation point on high ground. Stukas went in first to bomb various positions, and our artillery supported the advance with a barrage. Considering the mixed nature of the group, Schräpler's troops displayed first-rate co-operation in the advance. The guns of Tobruk hammered away at them. Well-placed Australian sharp-shooters also did their best to hinder their advance. It was late afternoon before they reached the barbed-wire and the minefield.

Rommel had kept his glasses glued on the scene of battle. Now he beckoned to me. 'Schmidt, work your way forward to Schräpler. He must consolidate and hold his present positions. The attack will be reinforced and continued to-night.'

It was a hazardous task to proceed alone and swiftly over the open ground which it had taken the infantry almost all day to cross. But I made as much speed as I could, feeling every time I slowed down that Rommel's glasses were blistering the seat of my trousers. I reached Schräpler just before dark.

During the night Pioneer combat groups with flame-throwers were sent into the attack. After a hard struggle in the darkness, a number of concrete strong-points were taken. 'We have succeeded in removing a portion of the defence,' said Rommel in his formal report.

Daybreak brought us a new ally, but a questionable one—a light sandstorm sprang up and cut down visibility. The dust both helped and hindered us. The spearhead of the combat troops had broken through immediately in front of Ras Medawwa, and were finding it difficult to see what they were doing or where they were going. The Australian strong-points were not easily distinguishable on the flat ground, and they were sited in depth. Frequently our men worked their way forward between two bunkers without noticing either. Unexpectedly, they would be fired upon from behind. 'Don't fire, we are Germans!' they would shout desperately, thinking they were being attacked in error by their own comrades. Too late they would discover that the troops behind them were not friendly, and only too glad to hear them confirm that they were Germans.

The combat engineers had now cleared a gap in the minefield, and, under cover of the dust, vehicles brought up reinforcements, anti-tank guns, munitions, and supplies.

'The strong-points taken will be held at all costs,' Rommel ordered.

He himself was one of the first into the captured positions in the morning. Next to me, the General crawled along like any front-line infantryman. He wanted to reach one particular trench ahead. We had not far to go when we sighted a group of combat engineers lying behind a heap of stones.

'Where the hell are you going?' their sergeant-major called. I shouted back, giving the map-reference of the strong-point.

'Don't be stupid,' he called back genially. 'Tommy has occupied it again.'

Lying prone, I pointed meaningly at my shoulder-straps and at Rommel. The sergeant-major then recognized the dust goggles on Rommel's cap, and his conversation melted away.

A burst of machine-gun fire made us decide that it was inadvisable to prolong our stay. We crawled back carefully.

4

The Australians launched a counter-attack and recaptured some of their strong-points. The Middle East High Command announced that on May 1 an enemy attack had been made on Tobruk and continued next day, piercing the outer defence perimeter, but that the position had then been stabilized. This was an accurate report. From that day the positions we held after the counter-attack formed the forward localities of the German line at Tobruk.

CHAPTER EIGHT

HURRICANES STRAFE ROMMEL

In the days that followed, the rest of the motorized infantry of the new 15th Panzer Division were landed from Junker 52's at Derna. Troop-carriers were waiting at the airfield to meet them, and before they knew where they were, they found themselves in the front line outside Tobruk. Where, they wondered, were the shady palms of Africa—the insignia of the German Afrika Korps to which they now belonged?

They hated the Africa they saw. Flies, millions of flies, confined movements, short and monotonous rations, and shortage of water, did more to brown off the troops during the passing weeks than all the incessant barking of the Tobruk guns.

Rommel thought the Australians who lay opposite us 'the best of soldiers, with their cold-blooded ability to carry out reconnaissance raids night after night.'

I remember an occasion when a machine-gun opened up on a trench occupied by Australians just forward of us. Our troops stared in astonishment when one Australian coolly seated himself on the parapet and waved his broad-brimmed hat at us as a stream of machine-gun bullets splashed by.

We were puzzled by their uncanny gift of working so silently into our lines by night, until one night a raiding-party were captured and found to be equipped with patrol boots—Desert boots with extra-thick crêpe-rubber roles.

Rommel came to the conclusion that Tobruk was a tough nut to crack. If it could not be taken easily, what else might he do? He prepared to consolidate and strengthen his positions in siege, but, as few German troops could be spared, the beleaguering garrison had perforce to be largely Italian. He decided to acquaint himself with the Sollum front and to view the 'Promised Land' across the barbed-wire on the frontier.

Meanwhile, the Knight's Cross had arrived for von Wegmar, the hero of Bardia and Sollum, and Rommel announced that he would make the award in person. This provided the ostensible reason for our journey east. We left the White House with a considerable column on April 19, led by my car and Rommel's Mammoth. A wireless truck accompanied us to maintain contact with G.H.Q. The Propaganda Company was also represented: with us were my old friend the war correspondent, von Esebeck, and a colleague of his named Ertl,[1] a typical mountaineer-type of a man, who was equipped with a movie camera and took his instructions about publicizing Rommel from Berndt.

We drove round Tobruk enveloped in a cloud of dust. Our eyes burned, our teeth crunched on sand, and faces, hair, and uniforms were all camouflaged into a dun anonymity.

As we crossed the road from Tobruk to El Adem, one of the vehicles drove into an area over which were scattered 'Thermos' mines dropped from enemy aircraft—dangerous little anti-personnel booby-traps which we soon learned to recognize. Chivvied by only a few salvoes from the Tobruk artillery, we reached the Via Balbia without mishap, and bowled along the coastal road so swiftly that we arrived at Bardia earlier than we anticipated.

Rommel gave von Wegmar a very warm greeting, and, while the movie camera purred, hung the Knight's Cross at his throat.

Now Rommel was in his element. He had von Wegmar recapitulate every phase and stage of the fight around the heap of stones that was Fort Capuzzo. He scanned the barbed-wire entanglements that rolled away into the hazy south along the Libyan–Egyptian frontier. He gazed eastward through his glasses for a long time at Wavell's armoured reconnaissance cars, which could be picked out lurking in the distance, their glasses no doubt on us, too. He was almost boyishly amused at the Italian coastal-defence guns. Tirelessly he crept into every defensive position and communication trench, and noted that the Italians had built them in the same style as those at Tobruk. At the end of the day everybody was tired but Rommel. He had kept himself and everybody else on the go, doing everything in a hurry, yet thoroughly.

Towards evening we began the return journey. Again I led the

[1] Ertl produced the famous Cape Horn film, *Robinson*, and was a distinguished Alpinist who won fame in an expedition into the Mount Everest *massif*.—H.W.S.

column. We were half an hour's drive west of Bardia, not far short of Gambut, driving into the blinding rays of the setting sun, when suddenly I spotted two low-flying aircraft. Were they Germans or Tommies?

They swooped towards us. There was no longer any doubt. 'Air alarm!' I yelled at the top of my voice. I pointed at the air-craft, then dived for whatever shelter the side of the road might afford. My driver was even swifter: he was flat on the ground before I could throw myself down beside him. A moment later the Hurricanes were spitting at us. They swooped and circled tightly to dive again, returning twice to the attack. One of them in particular showed decided ill-feeling towards my driver and my-self. I tried to worm myself into the sand.

When at last the aircraft broke off and flew away north towards the sea, I picked myself up, bleeding from scratches on my face. I noted rather irrelevantly that the sun was just sinking. Con-forming to routine, we took up positions by our vehicles. I counted over a dozen bullet holes in my car. The motor-cyclist dispatch-rider travelling just behind me had evidently not leapt from his machine in time: he lay next to the sprawling motor-cycle. He had a bad head wound and was obviously dying.

Rommel climbed out of the Mammoth. Before his driver had been able to pull down the armoured shutter, an enemy bullet had found the opening. It had passed through the driver's chest, narrowly missed Rommel's head, and splashed against the inner bulkhead.

A number of other vehicles had been hit. The wireless van was damaged so severely that it had to be abandoned. We buried the dead soldier beside the road without delay. Rommel's driver behaved with exemplary quiet courage. A blanket was wrapped round him, and he was placed on the leather seat at the back of the Mammoth. He gave no sign of pain.

Rommel took the wheel of the Mammoth himself and drove all night. Despite requests by Aldinger and Schräpler, he refused to be relieved. We did not reach the White House until morning.

CHAPTER NINE

PAULUS OF STALINGRAD—AND MY ERITREA STORY

OUR first 'big shot' visitor from Berlin dropped in—Lieutenant-General Paulus, acting chief of the O.K.H., the Army High Command, who was to surrender at Stalingrad in February 1943 in the greatest defeat the Wehrmacht ever sustained.

Rommel showed no signs of enthusiasm over Paulus's visit. I felt that he suspected that it might be the prologue to some intrigue in high quarters, possibly even to his own supersession. Paulus expressed a wish to see the Tobruk front at first hand, so I presumed we would make one of our usual trips the following day. But my assumption was false. Rommel stayed at headquarters.

'Schmidt,' he ordered. 'To-morrow you will accompany the General to the Tobruk front. You know the dispositions of the staff and will be able to give all necessary information.' He addressed me immediately after introducing me to Paulus. His words seemed meant not only for me but for Paulus.

We set off down the familiar dusty track the following morning with two cars. Paulus seated himself alongside me in the back of my own open car, remarking: 'Now we shall be able to talk more easily.' Unlike Rommel, he adopted a personal note at once, and I soon felt at ease.

'How long have you been in Africa?' Paulus asked.

I had to figure out the number of months, and meanwhile replied, 'Since January, Herr General.'

'Since January? But how, with the Afrika Korps not here . . .' He glanced at me questioningly.

'I was in Eritrea for a while before the Afrika Korps first landed,' I explained.

'Interesting. Please proceed.'

While the car whirled up clouds of dust on the Acroma by-pass, and as there was nothing of military importance to point out or describe to Paulus, I told him my story.

'As you know, Herr General, when war became certain in

August, 1939, all German ships received orders to make for the nearest neutral harbour. Nine German cargo vessels in the Mediterranean reached Massawa. They were mostly German Far East Line ships of between 6000 and 9000 tons. They ranged from the yacht-line *Coburg*, which was provided with all modern equipment, to the dirty little tramp called *Schwan des Ostens*, the "Swan of the East."

'In June 1940 Italy declared war, and Abyssinia and Eritrea became a theatre of war. Most of the sailors aboard the German ships in Massawa banded themselves together as a company of volunteers. They were armed and equipped by the Italians, and wore Italian uniforms, but with Swastika flashes on their helmets and armbands. The uniform was not exactly smart in appearance, but the high enthusiasm of the sailors made up for any shortcomings.

'A passenger reported himself as a Reserve Officer and a veteran of the First World War, and he was appointed company commander by the Italians. But the first time the company went into action, it was clear that he would not do. So a request was sent to Berlin for a suitable officer to take over command. I was detailed for the job, and flew from Rome to Eritrea. At that time the Italians flew regularly across Libya and the Sudan.

'Though my company was untrained and poorly equipped, it fought enthusiastically in Eritrea at Agordat and at Keren. But the Italian East African Empire was doomed, and the little we could do would not help. My company was withdrawn. It was in the Massawa area when instructions came through from Berlin that the company was to be disbanded immediately, the soldier-sailors were to report to their ships, while I personally was to hold myself in readiness to fly to North Africa and report to the German Expeditionary Force that had landed at Tripoli.

'I left the *Coburg*, in which I had made myself comfortable, and went back to Asmara, where the Italians had been instructed to place a machine at my disposal for the flight to North Africa. I made inquiries daily, but was repeatedly given the reply, "*Domani forse dopodomani*," "To-morrow, perhaps the day after to-morrow."

'The front at Keren was dangerously near, and it was obvious that the British would soon be in Asmara. One Sunday morning as I was leaving the Hotel C.I.A.A.O., I learned accidentally that

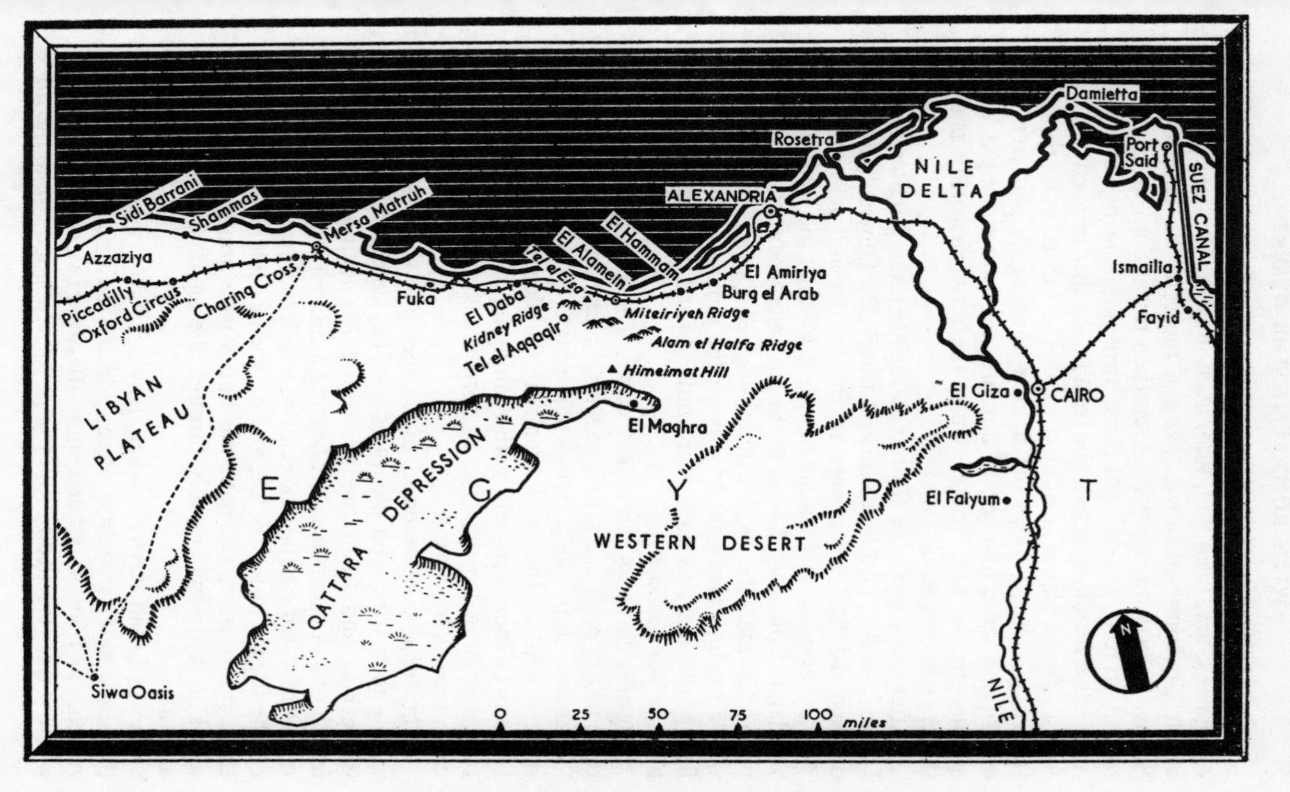

MAP 1: PORT SAID TO SIDI BARRANI

a plane which was to take off in half an hour was then at the aerodrome at Gura, twenty minutes away by car. Without bothering about kit, I jumped into a taxi and raced to the aerodrome. A Savoia 87 was on the field, even then revving up its engines. I rushed up to it, but as I got there, three pilots leapt out and past me to dive headlong into a slit-trench. At that moment I sighted South African planes heading towards us. I dived in on top of the Italians. In low swoops the fighters thoroughly plastered every one of the large number of aircraft—all long since put out of action—on the aerodrome. Ours, the only airworthy machine there, escaped untouched.

'After our stay in the slit-trench together, the Italian pilots and I were friendly. I explained my purpose. The fighters had scarcely disappeared before we were in the Savoia and had taken off. We flew down a deep valley eastward towards the Red Sea coast and landed on what I took to be an emergency air-strip on the plain. The machine was swiftly, though temporarily, camouflaged with a net and ready-cut bushes on the ground. Before dusk we flew out to sea and then over land, which I presume must have been Sa'udi Arabia.

'By now darkness had enveloped us. The three pilots were all in the cockpit, each one provided with a parachute and prepared to "abandon ship" at a moment's notice if necessary. I need scarcely say that their solitary ally in the plane had no parachute. I had the cabin to myself, with nothing for company but a small bag containing dispatches and a perpetually clanking chain on the cabin wall alongside me.

'The three pilots seemed to be spending their time drinking wine—good wine, and plenty of it. They emerged in turns from the cabin, and undoubtedly were doing themselves well. At length one of them came aft bearing a full bottle and offered it to me. I reflected on the ack-ack fire which had harassed my plane on the flight out to Eritrea, and on the possible condition of my three pilots later, accepted the bottle with gratitude, promptly drank it, and slept soundly through the night. I woke up alive after all.

'It was broad daylight when I awoke. We were flying over the sea and approaching land, which I assumed to be North Africa. The Savoia landed soon afterwards west of El Aghelia, where it was refuelled. I said thank you and good-bye to the three pilots, who then flew on to Rome, where they were received by Mussolini and congratulated on their daring escape from Eritrea. A small machine from a neighbouring landing-ground was made available for me, and I flew on to land at Tripoli that afternoon. I reported to General Rommel that my mission in East Africa was at an end.'

'Really,' said General Paulus. 'Very interesting indeed. And what happened to your seamen?'

'As far as I know, Herr General, one or two Italian submarines succeeded in rounding the Cape, and on them were some members of the German Volunteer Company and also the First Officer of the *Coburg*. I believe the other ships were all scuttled by their crews, mostly in Massawa harbour. The *Coburg*, so I heard in Tripoli from the English radio, was scuttled near Mauritius.'

Paulus asked further questions about the Abyssinian and Eritrean campaigns, while we left Acroma on our right and swung towards the Tobruk lines.

I indicated to General Paulus the most important positions, but purposely did not take him to visit them. Even at a distance the enemy's steady artillery fire was sufficient to convey a picture of what everyday life was like in our forward positions. I did not need to take Paulus in among the shell-bursts for him to see that this front was no picnic.

As we drove rapidly from sector to sector, Paulus displayed keen interest in the general situation and had lively discussions with the tactical commanders. He was particularly concerned about the positions in front of Pilastrino and Medawwa.

'How are the men of the 115th Rifle Regiment over there supplied with provisions and ammunition?' he asked when we had approached as close as we could with safety in broad daylight.

'Provisioning is possible only at night, Herr General,' I explained. 'Every night the kitchen personnel of the companies drive a truck filled with warm food, coffee, bread, and the like, as well as ammunition, into the line.'

'When is this done?'

'Usually not before midnight. The positions are so placed that the Australians are able to observe all movements by day and on moonlight nights.'

'That means that by day every man must remain in his shelter almost without movement?'

'Yes, Herr General. The unbearable part of the life is the aggression of millions of flies. They settle on the food in thousands, and are probably the cause of dysentery and other diseases among the men.'

'But isn't that due to the nature of the food?' asked Paulus. 'What do the troops generally eat?'

He had opened up the subject that is the commonest topic of conversation and a sore point among the men.

I did not gloss over the imperfections of the food, for I hoped that this influential general might be in a position to improve our common lot.

'Fruit and vegetables are unknown to the soldier. They miss their potatoes especially. The usual rations consist of sardines in oil, bulky tinned-meat sausages (*Bierwurst*), and "Alter Mann."'

The General looked at me questioningly. 'Alter Mann?'

I remembered that Paulus had been on African soil for two days only, otherwise he would have known, as Rommel did, that the small round Italian tins of tough beef were all marked A.M. I have heard it said that the German troops in North Africa took this to stand for 'Asinus Mussolini,' but I never heard that. I explained to Paulus about the inscription 'A.M.,' and said that the men declared this stood for 'Alter Mann,' or 'Old Man.'

He laughed, and was silent for some time. Just before we got back to headquarters he said: 'The troops around Tobruk are fighting in conditions that are inhuman and intolerable. I am going to recommend to Berlin that we withdraw to a strong position at Gazala, where our supply lines will be shorter. The troops will live under better conditions, and we shall be ensured greater reserves. . . . As I see it, every man here is on duty without a break. Reliefs and the freshening up of troops is not possible. We must do something to remedy this state of affairs.'

I could see that a case could be made out for Paulus's idea that we should hold a safe defensive line at Gazala. But I was certain that Rommel, the aggressive, would never agree to such a negative role in the Desert. And, in truth, we noticed no important changes during the weeks that followed Paulus's inspection. We did not fall back to Gazala, and we still ate 'Old Man.'

CHAPTER TEN

'BATTLEAXE' ON THE BORDER

AFTER our visit to Sollum Rommel's interest shifted from Tobruk to the frontier.

'Tobruk is a hard nut to crack, and it will require careful preparation,' he said. And he did not expect Wavell to allow him to prepare undisturbed. So he planned to consolidate all positions not only round the perimeter of the fortress, but on the frontier as well. The heat had increased considerably in the Desert as May wore on. A rumour was current among the troops that operations would be suspended during the hot summer months, and the wish was father to the thought. Indeed, most troops who had experience in armour thought that they were out of the question. But they did not know that Wavell felt aggressive.

British air reconnaissance now discovered the location of our Advanced Headquarters. We shifted from the White House area northward to the coast west of Tobruk. I was grateful to the R.A.F. reconnaissance planes, for conditions here were almost idyllic after the bleak White House area. And it was refreshing to return to the sea after our dusty Desert trips.

I drove frequently with Rommel to the frontier. We were building up a defensive line from the coast at the foot of Halfaya Pass inland to Sidi Omar. This was rapidly being strengthened with German 88-mm. guns and Italian artillery. The Panzer Reconnaissance Group was now lying between Fort Capuzzo and Sidi Omar as mobile reserve.

I enjoyed bathing whenever we came back from the frontier. Rommel, allowing himself to relax for the first time since I had met him, lived in a small truck, and Berndt and I shared a tent close to it. On the other side of us our neighbours were the war correspondents, von Esebeck, Ertl, and Borchert. They were often our guests at dinner, especially when I prepared a mixture of rice and condensed milk. Esebeck liked his rice fairly dry, and I always did my best as a host to please guests. The Desert was an all-male preserve, so the socially accepted dress at our headquarters by the sea was, by day, Adam's; evening dress consisted of bathing-trunks and a tunic.

2

'Schmidt, get up!' Berndt shouted at me through the open tent door early one morning. 'Get up quickly—a large ship, quite close out at sea, is being attacked by Messerschmitts.'

'Oh,' I said, thinking my leg was being pulled. 'I suppose we're busy sinking the *Ark Royal* again?'

'No, really, Schmidt, have a look through the opening. There's a ship probably trying to get through to Tobruk. Get up, man!'

I was on the point of advising Berndt to think of something better if he wished me to abandon my blankets, when I heard the firing of distant machine-guns.

'Listen! The Messerschmitts are pumping lead into the ship, but if you don't believe me, stay where you are.' Berndt's massive head disappeared from the tent opening.

I slipped on my bathing-trunks and in a few strides crossed the little sand dune that shut off the view of the Mediterranean. Yes indeed, there was the ship—not a large one as Berndt had said, but at any rate a ship with three sails and a motor. Three German fighters were diving down and peppering the ship for all they were worth. Light anti-aircraft guns on board were replying bravely. The ship was some miles out, but everything could be seen clearly.

A crowd quickly gathered on the beach. It included Rommel and several other officers of the staff. The war correspondents, von Esebeck and Ertl, also rushed on to the beach. Ertl was hugging his inevitable cine-camera.

The fighters apparently had no bombs to drop. They could scarcely be expected seriously to interfere with the progress of the ship. But no! Suddenly the unexpected happened. In seconds the ship was aflame, first amidships and then astern. We watched the crew scramble into their lifeboats. In a few minutes they were pulling away from the ship for all they were worth. They were not two hundred yards from the ship when it exploded. There was a lightning dart of flame, immediately followed by bright sheets of fire that spread out on all sides. Only then did the sound of the detonations reach us. A pillar of smoke had mushroomed high into the air. Next to me I watched Ertl, with the cine-camera viewfinder glued to his eye, panning upwards to follow the rising column of smoke. A few beams splashed back into the sea. When the thick smoke dispersed a few minutes later, there was nothing to see of the ship.

The lifeboat appeared again through the smoke. The crew were pulling hard for the shore. Several attempts to pull towards Tobruk were frustrated by the fighters zooming in the opposite direction, a foot or two above the heads of the rowers. For almost two hours the boat edged away from the shore and then towards before they landed at last, quite close to our tents, at the exact spot where a British raiding-party was later captured.[1]

The crew were exhausted. Two severely wounded men died shortly after landing. They were mostly Greek civilians, apart from the detachment who had manned the anti-aircraft gun aboard the doomed ship. She had been a small Greek freighter and had left Alexandria to run munitions into Tobruk. The captain had missed the harbour entrance during the night. At daybreak he had realized that he was a few miles too far east. Then the fighters came on the scene. One shot had been fired through the open cabin door and had struck a burning primus stove on which early morning tea was being prepared. In a matter of seconds the cabin was afire. The flames spread farther when a petrol container ignited. There was only one thing for the crew to do—abandon ship.

3

But we could not expect this idyllic spell in a war to last. Behind us the British Navy bombarded Benghazi in an effort to interrupt the build-up of the Afrika Korps. A day or two later Wavell struck back at Sollum. At the same time the Duke of Aosta was surrendering at Amba Alagi,[2] and the last important resistance in East Africa had ended; but within a couple of days

[1] See p. 69.

[2] A stronghold 11,000 feet up in Abyssinia. Here, on May 19, the Italian Viceroy—the Duke of Aosta—and the garrison surrendered 'with honour' to the 5th Indian Division (Major-General A. G. O. M. Mayne) and Brigadier Pienaar's 1st South African Brigade.

Germany was to invade Crete with airborne forces and to inflict a severe blow on Wavell.

'Battleaxe' was the code name for Wavell's attack, though we did not know this when the first reports came through from the Halfaya front telling us of 'a strong tank assault.' Most of the British tanks were Mark II's, which were specially armoured in front and had their tracks protected by flank skirts of armour-plate.

Infantry supporting the tanks made determined advances in the deep gullies of the escarpment at Halfaya Pass and along the coast into Sollum. Rommel was most anxious about our defences there, for they were still being built up. He flashed orders that elements of the 5th Panzer Regiment should advance as swiftly as they could along the Trigh Capuzzo, one of the best-defined Desert tracks south of the coastal road.

The situation was in doubt on the second day of the British attack. Wavell's spearheads were stabbing at Sollum. Rommel decided to visit this sector in person. Aldinger, Berndt, and I went with him. We could not use the coast road because the R.A.F. was so aggressive, and we were forced to take to the Trigh Capuzzo.

It was bonny fighting that we saw. Wavell's tanks broke into a number of infantry positions, despite the intensive fire of our 88-mm. guns, which they had scarcely expected to meet. The crews manning the 88's sat high up and unprotected at their sights. When one man fell, another of the crew took his place at once. The Italian gunners, impressed by the courage of the Germans, also began to develop a praiseworthy fighting spirit. But despite the heavy losses caused by the artillery, the British infantry with rare gallantry pressed forward across the Halfaya wadis.

After days of struggle, the battle ended in Rommel's favour. The battle was not reported as extensively as other Desert encounters; in fact, many veterans of the Libyan campaigns scarcely remember 'Battleaxe.' So much else was happening in the European and Mediterranean theatres at the time.

I accompanied Rommel on a personal inspection of the battlefield along the frontier from Halfaya to Sidi Omar. We counted 180 knocked-out British tanks, mostly Mark II's. Some of them were later recovered from the battlefield, repaired, marked with

ROMMEL DISCUSSING THE IMPENDING ATTACK ON TOBRUK WITH A GROUP OF YOUNG OFFICERS

The author stands on the left.

ROMMEL WITH MAJOR THE REVEREND BACH

Imperial War Museum

[*See p.* 77]

the German cross, and in due course sent into battle against the men who had manned them before.

Rommel's victory was largely due to his use of the 88-mm. guns, which were primarily designed for anti-aircraft work, as anti-tank weapons. They were effectively sited as the core of every defensive position.

A few of the enemy were captured. I overheard in passing a conversation between a staff interrogator and a young English tank driver.

'In my opinion,' said the Englishman, with an unfriendly glance at a near-by 88, 'it is unfair to use "flak" against our tanks.'

A German artilleryman who was sitting on his haunches near by, listening to the interpretation, interjected excitedly: '*Ja*, and I think it most unfair of you to attack with tanks whose armour nothing but an 88 will penetrate.'

I smiled at the exchange. But there it was. The 88-mm. flak gun had been proved incapable of stopping a Mark II with a frontal shot; and the Mark II had been proved completely vulnerable to a flank shot.

Everywhere that Rommel went now the troops beamed at him. He was already in the process of becoming a hero. He made short complimentary speeches to many groups of men, and did not omit to praise the Italians, who had indeed fought well. Berndt knew how to turn Rommel's success into excellent propaganda, and he did a good deal to further Rommel's popularity in the field. His exploits were publicized in Germany as well.

Soon afterwards an English Press report referring to Halfaya Pass as 'Hellfire Pass' fell into our hands. Berndt studied it with interest and passed it swiftly back to Goebbels in Berlin.

Already a legend was growing in the Desert—the legend of 'the Desert Fox,' cunning, ubiquitous, fast-moving.

4

Rommel concentrated his attention more and more on the frontier. Our observers on the highest points along the coastline from Bardia to the Tobruk perimeter kept an eye on seaborne traffic, and they reported the arrival of replacements and supplies at the besieged port. But there was no sign of troop reinforcements, and there appeared to be no reason to expect trouble in the way of a break-out from Tobruk. Rommel estimated that a fresh British offensive would not be possible for three months.

He recognized the Sollum front as the likely scene of any operations in the coming months, and so decided to move his main battle formations farther east towards the frontier. He chose Bardia as his own operational base. His new H.Q. and living-quarters was a slightly damaged house just below the village church—a building no doubt known to thousands of South African, Australian, and British troops.

Rommel at this time was G.O.C. of the Afrika Korps only, and though every soldier in the field accepted him as the real commander, in theory the supreme command of operations in North Africa was vested in the Italian, General Garibaldi.

Rommel invited him to visit the front when the Sollum defences had been satisfactorily strengthened. Garibaldi accepted the invitation and shortly afterwards turned up in Bardia. Here he presented to Rommel the Italian Silver Medal for Bravery. I was more than surprised when this distinguished Italian decoration was pinned on my chest also. Garibaldi treated us all with a fatherly goodwill.

Rommel rapidly put Garibaldi in the picture, and when he had explained the situation and troop dispositions, drove with him down to the Sollum front. Characteristically, Rommel intended to take the Italian general on a thorough inspection of our positions. But I noticed that throughout Rommel's explanations, which were translated to our Allies by Dr Hagemann, the Italian officers with Garibaldi showed ill-concealed impatience. We had only just reached Halfaya Pass when one of the Italians came forward and said to the General: 'Excellency, may I remind you that very pressing conferences demand our presence at Cyrene?'

'*Si, si,*' said Garibaldi, and he talked of the importance of his immediate return. This did not accord with the programme Rommel had planned, for he still had a good deal of the front to show to his nominal chief. But I caught a gleam of ironic amusement in Rommel's eye when Garibaldi took his leave with a kindly: 'Thank you for your wonderful achievements. All the measures you have taken are correct. I would have done exactly the same.'

The Italians drove off. Without our Allies, we called on Captain the Reverend Bach, the senior German officer in the Halfaya Pass defences. A clergyman who had become a fighting soldier, Bach, then a major, was to surrender the German forces at Halfaya to Major-General I. P. de Villiers, of the 2nd South African Division the following January.

Then we set off back to Bardia. Rommel's eyes twinkled, and he suddenly said with a mischievous smile: 'I wonder what it is that is so urgent at Cyrene?'

5

Ehlert had left Rommel's staff now and been succeeded by Major Wustefeld as I a. Putting him in the picture, Rommel gave a clear exposition of the aims he hoped to accomplish before the end of November.

First: to complete a line of strong-points from Halfaya Pass to Sidi Omar which were to be provisioned adequately to withstand without replenishment an enemy attack lasting three weeks or more.

Second: behind the screen of this defensive front, to launch a well-prepared attack on Tobruk and to reduce it.

'Yes, Wustefeld,' Rommel mused. 'That means another half year through which we shall have to maintain our supply lines to the positions at Tobruk, and round Tobruk to this line. . . .'

'Yes, Herr General, that I suppose is unavoidable,' Wustefeld remarked without enthusiasm, probably thinking, as I was, of the churned-up tracks through the dust skirting the Tobruk perimeter.

'Yet something could be done about that,' Rommel added. 'What would you say to a proper road—round Tobruk? Then we should not miss the coast road through the port, which those damned Australians now deny us.'

Rommel's plan was greeted with enthusiasm. It swiftly became concrete. Conferences were held with the Italian divisional commanders, and as a result troops were made available at short notice to begin building the loop road. German battalions were also detailed for the work, but they preferred front-line duty and, after appeals, were all allowed to replace other Italians who were at combat stations.

The road was speedily surveyed and marked. There was an

ample supply of stone in this rocky desert, and no especial shortage of sand. Soon 3000 Italians were working hard and enthusiastically at a task which seems to suit their talents admirably. Travelling along sections of the road that were partly completed, I ceased to be surprised to find large Chianti bottles and barbers' establishments.

The road was finished in three months. An Italian general performed an official opening ceremony and named it '*Achsenstrasse*'—Axis Road. It was a feature of life in the Desert for both sides, from then on until the end of 1943. I suppose it is still used in Cyrenaica to-day.

CHAPTER ELEVEN

THE GENERAL'S LETTERS

BARDIA is perched on the edge of a precipitous cliff overlooking the Mediterranean, with an almost land-locked bay—the resort of ancient pirates a thousand years ago—far below on its eastern hand. In peace-time I can imagine Bardia delectably restful. Rommel found it a good Advanced H.Q., for it provided comfort for strenuous work and was convenient for a commander who believed in close contact with his troops.

We had received some reinforcements. A third division was created out of a varied assortment of troops and named the 90th Light Division, but the formation was still without transport. The 5th Light Division was reconstructed as the 21st Panzer Division, now commanded by Major-General von Ravenstein in place of Streich. Major-General von Esebeck, a cousin of my war correspondent friend, took over command of the 15th Panzer Division, but was wounded a few days afterwards during a British air attack near Acroma.

Thus the main elements of the Afrika Korps as it was to win renown were now in being—the 15th and 21st Panzer and the 90th Light Divisions.

We were all much at home at Bardia and were not really disturbed, even when we learned one morning that a British raiding-party had made a landing below the cliffs at our bathing beach. Two of the raiders were captured, but the rest appeared to have escaped.

Some days later Rommel, accompanied by Berndt and I, was inspecting the ground near the Bardia trenches in our western coastal area when, with not a soul in view, we were suddenly subjected to well-aimed rifle fire from isolated snipers. Armed only with pistols, we took refuge behind a stone wall. For half an hour we could not raise our heads without the 'ping' of a bullet close by. When the sniping ceased, we hurried back to our cars. Half an hour later I returned with thirty soldiers to comb the whole area and search every trench. Everywhere we came across old blankets, hand-grenades, and other debris dating back to before the Italian defeat in December. But it was impossible to determine whether any of the hide-outs we searched had been occupied half an hour before. We gave up after two hours of fruitless searching, as it was clear that anybody who planned to hide in this maze of rocks could do so with little fear of discovery.

This was the second time that the enemy had tried to 'knock off' Rommel. The first had been made when our headquarters were on the coast west of Tobruk. The raiders were captured only a few hundred yards from Rommel's truck; this was fortunate, because we had been most remiss about establishing a headquarters guard. Rommel was as easy to get at then as a subaltern in an outpost—or easier. We did not realize it was the General they were after, but thought at the time the raiding-party were merely on a sabotaging foray.

Rommel was not perturbed by the Bardia raid. He laughed: 'I must be worth quite a lot to the Englishmen.'

2

Our supply position also improved gradually. For the first time in the Desert we were receiving fresh vegetables from the Jebel Akhdar region and from Tripoli. Then came a red-letter day when we dined on liver fried in butter. When the Messing Officer called out: 'Who among you gentlemen wants a second helping of liver?' we were greatly surprised at his liberality, and none refused. But at the next meal when he called out: 'Who among you gentlemen wants another helping of camel liver?' our faces dropped.

Rommel himself was modest in his appetite and uncomplaining about his food. He believed in living on the same rations as the men, and most of the time we had little but tinned sardines, a poor-quality tinned sausage, bread, and, of course, 'Alter Mann.' He permitted himself a glass of wine only when a special occasion called for a show of sociability. He never smoked. Indeed, he and his arch-opponent Montgomery were singularly alike in their Spartan attitude to life.

He went to bed early for preference, but he was always up

betimes and hard at work. He loved hunting and occasionally allowed himself the relaxation of a gazelle hunt in the Desert. Then, indeed, one saw the hunting instinct emerge sharply from beneath his unemotional exterior. Otherwise he had just one recreation—swatting flies. Daily during the lunch hour he dedicated himself to the task of systematically destroying as many of these pests as possible.

3

Berndt and I lived in a small building close to Rommel's quarters. It was right against the cliff and was reputed to have been a stable in days gone by.

I got to know Berndt very well in those days. I saw then that he was contributing more than most people realized to the steadily growing Rommel legend. He took every opportunity of arranging for photographs to be taken of the 'Desert Fox,' for publication at home and in neutral countries. Rommel himself, as war correspondents will testify, readily allowed himself to be photographed. I noticed that he often deliberately fell into a pose that would make the photographer's task easier and more effective.

Berndt and I were friendly, although we had frequent political differences. This burly man with his great bowed head often reminded me of a bear. His speech was calm and confident, but his imagination was less sober, and his reports about our experiences—or rather his own—were not always strictly true. Although he wore the uniform of an ordinary lieutenant, he liked to give the impression that he was still an influential figure in the Ministry of Propaganda. Was it, I wondered, merely a desire to hold the limelight, or was he really a big shot?

One day, at any rate, he confided to me that he had at one time been the organizer, in Czech uniform, of frontier incidents which were described officially as 'anti-German provocations.' You know the sequel. As a soldier at the time I had not heard of any deliberately staged incidents; and had I done so, I should have dismissed them as mere propaganda cooked up by Germany's enemies and hence unworthy of notice. Thus I was somewhat shocked by Berndt's boastful statements.

I remarked frankly that I thought such conduct not only dirty work but highly dangerous, in that if it had misfired the blame for genuine provocative behaviour by Czechs might well have been thrown on to his own provocateurs alone.

Berndt lost his usual calm and shouted at me in high dudgeon: 'Schmidt, you are typical of many unfortunate Germans whose ideas are based on an idiotic stupefaction caused by emotionalism.' He went on: 'We must adopt the Englishman's motto, "My country right or wrong."' I had not heard the saying, and thought that Berndt seemed to be misinterpreting it anyway. I angered him still more by saying that the methods he condoned were a deception not only of other countries but for that matter of the German nation and particularly of the troops.

Berndt looked at me pityingly and remarked: 'Yes, politics are not everybody's province.' For the sake of peace I agreed, 'Quite,' but where he was applying the statement to me, I was unspokenly applying it to him.

In spite of such disputes we lived as placid a life—almost the life of an all-male family—as war conditions would permit. But changes now took place which not only altered the routine but brought me much closer to Rommel.

Aldinger's constitution was not as robust as Rommel's. His health cracked up, and with a heavy heart he had to give up his post as Rommel's right-hand man, his confidant for many years, and leave North Africa for Europe.

His duties were handed over to me, and I moved into the room next to the General's.

Berndt also asked for 'duty leave' to return to Berlin and a six months' posting to the Ministry of Propaganda under Goebbels.

My responsibilities were now tremendously increased. Preparations for and details of the daily front-line tours were now among my personal tasks. Every wish and every order given by the General had to be accurately recorded in writing, and there were endless memoranda on exact times, names, localities, unit strengths, and so on.

I spent the evenings acting as a sort of private secretary. At this time, though Rommel was not yet at the height of his fame, thirty to forty letters a day reached him from all states and all social levels in Germany. Many came from hero-worshipping boys, but the majority were from girls and women. They all verged on adoration. Nearly all asked for a photograph. To answer this demand we kept a large carton of postcard portraits taken by Hoffman of Munich, Hitler's official photographer. Replenishments of stock were received regularly, and Rommel personally autographed every photograph I sent out.

I had also to reply personally to letters received from Rommel's slight acquaintances. This was not always easy, as I did not know the writers nor the degree of their acquaintanceship. But we had little time to spare, and I soon evolved a number of more or less stereotyped replies which went off from the General's office as a matter of routine. Other replies I dictated to a stenographer-clerk, Corporal Böttcher.

I would hand Böttcher a handful of letters and say: 'Eighteen boys and girls wanting photos—please get them ready with the usual covering replies.'

Then I would fish out a couple of other letters. 'Here are two from First World War comrades. Please write: "Dear Mertens, My best thanks for your letter of . . .'" and I would go on in as close an imitation of Rommel's manner as I could manage. But Rommel always scrutinized these letters and would not sign them if they did not ring true.

I was always amused when he signed letters to see the tip of the General's tongue protruding and comically following in the air the outline of the unusually florid flourish of his pen when he completed the bold 'R' in his signature.

Sometimes I would find a familiar hand among the letters and say, 'Ah! Another from *Die alte Schachtel*—the Old Hag—of Leipzig.' This correspondent, apparently a woman of ripe age, always signed herself 'The Old Hag.' Her first letter had begun '*Sehr geehrter Herr General*—Most Honoured General . . .' But by her fifth letter she was opening gaily: 'Dear Rommel, and Rommel's men . . .' She used to write straight from the heart, and had neither inhibitions nor respect for persons in high places. For instance: 'Hans Fritsche is again busy over the radio—I can't bear his twaddle and ironic sarcasm.' But her letters always carried a great deal of cheerful news and, although addressed primarily to Rommel, gave much pleasure to all of us. We agreed that, even if queer, she certainly had spirit, the Old Hag.

One day a large parcel of books arrived from her. Rommel asked me to take them to the troops at Halfaya. I examined the books first and was amused to note that they consisted entirely of 'trashy literature' of the type that those who managed the Third Reich had condemned as fit only for the bonfire or the Decadent Democracies.

I would find that the next letter began, 'We are so proud of you, my famous brother,' and hand it unread to Rommel, assuming that it came from his own sister.

I found especially interesting the letters that were received from Rommel's Swabian[1] countrymen. They clearly revealed the characteristic qualities of loyalty, obedience, and courage that make these people such excellent soldiers. But the Swabians have, in my opinion, one weakness: they are often too vehement in their provincial pride. Thus I would read a letter running: 'We have read with joy of your successes. It is really grand that a Swabian leads the Afrika Korps, and we have heard that a large proportion of your troops are Swabians. Yes, there is no doubt that after all the Swabians are the best soldiers. . . .' I would try to reply as tactfully as possible to such Swabian enthusiasts, and gently state that all German states were represented in the Afrika Korps, 'even the *Saupreussen*, the Prussian Sows.' Rommel hesitated a little over that one before, with a smile, he signed it.

Every evening the Senior Staff Officer gave, in Rommel's office, a summary of the day's events in Russia. A large situation map hung on the wall. Rommel was especially interested in the progress of the 7th Panzer Division, the 'Ghost Division,' his former command, which to his pride was then figuring prominently among the spearheads in the thrust towards Moscow.

He also displayed, quite naturally, the greatest interest in the seizure of Crete by Axis parachute troops at the time it happened, for the Luftwaffe was thus provided with a most favourable base for operations against the enemy in the Desert and the Middle East as a whole. But he felt that the occupation of Malta would have been of far greater value, as this little island was, throughout the North African campaign, a constant menace to our vital shipping. Would Britain ever have won the war in North Africa if Malta had been attacked and taken in 1941? I think not.

[1] Swabia, an area in south-west Germany, on both sides of the Black Forest, and between the Neckar and Lake Constance.

CHAPTER TWELVE

FRONT-LINE DAY

ROMMEL was building up the Sollum front feverishly. Let me give you a picture of what that meant in our everyday lives.

Punctually at 7 A.M. we leave on one of our customary front-line visits. As distances are short, the Mammoth is left at home. In two open cars our party sweeps through the only entrance to Afrika Korps Headquarters, the boom across the road drops behind us again, the sentry salutes. Since Aldinger's going, I travel with Rommel. He sits in front with the driver, I sit behind with Dr Hagemann, the interpreter.

We drive past Capuzzo and through a gap in the wire entanglement on the frontier, and rapidly head out into the Desert far beyond our front-line positions. On the horizon in no-man's-land we often spot enemy patrol cars. They cannot guess how fat a prize is moving within eye-shot of their binoculars.

Rommel studies our own positions from vantage points on the enemy's side. He examines them through his field-glasses with the painstaking care of a scientist using a microscope. He snorts: he has seen something that displeases him. We leap into the car after him. He stands up as we head straight for the strong-point he has surveyed.

The sentry on duty stares at Rommel wide-eyed. 'Why don't you salute?' the General barks. The soldier jumps to attention, petrified, speechless.

'Where is the outpost commander?' Rommel demands angrily.

'He is asleep, Herr . . . er . . . Major!' the sentry stutters.

He is a recruit, new to the front, and has not seen Rommel before. The insignia of rank are confusing. He thinks anybody so authoritative must be of field rank: he takes a gamble on 'Major.'

'*Ja, Herr Soldat,*' snaps Rommel. 'It seems as if everybody is asleep here. Please wake this—gentleman.'

The sentry need not move. The flushed face of a young officer appears at the entrance of a dug-out near by. When he sees the General he comes smartly to attention, salutes and reports: 'Outpost Franke—nothing special to report.'

'How do you know, Herr Leutnant?' Rommel raps out at him. 'You have been sleeping—and beautifully, too.'

The lieutenant has nothing to say. There is a grim pause. Rommel says: 'Herr Leutnant, your post is not being run in accordance with my instructions. Your shelter is too prominent. The post is not camouflaged. Your men are running about—while you sleep! I shall return to-morrow and satisfy myself that my requirements are satisfied in every particular. Good morning, Herr Leutnant.'

He signs to the driver to start. The young officer stands rooted to the spot. Rommel has gone before he can ejaculate the customary '*Jawohl, Herr General.*' If ever he thought he would find the North African Desert romantic, he has received a rude shock now.

Our cars have been recognized before we reach the next outpost. which is named 'Cowa.' The strong-point is alert. The lieutenant in command is on the *qui vive*. Rommel's manner changes completely. But nevertheless he delivers a little homily.

'A well-selected position, and good dispositions,' he comments. 'This is of the utmost importance. We cannot take chances. The problem of our supply lines over the Mediterranean make it difficult for us to provide equipment and rations for more troops than we already have in Africa. For this reason we must take the fullest advantage of natural features and whatever else we have at our disposal. One good strong-point must serve as well as two indifferently planned and manned. . . .'

'*Jawohl, Herr General.*'

'How are you off for ammunition and supplies?'

'We have plenty of ammunition, Herr General, and food for three days.'

'For three days, my friend? You require provisions for three weeks. But . . . never mind, we will see to that.'

With a short 'Thank you!' Rommel is on his way again.

At every outpost the General leaves his car. Although nearly twice my age, he shows no sign of fatigue; my legs are sore and heavy as lead, for it is heavy going in the sand. I make endless notes and write down every request, every order, every observation. When we get back it is my duty to bring everything relevant to the notice of the Chief of Staff or the Chief Staff Officer.

We visit one of our wireless listening-posts. Two of them are on the Sollum front, a measured distance apart. They tune in on the enemy's wavelengths, take bearings on direction-finding aerials, and, by triangulation, pinpoint the location of the enemy's fixed and mobile transmitting stations.

The listener at one post reports that intercepts now indicate that the enemy is shifting his wireless stations northward towards the sea. 'No wonder,' grins Rommel, 'in this weather. Do you imagine that the English do not like sea-bathing?'

We often visited Halfaya. This day we came to it after a lengthy tour of outposts. Captain Bach, limping with a walking-stick, came up to meet us. No other officer but Bach was allowed the privilege of a walking-stick, but he was no longer young. A pastor in civil life, he was beloved by his men because of his considerate treatment of them. In spite of his unsoldierly profession in peace-time, he ran his sector more efficiently than many professional officers ran theirs. Rommel had the highest regard for him.

Halfaya had been the scene of action before. Rommel recognized its obvious strategical importance, for it commanded the coast road from Egypt into Cyrenaica. Denied the road past Sollum and Halfaya, the enemy would be forced far south into the Desert if he aimed at an attack inside Cyrenaica. So Rommel was strengthening this sector as fast as he could, and had just sent to it the elements of the 90th Light that were still immobile through lack of transport.

Bach had just called the company commanders together for a conference. Rommel took the opportunity of giving a little talk on tactics.

'Gentlemen,' he said, 'the struggle in the Desert is best compared with a battle at sea. Whoever has the weapons with the greatest range has the longest arm, exactly as at sea. Whoever has the greater mobility, through efficient motorization and efficient lines of supply, can by swift action compel his opponent to act according to his wishes.

'Your troops here at Halfaya Pass are immobile. They are of value against motorized troops only when they are in strong and well-prepared positions. But here again the "longest arm" has the advantage. We have it—in the 88-mm. gun. It is essential for you, as immobile troops, to have the best-prepared cover, the best camouflage possible, and the best field of fire for the 88's and other pieces.'

Rommel paused and then went on, speaking with characteristic forcefulness: 'It is my intention to occupy a long defensive line stretching from the sea to Sidi Omar. The outpost positions, up to company strength, must perforce be fairly far apart; but the whole line must be planned in adequate depth towards the rear.

'Every defended point must be a complete defensive system in itself. Every weapon must be sited so that it is able to fire in every direction. I visualize the ideal arrangement of such defensive points on these lines:

'One 88-mm. "flak" gun should be sunk into the ground as deeply as the field of fire permits. From here trenches should radiate in three directions to three points—one a machine-gun position, the second a heavy mortar position, and the third a light 22-mm. anti-aircraft gun, or to a 50-mm. "pak" (anti-tank) gun. Sufficient water, ammunition, and supplies for three weeks must always be available. And every man is to sleep prepared for action.'

Rommel warmed to his subject.

'Gentlemen, a few words in regard to battle tactics. In case of an enemy attack, the fire of our arms must completely cover the gap between the defended points. Should the enemy succeed in breaking through the gaps, owing say to bad visibility, every weapon must be in position to engage towards the rear. Let it be clear that there is no such thing as a "Direction, Front," but only a "Direction, Enemy."'

He added another pronouncement: 'The final decision of any struggle if the enemy attacks will probably rest with the Panzer and motorized units behind the line. Where this decision is reached is immaterial. A battle is won when the enemy is destroyed. Remember one thing—every individual position must hold, regardless of what the general situation appears to be. Our Panzers and motorized formations will not leave you in the lurch, even if you should not see them for weeks. . . . I thank you, gentlemen.'

The officers were dismissed. Bach accompanied us as we moved on to visit an Italian battery. Here, too, Rommel's concern was with ammunition supplies. Dr Hagemann translated the conversations with the Italians; but I noted that Rommel was swift to spot if the translation did not convey precisely the shade of meaning he intended. He knew more Italian than he cared to allow the Italians to perceive.

I remember that we were shelled from the east that day as we drove down 'Hellfire Pass' towards the coastal plain. The General reckoned that the fire came from self-propelled field-guns which the enemy had temporarily sent forward.

On the flat coastal plain Rommel noticed that at some defended points captured British Mark II tanks had been sunk deep in the ground with only their turrets above the surface. This intelligent employment of enemy material pleased him greatly, and we went on in high good humour.

When we reached the shore, I suggested a dip. We had no bathing-trunks, but who was to worry about that in the Desert front-line? Rommel and I plunged into the cool Mediterranean. It had the lively sparkle of a blue champagne. Rommel splashed about with the gaiety of a schoolboy.

The road now led us up the Serpentine Pass towards Sollum Barracks on the escarpment lip. Halfway up we saw sappers blasting a tunnel-like hole into the steep slopes to house an Italian coastal-defence gun. We stopped to examine the work. As usual, Rommel swung round, his glasses probing the hazy east where the enemy lay.

And so, late in the afternoon, back through the boom and into Bardia. No meal all day, but a mass of office work waiting for me. And, for Rommel, the multitudinous tasks that accumulate on paper round even a fighting general.

This, then, was a sample day in my life with Rommel.

CHAPTER THIRTEEN

THE PANZER GROUP IS BORN

In mid-1941 changes were made in the Italian High Command in Africa. General Bastico replaced the genial General Garibaldi.

A coded wireless message reached Bardia instructing Rommel to report immediately to Bastico at Cyrene. We arrived at Cyrene the following day, tired out and dusty from the long journey, which of course included by-passing Tobruk. We who were accustomed to the battered little house at Bardia felt as though we were entering some sumptuous imperial palace when, after passing through a gracious park, we were admitted to a large marble-pillared building.

It was good to be in the green Jebel Akhdar; for the first time in months our eyes beheld not sun, sand, and flies, but green fields, fleecy clouds, wooded hills, and even lovely women. But Rommel and I, dusty and sweating, our vehicles riddled with bullet holes and covered with the accumulated dirt of months in the Desert, did not feel at home in these marble halls and cultivated surroundings. I sensed that the Italian General Staff also felt that we were misfits.

Rommel at once reported his arrival for the interview with Bastico. The new Italian Commander did not find time to receive him until half an hour had passed. When Rommel left Bastico's office after a short talk, he was in an ill-humour. We always referred to Bastico thereafter as 'Bombastico.'

Actually, Rommel now achieved a higher command and more authority. A new headquarters group of German officers had arrived at Cyrene. Rommel's early inquiries yielded the information that this staff was earmarked for a Panzer Group which was 'to be placed at the disposal of' the D.A.K., the Deutsche Afrika Korps. Rommel, I saw, speculated on the precise intention behind this move. Was the new staff to serve as a direct link with the German High Command; or was it intended that a senior German general would include the Afrika Korps in his overall command?

The situation was cleared up during the Cyrene visit. While I waited for my chief I met several officers of the new Staff. One was a lanky orderly officer, a Lieutenant Dickmann, who greeted me with a superior and almost condescending friendliness that made me feel all the more that in this rarefied atmosphere we roughnecks from the front were looked on as oafish though well-intentioned creatures. But after seeing Bastico, Rommel ran into General Gause, chief of the newly arrived Staff. Gause, pleasantly respectful, obviously a man of balance and strength, made it quite clear that the new Staff was to be attached to Rommel.

Thus it emerged that there was to be a Panzer Gruppe Afrika, with effect from August 1941, commanded by Rommel. It was to include for practical reasons the two Italian Corps outside Tobruk as well as the German Afrika Korps, which would now be commanded by General Cruwell under Rommel's direction.

Despite the creation of the new Higher Command, there had been little reinforcement of our strength in the Desert. It was clear indeed that effective reinforcements could not be expected for some time. Rommel himself had insisted that his supply lines in the Desert be strengthened sufficiently to maintain adequate services to the existing three German divisions before further German combat troops were transported to Africa.

During the hot summer months the Sollum front was built up as Rommel ordered. Heavy defence guns were sited and more minefields laid. When these preparations were complete he concentrated on the Tobruk front. Systematically he prepared for an attack in late November. He ordered troops in some sectors to occupy more advanced positions. New battle outposts ahead of the existing line were constructed by night, despite the aggressive raiding of Australian patrols, and these posts were to be occupied when completed.

This time Rommel intended to forget the Medawwa sector, and to launch his attack through the El Duda sector in the south-east—the sector for which I had always had a fancy.

Our lack of information about the nature of the defences in April and May had now been overcome by the diligent preparation of air photographs. Every picture was minutely studied. Every regiment, every battalion, and even every company that was to take part in the attack was provided with detailed photographs of the area which it faced.

The main weight of the attack was to be borne by the two Panzer divisions. They were both withdrawn from the front for rest and special training. The 21st was quartered between Bardia and Tobruk. The 115th Rifle Regiment of the 15th Panzer had occupied the trenches south-west of Tobruk ever since their arrival months before. (I had pointed out their positions to General Paulus.) They were withdrawn from this uneasy sector for recuperation and specialized training near the sea, east of Tobruk. The physical reaction among the men was immediate and patent. About 70 per cent. of the unit went down at once with diseases such as dysentery and jaundice. The fighting strength of the unit, which had always been about normal in the Tobruk line, was at once reduced so gravely that companies were only of platoon effectiveness.

In order to disperse the enemy's artillery fire, Rommel gave orders for the creation of dummy positions in unoccupied areas. He directed that within fourteen days hundreds of fake observation posts made of wood and sacking were to be erected all around the perimeter. He trusted that these would cause the besieged garrison to waste hundreds of rounds of precious ammunition without doing any damage to our troops. After the enemy had duly expended his shells without result, a number of the dummy posts were actually used as O.P.'s.

I appreciated the soundness of the scheme when Rommel planned it, but when he was out of earshot I used to find harassed officers saying: 'Heavens, Schmidt, what are you people thinking up? You tell us to build twelve towers in our sector alone. Where do you expect us to find the wood and the sackcloth in this Desert?'

Rommel at all times—and never more so than now—demanded initiative and energy from his troops. 'Sustained positional warfare,' he growled, 'must not cause them to get rooted to their seats.'

To make available for the attack as many fresh German troops as possible, the defensive lines were taken over wherever feasible by Italians. Rommel's order was: 'A few German companies only are to be focussed at certain points of the front in order to act as "corset stays" to the rest of the line.' I do not know how the Italians liked that.

Not that Rommel was tactless with them or overbearing. We drove along the Axis Road one day when it was nearing completion, and he was genuinely pleased with the accomplishment of the Italian road-builders. As protection against enemy air attack, the Mammoth accompanied our usual two open cars. The party included the Italian General Calvi's Staff Officer, Major Tuzzi, a Lieutenant Turini, and Dr Franz, who had replaced Dr Hagemann as our interpreter. Rommel called on a fat Italian major who was commanding one of the road-construction battalions.

'Tell him, Dr Franz, that I am extremely pleased with the excellent work that has been accomplished.'

The rotund major's face beamed with pleasure at the compliment. He was a gay and vivacious fellow, and kept us smiling. Rommel asked him whether there were any complaints. The major replied excitedly: '*Si, si, Signor Generale*, the food is very monotonous and the *vino* is not good.'

Rommel looked with a mischievous smile at the fat little figure and murmured gently: 'And yet it does not seem to be doing you any harm!'

2

When Cruwell was appointed to take over the Afrika Korps and Rommel the Panzer Gruppe Afrika, the latter left his staff to the new commander at Bardia—all but myself, his batman, Gunther, and the clerk Böttcher. We moved back into the Jebel Akhdar and for the briefest of spells lived in the lovely green surroundings of Beda-Littoria.

CHAPTER FOURTEEN

HOW ROMMEL IMPRESSED HITLER

Do you remember green Beda-Littoria in the Green Mountains? I do, with brief affection. But Rommel, although a little cottage was prepared for him there, in all possible contrasting comfort to the Desert, did not like it. He was wrenched away from the front-line troops whom he loved even when he bullied them.

And now, with the Panzer Group under his hand, he was in a sense mastered by his subordinates. For the first time he had two first-rate staff officers as his immediate assistants, and they swiftly proved of the greatest value to him. They were Major-General Gause, the Chief of Staff, a placid, sturdily-built man of reflective and thorough habits, whom I mentioned a little earlier, and Lieutenant-Colonel Westphal, the General Staff Officer, wide-awake, competent, and a strict disciplinarian. I presume that in British military terminology they would correspond to the Major-General, General Staff and the G.S.O.1 Operations, and that our Panzer Gruppe (an elastic term) would be slightly weaker in infantry but perhaps stronger in armour than the equivalent of a British 'Army.' Certainly the Panzer Gruppe Afrika did not correspond to an Army Group.

The new Staff subtly persuaded Rommel that his value lay now not so much in personal contact with his front-line troops as in his diplomatic and supervisory activities. As a soldier with a predilection for the front-line—I was young then, you will remember—I regretted this obvious development, for I became steadily more certain that we should see less of the vigour of the day when the lid blew off the Desert, as blow off it must—because we were certainly 'cooking,' and nobody who knew this enemy we faced in the Desert could conceive that he had cooled off.

Gause and Westphal with tact convinced the Chief that the new relationship with the Italians—after all, he now commanded their principal fighting elements in the field besides his own Germans—demanded that he allow himself to be 'represented,' that he concentrate more on staff work, which in the end would be all-important, and on preserving sweet relations with our Allies.

Rommel and Gause became fairly friendly, but Rommel never became really intimate with anyone. I remember many an interesting conversation, to which I was privy, during our boring drives between our own H.Q. and the Italians.

One day Gause asked, 'Herr General, how did you first gain contact with Hitler?'

I pricked up my ears. Rommel sank back into his seat in one of his rare reminiscent moods.

'I was actually attached to the Führer's Headquarters when Hitler first noticed me, though I had been on the Staff for a considerable time—just an unimportant lieutenant-colonel,' he said. 'Really I was small fry—something corresponding to a camp commandant of a headquarters camp out here in Africa. That meant I was responsible for transport, security measures, and other dull organizing jobs.

'Then on one of those worrying occasions—a "Party Day"—I received an order from Hitler that he wished to leave his headquarters on the following day accompanied by not more than six vehicles, and that I was on no account to permit any vehicles in excess of this number to accompany him. Next morning when the Führer was about to leave I saw that the square in front of headquarters was full of vehicles all carrying ministers, generals, gauleiters, and other "high animals." But I was prepared for a show like that.

'When the column moved off I allowed the five vehicles following Hitler to pass, and then stepped in front of the next. It stopped of course, and I delivered Hitler's orders. The occupant—a Minister or something—bawled at me and bellowed about the "presumption" of a mere lieutenant-colonel attempting to hamper the discharge of the duties of an important executive on whom rested the responsibility for the efficient execution of tasks in the Führer's entourage. Pompous, by God!

'Before I allowed him to proceed, I explained calmly: "I cannot stop you from going on, but at each of the next three cross-streets you will be held up by two Panzers." The man became livid with fury. "Confounded insolence!" he roared at me. "I shall make a point of reporting this matter to the Führer, Herr Oberstleutnant!"

'I had placed two Panzers, one right and one left, in each of the three narrow intersecting streets ahead. My orders were to allow the six leading vehicles of Hitler's column to pass and then to drive up face to face across the street, thus blocking it to any vehicles following.

'Hitler heard of this—no doubt from the infuriated dignitaries who, time and time again on the route until they tired of it, found the Panzers checking them. But instead of reprimanding me he called for me that evening to express his appreciation. He had not expected to have his order strictly carried out and to be free to move without the "impedimenta" as he wished. After this personal meeting I was more frequently invited to join his parties, and he used to speak to me about my book on the First World War, *Infantry in Attack*, which he had read· closely. After that, he seemed to think I was a bright fellow.

'Then when war broke out Hitler asked me what command I desired, and without hesitation I begged him to give me command of a Panzer division. That was an immoderate request on my part: I did not belong to the armoured branch of the service, and there were many generals who had a much stronger claim to a command of this nature. But still, as you know, I got the command of the 7th Panzer Division. The appointment, as you possibly also know, did not suit the gentlemen at the O.H.K.'

Gause had listened intently to the story. He made polite remarks—'That's interesting, Herr General'—and went on to ask: 'But weren't you at one time a sort of liaison officer to the Hitler Youth?'

'Yes, that is so, to some extent,' Rommel answered. He talked, though without particularly quotable detail, about his work a the Potsdam Military Academy on the pre-military training of the Hitler Youth Movement. But I gathered that his ideas on the training of the German Youth had not coincided with those of Baldur von Schirach, whose province this was. He had found Schirach overbearing and tactless, and had indeed called him flatly, '*Dumme Junge*—Stupid Boy.'

Rommel lay back in his seat in the car and remarked rather wistfully: 'I think the happiest period in my life—and for my wife as well—was when I was commandant of the Military Academy at Wiener-Neustadt.[1] And now? What is one doing? It is good

[1] A town some 40 miles south of Vienna.

to have command. There is a great chance here. After all, we of the profession are trained for war. . . . What are we to do? It is simple. We must beat the English. They are opponents fit for our own steel. They pretend they are not trained for war, and indeed one sees it is true. But they are good men at the art of war, or the game of war. Our task is clear. Every man in the Desert must realize this simple fact. We are here to win. There must be no doubt as to our purpose. The task to which we, as men, are committed is battle in the Desert.'

Gause talked to Rommel of his own military career. I was most interested to hear him tell of his work as one of the staff officers entrusted with planning 'Operation Sea-lion'—the invasion of England in 1940. Gause said that he personally had discounted the projected operation as unlikely to succeed.

'In the first place,' he said to both Rommel and myself, 'the tonnage of shipping available was far from adequate. Then, after the air battles over England, it became obvious that in spite of Goering's optimism, air protection could not be relied on. And the German Navy gave full support to the project, but insisted that there was no doubt that the powerful British Navy would be thrown into the struggle to the last sailor, and that this unequal struggle could result only in the complete destruction of the German Navy. There you are!'

I remember that at the end of this day when we reached Beda-Littoria we still had a conference to attend with the Chief of the General Staff of the Italian Army, General Cavallero. After that there was the first dinner ever attended by Rommel at which representatives of both Axis Powers formally sat down. As an insignificant lieutenant I took small part in the conversation; but I remember being impressed by the idea that I was most privileged to spend the evening in the company of such distinguished men, and partake of such unaccustomed fare. The food was, of course, good.

CHAPTER FIFTEEN

ROMMEL KILLS A GAZELLE

ROMMEL was a hunter. Now that he had more leisure, he found more opportunities for indulging in his favourite sport. He would, I know, rather have been forward with the troops planning the hunting of bigger game; but he had to be, at least within limits during this static period, a 'good boy,' and gazelles on a day off were his quarry.

'I am looking forward to a spell of leave in Europe and a chance to do some hunting with Manfred,' he used to say to me. (He was most attached to his son, then aged twelve.) He seldom mentioned his family or his private life, and, indeed, was almost reticent about intimate affairs of any sort. It was months before he called me anything but the formal Leutnant, and only after he had decided that I was more than a necessary additional limb did he address me by name, bother to find out my age, whether I was married, whether I was happy, or, indeed, even to think of me other than as something that filled a uniform and answered a command. It was, in fact, almost strange, after a long acquaintance, to find the impersonal General actually human.

The country south of Gazala, where we set up Panzer Group Headquarters after Rommel had swiftly decided that Beda-Littoria was much too far back, was fairly wild. As its name implies, it was noted for its gazelles.

I remember a day when we drove far into the Desert with two cars, seeking relaxation.

Rommel had a service rifle and a sort of light Tommy-gun which an Italian unit had presented to him. But though his weapons were not remarkable, the chase which we undertook was organized like a military operation, and both strategical and tactical plans were made to intercept escaping game in the rear.

In the back seat of my car was an Italian captain, who acted as a kind of master-of-the-chase because he had known this territory for years. He led us without hesitation to gazelle country. We put up a herd of them. Both cars tore after the buck. But the frightened animals just fled the faster. Our drivers stepped on their accelerators, and slowly we overhauled the gazelle.

Rommel's car skidded to a stop in the coarse sand and stone. He shot standing. He missed: we saw the spurt of the shot in the sand, despite the dust of the gazelle's hooves. And on went the quarry. On went Rommel.

My own car meanwhile had not halted. We were close on the heels of the animals and tried to head them off. But within seconds the General's car was close behind us. On a rise I shouted to my driver 'Stop!' He did so abruptly—so abruptly I was almost thrown over the windscreen. Through the dust I took a quick shot at one of the gazelle. Rommel's car charged past in swift pursuit.

So the hunt went on for some time. I could not help feeling sorry for our quarry. They employed tactics that were extremely effective. After every shot the herd split in two. One group swung left, the other right. Always we followed the larger group. And eventually the larger group consisted of only three animals. 'You may destroy us in detail,' they seemed to say, 'but, brother, only *this* detail. You have been misled by a succession of demonstrations into forgetting your main intention. . . .'

But had the hunters really been deprived of their quarry? On this field of battle the plan was not to destroy all, but, alas, merely to assert one's tactical superiority. Indeed, the herd won strategically; but tactically there must always be a loser in this fight.

I was amazed at the endurance of the three gazelle who still drew us onward. They swerved sharply to the right and gained some ground. You would have thought that they had planned the manœuvre deliberately and with a map, for the ground on the right grew rockier as it extended.

'Draw the enemy's tanks into ground of your own choosing and destroy them there!' Rommel growled, I'll bet—it was an axiom of his.

The ground was pitted with fox-holes. It grew ever more rugged. The mad tempo of the chase became a danger to life and limb. What if Germany's top general in Africa broke his neck in a senseless pursuit of a buck? The hunting spirit had possessed Rommel. The wild chase went on.

At any rate, I think, it is now at least fair sport. We are at least risking our lives equally with the hunted game.

The cars rip to a halt for another shot. I am almost bowled over by a thunderous report and a hot, stinging pain in the right ear. What would you? An Italian officer behind me in my car has taken a pot-shot and in his excitement has failed to note that the muzzle of his short infantry rifle is one inch ahead of my right ear. But it seems one can still hunt even though deafened.

The chase went on. It looked as though the game would escape. The ground got rougher and rougher. But Rommel grew more and more determined, and kept urging his driver to step on the gas. I did likewise. In this suicidal manner we again caught up with the gazelle. Rommel thrust his rifle into the hands of Major von Mellenthin, the Intelligence Officer, in the back seat. He whipped out his automatic and fired a shot. One gazelle dropped.

We stopped. Before us lay a sleek and beautiful animal. Somehow most of us felt depressed to see the life gone from that vivid and bounding thing. Nobody spoke. I had never hunted in my life before, and did not know what one did now. But Rommel did not hesitate. He flashed out a large hunting-knife and finished the job. He eviscerated the animal expertly, sawed off the horns, and had the carcass loaded.

When we got back to headquarters the cook was pleased.

Well, there it was. On the credit side, a handsome hunk of venison. On the debit side, two broken springs, a shattered windscreen, a deafened ear, and one uneasy conscience. Whenever we hunted again, we used a more sporting technique, and stalked the game.

And yet . . . After all, we were at war. Rommel was the master hunter. He was in the business to kill or be killed. For that matter, so was I. Was I to be squeamish behind the sights of an anti-tank gun?

CHAPTER SIXTEEN

ROMMEL ON A RAID: STRANDED IN NO-MAN'S-LAND

ROMMEL was not satisfied with the location of his Panzer Gruppe Advanced H.Q. at Gazala. It was too far from his soldiers, and a visit to the front which had required only a few hours when we were at Bardia now took an entire day. It was almost as bad as being away at Beda-Littoria. The road engineer's house which we used as headquarters—the 'roadhouse,' we called it—had also been attacked several times recently by British aircraft which came over in the early hours of the morning; we suspected that the British had located the 'Desert Fox's' earth.

An officer was detailed to explore the area between Tobruk and Bardia for a new H.Q. He chose the 'roadhouse' at Gambut.

We drove forward to examine the new H.Q. site, and also to visit Major-General von Ravenstein, the commander of the 21st Panzer Division. We were able to by-pass Tobruk in half the time it had taken before, because the Axis Road was now complete.

Von Ravenstein had moved his headquarters to an area west of Bardia, almost on the beach. He loved beauty, and his Mammoth was parked in a picturesque spot among a grove of palm-trees which despite the Africa Korps insignia were almost as rare as women in this region. It was evening when we arrived. Von Ravenstein and his officers were just about to sit down to their meal in the large, well-equipped marquee that served as their mess. They received us hospitably.

I noted a little enviously that no other staff mess in North Africa was equipped and run as modestly as Rommel's H.Q. Here there were delicacies, including fresh eggs and cold beer, of which we never dreamed. It seemed such a long time since I had eaten a fresh egg that I polished off mine with concentrated enjoyment. As I finished I noticed von Ravenstein twinkling at me. 'Hmm! Tastes good, eh, Schmidt?'

We had known each other—or more correctly, I should say I had known von Ravenstein since 1937, when at Iserlohn[1] he had

[1] Town in Westphalia.

commanded the battalion in which I was doing my peace-time training as a young cadet officer. Now von Ravenstein silently pushed his own untouched egg across the table towards me. I protested, but he insisted with friendly firmness that I should have it. So I enjoyed the General's egg.

After the meal I went for a short stroll in the starry night. Von Ravenstein joined me and we walked to the top of a sand-dune. 'I often come up here of an evening,' he said, 'and enjoy the beauty and serenity of the surroundings.' He took a deep breath of the fresh Desert air. 'In this bright moonlight the dunes create the illusion of a snow-covered landscape.'

We drank in the loveliness of the scene in silence. I reflected on the different natures of the two generals in the Desert whom I knew best: von Ravenstein the lover of beauty, the gentle, the human, the considerate, for whom life contained poetry; and Rommel, supremely practical, hard, indifferent to the personal problems of others, concerned with personalities only in so far as they affected his military aims, for whom life was plain prose.

Despite the fundamental difference in their character, the two generals had a close understanding and saw eye to eye about the art of war. This was most apparent at the conference held the following morning. Von Ravenstein was versatile and resourceful, and tackled the most difficult problems confidently. He would not admit defeat and sought always for a way of overcoming obstacles. I felt, as the discussion continued, that here at least was a fighting General who was Rommel's equal, and it was clear that Rommel thought highly of him.

Together they were hatching out new schemes. We were aware that the British had set up certain advanced wireless observation posts on the Sollum front. We also suspected that they had a hidden supply-dump in the Desert to serve the armoured cars that constantly reconnoitred the forward area. The Generals now planned that von Ravenstein should, in mid-September, make a sharp raid into the forward area with a highly mobile, motorized battle group supported by Panzers and a few 'flak' guns.

The raid was to be made from our own lines, south of Halfaya. The element of surprise was essential, and lightning speed was also insisted upon for the success of the operation. The battle group, about half a regiment in strength, was to carry out demolitions and attempt to return with prisoners before the enemy could rally for a counter-attack. Rommel and von Ravenstein were as gleeful as a pair of boyish rascals over their little plot. 'I'm coming with you,' Rommel announced. 'Now try to make sure about one thing—that British air reconnaissance gets no premature indications that anything is in the wind.'

We went back to Gazala. On the way we paused to examine the Gambut roadhouse which was to be our new Battle H.Q. It was not particularly encouraging to learn that British bombers had dropped several sticks of bombs across the house a few hours before our arrival; we wondered whether the enemy had learned that this was to be Rommel's new home.

2

The September raid appealed to the imagination of Rommel's staff. It was a welcome diversion, and more of them than usual asked for permission to accompany the General. The Mammoth also carried General Calvi and Italian staff officers.

We reached the Capuzzo area the evening before the attack. Von Ravenstein reported that all preparations had been completed but deplored the fact that against his orders a number of Panzers had moved into position during the day and might have been spotted by the British aircraft.

At dawn next morning we passed through a prepared gap in our minefields and drove east. Rommel, looking like a U-boat commander on his bridge, was perched high up on the edge of the Mammoth's 'sunshine' roof. He was in an unusually jovial mood and shouted out with an even more unusual boisterousness: 'We're off to Egypt!'

It was agreeable to drive into an unknown part of the Desert, and I had a pleasant expectation of adventure to come. We sped on for some distance until we were not far west of Buq Buq. But the cisterns that we expected to find occupied here were empty. We saw no sign of a secret supply-dump. There was nothing to see but a few empty bully-beef tins and a few ale bottles, also empty, unfortunately. Our dreams of booty—notably of canned fruit and Scotch whisky—faded like a Libyan mirage. I noticed suddenly that my mouth was parched.

One of the mobile columns of our raiding force swung back to us now, with a captured British truck. The driver and his companion had been taken prisoner. The truck was examined and found to contain a large quantity of written material, including several important copies of codes. The more the material was studied, the more important it seemed, and Rommel sent it back west for detailed scrutiny. Von Ravenstein was delighted. He said to Rommel: 'Herr General, the capture of these documents alone is enough to have justified the expedition.' Rommel murmured agreement, but I never knew whether he fully concurred.

We had gone as far as we intended to go now, and our Panzers and motorized infantry were ordered to form into a defensive leaguer. The Englishman was reacting in a most unfriendly manner to our visit. He opened fire on us with his mobile and most effective 25-pounders, which we nicknamed 'Ratsch-booms' because of the sound they made.

Then came the R.A.F. The enemy planes swarmed over us, and I saw their bomb-doors open and bombs hurtling down above Rommel's Mammoth. I jumped into the armoured vehicle for protection, and noticed as I did so that Rommel and his driver were both darting away from it. They flung themselves flat. The bombs whistled down and crashed on the ground. Splinters spanged against the hard steel walls of the Mammoth.

The moment the first sticks burst, I leaped from the Mammoth and sprinted towards Rommel. The driver, I saw, was severely wounded. He was gory with his own blood. Rommel picked himself up. To my consternation I saw he was limping.

'Are you hurt, Herr General?' I asked.

'I don't feel anything,' he said, patting himself.

Then we discovered that a splinter had ripped the left heel off his fieldboots.

The driver was rushed to a near-by ambulance. We examined our vehicles. A splinter had deeply gashed a front tyre on the Mammoth, but the tyre was of first-class quality and we reckoned it would probably hold.

Our wireless now reported that the British had ordered further attacks. Before we were able to move off, the next bomber onslaught was made. The troops were ordered to form up for the return march to the frontier. Rommel stayed with the main body until they were ready to move. It was almost dark by the time we headed west again.

Rommel took the wheel, and I relieved him from time to time. The night was pitch black and we lost sight of the other vehicles in the column. Suddenly the damaged tyre went flat. We could not go on until that wheel had been changed or repaired.

I said to myself, 'Oh, heavens!' I did not relish the idea that, as the youngest, the most junior, and probably the most practical of the party in the Mammoth, I should have to try to carry out the repairs.

We hunted for tools in the dark. The jack was too short. We packed stones underneath the axle and dug away the sand with our hands. When I say we, I mean myself and a young Italian count on Calvi's staff. The others stood around as expectant, helpful, but critical observers. I had never in my life before repaired a punctured tyre, let alone a giant such as this.

The job had not been completed by midnight. Rommel and the other gentlemen now all gave a hand, which really just complicated the task.

Our wireless operator sat glued to his set. He reported that the British were hard on the heels of the retiring German columns. He could distinguish the call-signs of enemy armoured cars in our vicinity. It would have been fatal for us to send out a signal asking for help. Our troops were well on their way back to our own lines. Nobody suspected that we were stranded alone in the far Desert. A radio message would only have brought the British pouncing upon us.

We sweated away at the wheel. Perspiration poured off me. Rommel held a shaded pocket torch as I worked. I glanced at my watch. Two hours to go before sunrise. What a fat catch for Wavell we should be!

At last the wheel was fixed. We leaped into the Mammoth. Rommel took the wheel and drove the huge vehicle at a furious pace. As day broke we reached the frontier wire. Rommel found a gap in the minefields and whirled through. A group of Pioneers gaped at the solitary vehicle that had emerged at such speed from no-man's-land.

CHAPTER SEVENTEEN

KEYES HUNTS ROMMEL IN VAIN

SEPTEMBER merged into October, and active planning continued for the reduction of the Tobruk fortress in late November.

The troops who were to make the assault were still being re-formed and rested, and they engaged in regular training for their specific tasks. The attack this time was to be made from the direction of El Duda. Combat engineers were to achieve the first break-through with the close co-operation of the Panzers. The Luftwaffe was only to take part after the offensive had been launched on the ground. A dummy attack on the western defences was intended to mislead the enemy into concentrating his mobile reserve and counter-attack forces in that sector. Immediately the defences were breached, the 115th Rifle Regiment were to pour through the gap in their open armoured trucks and in co-operation with the Panzers were to thrust forward to King's Cross, where the Tobruk, Bardia, and El Adem roads met. From this point the next objective of the 21st Panzer Division was to be Tobruk harbour.

Every platoon received detailed instructions and their operations were planned down to the last detail. Air photographs were supplied to the smallest groups (sections of six men), so that the humblest soldier would have a clear picture of the battle area that was his own objective. The troops were painstakingly and systematically trained in 'rolling up' bunkers and in the art of attacking different trench systems.

Preparations were set back by outbreaks of jaundice, dysentery, and scurvy among the men. These diseases almost decimated the effective strength of some formations.

Our headquarters was near the Gambut landing-ground. The Jagdgruppe Neumann of the Luftwaffe were established here. Their officers had transformed an old underground *bir* into their mess. The ancient cistern was comfortable and bomb-proof, and was completely equipped with ante-room and bar-counter that had been moved from buildings at El Adem. When I dined there as a guest I used to be entertained royally, on iced drinks, fresh fruit, and cigarettes. 'One fetches the stuff,' the Luftwaffe officers explained, 'from Greece.' Their luxuriance was in sharp contrast to the meagre fare of Rommel's mess.

Wavell had gone, to command in India, and General Sir Claude Auchinleck had taken his place as the British Commander-in-Chief in the Middle East.

The airmen reported the extension of the Desert railway from Alexandria to Mersa Matruh onward towards the Sidi Barrani area. Behrendt, assistant to Rommel's I c, agreed that this was an indication of a coming offensive. I bet Dr Hagemann that the enemy would attack before the turn of the year.

My prediction was proved true, of course, when, three days after Rommel's birthday,[1] and five days before our own offensive against Tobruk was scheduled, the Eighth Army launched 'Operation Crusader'[2] under General Sir Alan Cunningham, the man who had driven our Allies out of Abyssinia.

2

An English Commando group, under Lieutenant-Colonel Geoffrey Keyes, son of the famous Admiral, were landed by submarine on the Cyrenaican coast in an audacious attempt to kill or capture Rommel on the eve of the offensive. The whole adventure was abortive and planned on false information, as I shall show.

Lieutenant-Colonel Keyes, Lieutenant-Colonel Laycock, five more officers, and about fifty other ranks, were sent to the Cyrene area in two submarines. Keyes and all except two of his men who got hurt were put ashore from one submarine, but Laycock only managed to get seven of his men ashore from the other. Keyes, two officers, and twenty-five other ranks met a British Intelligence Officer disguised as an Arab, and were told that Rommel's H.Q. was at Beda-Littoria. Arabs guided them through the rainy night on the first part of an eighteen-mile walk. Then they went on alone, and the following evening dumped all their surplus gear and food.

[1] Rommel was born on November 15, 1891, at Heidenheim, near Ulm in Württemberg.

[2] November 18.

A party of friendly Arabs whom they met told them that Rommel's H.Q. was not at Beda-Littoria, but in a house at Sidi Rafa'a. Keyes changed his plans.

The next night the Arabs guided him to the house, and at a minute before midnight they raided the house. They shot a sentry dead at the front door and lobbed a grenade in among the men in the first room they came to. In a second room the Germans switched out the light.

Keyes boldly flung open the door to attack, but fell mortally wounded by a volley of pistol fire. Another officer with Keyes flung two grenades into the room, which burst as he pulled the door shut. Keyes's two companions dragged him outside, but he died almost at once.

In their retreat a shot broke the leg of the officer with Keyes. He had to be left behind and was taken prisoner. Four German officers on the supply side—members of the Staff of Lieutenant-Colonel Otto, the I b—were killed, and were buried at Sidi Rafa'a with Keyes, to whom the British posthumously awarded the Victoria Cross.

It was a fearless exploit by the British, and the pity of it from their point of view was that they had been so badly misled. Rommel was not even in Africa at the time—he was at a birthday party in his honour in Rome, at which both Frau Rommel and von Ravenstein were present.[1] And the building which the Commandos attacked never had been Rommel's headquarters, which at the time was at Gambut, a couple of hundred miles away.

The house at Sidi Rafa'a which Keyes raided was in fact the one in which I had dined with Rommel, Gause, Cavallero, and others of my seniors when Rommel had first visited 'Bombastico' at Cyrene and learned of the creation of his Panzer Gruppe Afrika.

It had indeed been intended to serve as a private refuge for Rommel, where he could get away from even his own staff and the problems of war from time to time. It must be remembered that jaundice worried him throughout his tour in Africa, and he

[1] They attended the Opera. General von Ravenstein told me after the war that, as they emerged from listening to glorious singing, Rommel turned to him in the foyer and discussed not the opera but, at once, what had obviously been engaging his thoughts: 'Von Ravenstein, we must shift those battalions in the Medawwa Sector. . . .'—H.W.S.

was a sick man most of the time, for all his vitality and boundless energy in the front line.

Rommel did stop in the Sidi Rafa'a house once or twice. But British Intelligence slipped up badly in thinking that he was likely to be there most nights—and particularly at this time.

CHAPTER EIGHTEEN

'CRUSADER'

'CRUSADER' came as a surprise to us on the Axis side. Air reconnaissance had shown considerable bodies of troops moving in the deep Desert south of Matruh, but they had been taken for formations engaged in exercises. We did not expect the whole of the British 30th Corps,[1] containing the armour and Major-General Pienaar's 1st South African Division, to sweep in through the wire away in the south below Fort Maddalena and come up the Trigh el Abd track towards Bir el Gubi, aiming at El Adem. Indian troops went for the Omars[2] on the frontier. The British 13th Corps[3] with the New Zealanders and Army Tanks more or less isolated Sollum and Bardia. The New Zealanders pressed along the Trigh Capuzzo and the Via Balbia, and across the ground between them towards Gambut, menacing Rommel's H.Q. which, when the strength of the offensive was realized, became mobile. The 25th Bologna Division from the eastern perimeter of Tobruk was sent forward to meet the New Zealand thrust near Gambut. And after that the fighting was most confused, the object on either side being to destroy the opposing armour.

Our own assault was timed for November 23. That was now obviously 'off.' But Rommel debated whether perhaps this was not a lucky development. If the Eighth Army's offensive was met and neutralized over open ground, we might have more leisure to take Tobruk without fear of attack from the east. And, he said, perhaps it was as well that he was able to meet Cunningham's offensive with his formations fresh and rested, and not a little later, when they might have been weakened and wearied by their own assault on Tobruk.

[1] Lieutenant-General Willoughby Norrie.

[2] Omar Nuovo and Libyan Omar, captured on November 22 by Brigadier H. R. Briggs's 7th Indian Brigade (1st Royal Sussex, 4/16 Punjab, 4/11 Sikh).

[3] Lieutenant-General Godwin-Austen.

At all events, our plans were radically changed—and my own way of life with them.

2

Now that the attack on Tobruk was about to be launched, all sorts of materials and troops stuck away or detached in odd places were being collected in order to bring companies, battalions, regiments, and even divisions up to effective strength. Some units were short of vehicles, others of fuel and oil, others of ammunition; and most of them were considerably under strength in men and officers.

I had to lay before Rommel a report on the 15th Panzer Division. From it I noted that the formation was nearly 50 per cent under establishment owing to casualties and illness. And I made a decision which I had mulled over for some time. In the passing months a certain nostalgia had often taken possession of me. I remembered the pleasant days in 1940 when, as a company commander, I had been with officers and soldiers of my own age; with them I had shared fun and laughter as well as troubles and fighting; I had been independent and practically my own master. Now I was Rommel's A.D.C. I knew, of course, that a great many officers envied me my position and close contact with Rommel. But was I really so fortunate? Certainly it was interesting to have the privilege of being at the side of a spectacular general while he planned his operations, to watch the application of these plans, and the General's reactions in battle. But the majority of officers had a distorted idea of the nature of the job, which was not altogether 'beer and skittles.'

From first light to the last minute of the day, the General's affairs had to be arranged and his activities planned ahead. Through every waking hour one had to be on tip-toe and wide awake. Almost every word he spoke had to be noted and its import digested, and every detail of his orders, comments, and observations meticulously entered into his personal diary, together with exact times, places, and persons. Every verbal order given at the front had to be extracted from the diary and accurately passed to the staff officers concerned. While driving, I was responsible for knowing our exact location at any moment, and was expected to direct the General without hesitation to every lonely point in the Desert. It was also wearing to feel constantly responsible for the safety of his person and especially to make satisfactory arrangements for protection against the ever-present possibility of sudden or unexpected air attack by low-flying aircraft. At the end of the day's exacting duties, one carried on during the night hours and attended to voluminous correspondence, mostly private or semi-private. In short, there was no life of one's own; one was merely the shadow of a general.

But it was not the strenuous nature of my duties that led me to make my decision. It was a simple longing to associate with young men of my own age and to share our common woes and joys. I felt strongly that I would prefer once more to feel a measure of personal freedom and independence, even if it did mean service in a less exalted position. Remember, I had no professional ambitions in the army.

These thoughts were racing through my brain when I found myself unconsciously folding and refolding the report of the Division. I smoothed out the many folds I had made in the paper, took a deep breath, knocked, and entered the room. The General was answering a telephone call with his typically energetic 'Rommel here!' The communication was lengthy and apparently important. The delay gave me a minute or two to marshal my words. When the telephone conversation had come to an end, I placed the report on Rommel's desk. He took the report and read it silently. He shook his head, took a pencil, and endorsed the sheet 'II a—Speak!' He handed it back to me with one word 'Unbelievable!'

'*Jawohl, Herr General,*' I replied. Now was the time to come out with it.

'Anything else, Schmidt?' the General asked, scrutinizing me.

'*Jawohl, Herr General.* May I respectfully request that I be transferred back to a combatant unit?'

Rommel's eyes flickered for a moment and then he looked me hard in the eye. During this awkward moment the thought flashed through my mind: Is he thinking that this would never have happened with the faithful Aldinger who had been with him sinde the First World War and was now lying ill in Germany? Does he think I'm lacking in a sense of duty?

Still eyeing me sharply, Rommel asked in a half-jocular manner: 'Are you tired of working for me, Schmidt?'

'No, no, Herr General,' I answered quickly, if not quite truthfully, 'but as a young officer I should like to be back with the troops.'

'Quite right, Schmidt,' was Rommel's unexpected reply. 'As a lieutenant I should have done exactly the same. . . .' And he added with an unusual twinkle: 'A staff officer's life does not appeal to me either.'

He chewed the corner of his lip: 'There is certainly a shortage of Desert-worthy officers. . . . Very well.'

He added a further short endorsement to the 15th Panzer Division report. 'Go and interview the Chief of Staff regarding your successor.'

I was to train him to take over from me. I was also allowed to select the division to which I would go, with an appointment as a company commander. My choice fell on a heavy company of the 115th Rifle Regiment of the 15th Panzer Division. This company consisted of 50-mm. anti-tank guns, a 150-mm. gun, an infantry platoon, an 87-mm. mortar platoon, and a platoon of combat engineers.

My successor was an Oberleutnant Graf von Schweppenburg, a disabled young war veteran, as far as I remember minus his left forearm. I took an immediate liking to him. Later I heard he had stayed with Rommel for only three months, but I never knew what became of him afterwards.

3

I raced off at once to report to the 15th Panzer Division, in which I was promised command of a heavy company. The Division at the time was on the coast east of Tobruk. Heavy rain had fallen the night before in the regions near the coast, though not in the south. Those on the British side will remember how the sand turned into mud and hampered their movements on that first day of 'Crusader.'

My Division's area had been transformed into a muddy lake a foot deep, and it took the whole day for them to extricate themselves from the morass.

With Major-General Neumann-Silkow in command, the 15th were concentrated south of Gambut. R.A.F. machines in hundreds flew over us, but did not attack. We were puzzled at our almost complete immunity. Meanwhile our own aircraft were almost entirely grounded by the waterlogged surfaces of the landing-grounds.

I looked at the situation maps and decided that Rommel's position was not entirely unfavourable. The 15th and 21st Panzer and the 90th Light Divisions had been withdrawn for some time to prepare for the projected attack on Tobruk on November 23. The Tobruk lines were held by the Italian 21st Corps, strengthened by a few German infantry battalions. The 27th Brescia, the 17th Pavia, the 102nd Trento, and the 25th Bologna Divisions lay around the perimeter from west to east. The Italian 101st Trieste Motorized Division was at Bir Hacheim, the 132nd Ariete Armoured Division at Bir el Gubi, and the Savona Infantry Division at the Omars.

The Halfaya–Sollum–Bardia defensive triangle was manned mostly by Italians and by elements of the 164th Infantry Division, who included large numbers of elderly reservists and imperfectly trained recruits.

The 15th Panzer were formed into combat groups now. We marched south, still with British fighters buzzing overhead but no air attack developing against us. Suddenly we were subjected to artillery fire from the south-east. Gradually it grew in intensity. We dispersed over a wider stretch of the Desert, but continued our advance. We were in country which the enemy had already invaded: we found ourselves driving over coloured telephone lines which the British had laid on the Desert's surface. We cut them. In the distance we sighted tanks flying characteristic pennants—British. The 7th Armoured Division, we reckoned.

My own group was involved only in skirmishes during the chaotic days until November 23.

That morning we reached an area hard by Sidi Rezegh which was as flat as a billiard-table. As day dawned I sighted two large concentrations of enemy tanks, one to the north and one to the north-west. Our artillery opened up at long range against them. Tanks and Panzers clashed in the distance. We watched them through the morning hours, but were ourselves undisturbed. Once the tanks in the north started to roll down towards us. I had my guns deployed for action—five 50-mm. anti-tank guns. I had only just opened fire when our heavy artillery in rear of us joined in. The tanks veered off and joined another concentration, still away to the north.

CHAPTER NINETEEN

CHARGE AT SIDI REZEGH

I TRIED to puzzle out the purpose of these movements. It seemed likely that an attack was developing against us. Through the glasses I saw several batteries of British artillery emerge from the northern concentration of tanks. I gave orders to my men to dig slit-trenches. We should indeed have dug them earlier. The ground was stony and I had not got down a spit before the first shells were howling over our heads.

The battalion commander, an elderly Reservist major, was standing next to me, and not far away the lieutenant-colonel who was acting regimental commander. Both were calm. But even as I studied them, I sensed that the enemy fire was increasing in liveliness. Instinctively I grasped the arm of the Major next to me and shouted, 'Down, Herr Major!' Not a second too soon. We dropped into the same shallow slit just as a shell burst where we had been a moment or two before. Neither of us was hit by the splinters that sprayed through the dust over us.

The regimental commander sent out a call for his officers to gather. We had received Divisional orders. The whole situation was obscure. Rommel himself was uncertain of the enemy's strength, and he sent word that a dangerous situation was developing south-west of Tobruk on the high plateau at Sidi Rezegh. Rommel felt that he must soon cut the British lines of communication south of Sidi Omar. But at the moment the Sidi Rezegh situation had to be taken care of.

'The impending battle in this area will be of great significance,' the Colonel told us.

We received our orders standing, though salvoes were bursting steadily all round. When a fresh salvo landed even nearer and an officer fell wounded, several officers, as though moved by reflex action against their better judgment, went to earth.

'Gentlemen,' the Colonel called out reprovingly, 'a German officer does not lie down!'

In the din I murmured to the Major, 'For my part I consider this attitude exaggerated and inapplicable to modern warfare.'

The Major looked rather startled at my outspokenness, blinked, but nodded agreement. 'Yes, I think you're right.'

But still we stood there. More batteries seemed to have joined in the bombardment; more shells were falling round us. Two more officers dropped, wounded. Then we all took cover.

2

It was time to resume the march on Sidi Rezegh. Our orders were to attack Cunningham's tank formations at all costs—and to destroy the supporting infantry. Though we had not then identified them, these were the men of Brigadier B. F. Armstrong's 5th South African Brigade Group.

Our guns were limbered up, and the men took their seats. We dispersed over the wide plain and set off again towards the north-east.

They lay just south of the ridge at Sidi Rezegh. The day before they had made an abortive attack on our positions defending the landing-ground, rather more than three miles from the Muslim saint's tomb. The 3rd Transvaal Scottish and the South African Irish had suffered severe casualties, the Regiment Botha rather fewer. They had leaguered defensively for the night, and where they made their mistake was in putting the supply vehicles of their 'B' Echelon, with a mass of non-combatant and native auxiliaries, on their southern flank.

It is true that our threat seemed to lie north of them, but they should have realized that, in a fluid battle in the Desert, Rommel, whose tactics were by now clear even for the enemy to see, would hunt all round until he found a weak flank.

About half-past eight in the morning—Sunday, the 23rd—some of our Panzers had a skirmish with British tanks, got the best of it, and pursued them. The chase went right through the South Africans' 'B' Echelon. There was so much confusion and so little resistance, that our tank commanders, when they emerged from the ruck, reported a weakness in the enemy's defensive position. A plan was made at once to attack this vulnerable rear.

We were west of the South Africans at Sidi Rezegh that morning and moved somewhat farther south when the fire of their 25-pounders became embarrassing. More tanks that had been to the east were called up, and they joined us by travelling across the South Africans' southern flank, within easy range of their guns.

But surprisingly they were scarcely fired at. We learned later that they had been mistaken for a friendly column, possibly Pienaar's 1st Brigade arriving from the south. I never could understand this, as our Panzers were easily distinguishable from the South African motorized infantry columns. And, moreover, South African armoured cars came forward to investigate this tank column, and were driven off by gun-fire.

Rommel had observation posts on the ridge north of the South Africans, and in the early afternoon he began a bombardment to simulate the preparation for an attack from the north. But actually we were assembling our tank force, maybe 100 strong, to the south-west. I understand that reports of this actually reached the 5th Brigade H.Q., but apparently the threat was not discerned.

Ahead of us were the South Africans, and on our right front the 7th Support Group: the 7th Armoured Brigade had been driven away from the landing-ground in a tough tank battle the day before. West of the South Africans, on our left front, were all the tanks that the British 22nd Armoured Brigade had left.

The plan was that our unit, the 115th Rifle Regiment, should attack with the main force of our Panzers on our right. These would go for the British tanks, try to smash them up, then smash through them, and disorganize the South African infantry by tearing through their weak 'B' Echelon.

This we did. But the execution of the task was not as easy as it sounds.

About three o'clock we laid down a preliminary bombardment. Our attacking force got ready. Ahead lay a massed concentration of tanks—the 22nd Armoured Brigade. They looked almost as though they had formed a barricade. To their left were South African anti-tank guns and 25-pounders from (as we learned later) the 7th Field Battery. There were some 4.5-inch howitzers too.

Our motorized regiment fanned out into battle formation. The anti-tank weapons were thrust to the front. We noted with relief that a few of our Panzers had come up on the right flank.

'Attack!' The order was passed swiftly. The regimental commander led, standing erect in his open car. The Major's car followed, with me right behind him. We headed straight for the enemy tanks. I glanced back. Behind me was a fan of our vehicles—a curious assortment of all types—spread out as far as the eye could see. There were armoured troop-carriers, cars of various kinds, caterpillars hauling mobile guns, heavy trucks with infantry, motorized anti-aircraft units. Thus we roared on towards the enemy 'barricade.'

I stared to the front fascinated. Right ahead was the erect figure of the colonel commanding the regiment. On the left close by and slightly in rear of him was the Major's car. Tank shells were whizzing through the air. The defenders were firing from every muzzle of their 25-pounders and their little 2-pounder anti-tank guns. We raced on at a suicidal pace.

The battalion commander's car lurched and stopped suddenly —a direct hit. I had just time to notice the Colonel steadying himself. He turned sideways and dropped from the car like a felled tree. Then I had flashed past him. The Major was still ahead.

I recognized infantry positions in front of me. There was a tall, thin fellow out in the open, running backward as if impelled by a jet from a hose. I heard bursts behind me and followed the tracer as it whipped past me into the distance ahead. How slowly tracer seems to travel! The tall fellow dropped.

We had almost reached the screen of anti-tank guns and the tanks. A cold shiver ran down my spine. I saw small round holes forming in the windscreen of my car—just as though some invisible mechanic were drilling them there. Machine-gun fire! My driver huddled lower and lower over the wheel.

The Major's car lurched and went over on its side. I was alone out ahead in this inferno now. In front I saw nothing but belching guns.

Then suddenly there was a violent jolt, a screeching and a hiss, and my car stopped dead. I saw a trench immediately ahead, leaped from the car, and plunged towards the slit. My driver leaped out even as I did. But before he could dive on his face, he suddenly stiffened up erect, spun on his axis, and then dropped limp.

I wriggled down to the comfort of Mother Earth. I was

obviously in an outpost position abandoned by the Sidi Rezegh defenders.

I raised my head gingerly. Where was the horde of vehicles that had been pressing on behind me?

Stopped, by God!

What was my driver doing? Was he still alive?

He lay close by—dead.

The great fan of our vehicles stood well behind me, motionless. I discovered later that they had hesitated, wavered, and pulled up when they saw their officers one by one fall ahead of them. But a junior lieutenant was still on his feet. He rallied them and called on them to advance again, an achievement for which he was awarded the Ritterkreuz.

It had been a mistake for me to lift my head. Only too obviously, I had been spotted. Missiles whanged past now, clearly aimed at me alone. With every splash of lead I hugged the earth more closely. The slit-trench was, fortunately, not too shallow. Then I heard a fluttering noise, followed by an explosion. I knew the sound only too well. It was repeated again and again. Mortars!

Now I was certain that my fate was sealed. My mouth was dry, my lips parched. I thought of home. So this then, was the end, in a miserable hole in the dirt in Africa. But why, I reflected more philosophically, should my fate be any different from that of the Colonel or the Major,[1] or my driver?

Then I felt a severe slap on the rump, and simultaneously an avalanche of sand almost buried my head. I knew that I had been hit. But at once I felt strangely at peace. What did death matter, after all?

And with that the firing ceased. I lay motionless for a while—I have no idea how long. Then I cautiously moved first one leg, then the other. My right leg was painful, but I could move it. Spine and pelvis, hip and thigh bones must be intact. I had suffered only the indignity of a wound in the buttock.

What now? Would the enemy advance and find me? I could not help thinking of Australian bayonets. But were these men ahead of me Australians? English? South Africans? New Zealanders?

[1] Though wounded, the Major lived; I met him again in Italy at the end of the war.—H.W.S.

Why on earth were our troops not continuing their advance? Where were our Panzers?

They gave me an answer. Shells began to whistle overhead from the rear. Our shelling now far outweighed the reply from the men we were facing. Light 'flak' was rattling. The squeak and roar of Panzers grew steadily louder and nearer. When the roaring was practically upon me, I staggered to my feet.

'Here is one!' roared a soldier of my own regiment, leaping at me.

In a curious mixture of fury and relief I bellowed at him: 'You idiot. . . .' He hesitated, recognized me, sheered off, grinned, went on advancing. Limping, I followed.

British tanks flamed up and were knocked into silence. Others broke and raced back through the South African vehicles. Our Panzers followed them. Some received direct hits from the South African guns, but escaped damage, with the shot bursting harmlessly on the armour or bouncing off. A good number of the South African guns still seemed to be unready for action. They were not dug in, but were, some of them, still on their portees. It is, of course, possible that these were damaged or unserviceable guns, but even so they would have looked more dangerous if sited as though to meet our attack.

The South African position became one of complete chaos. Our tanks and infantry milled around among them. Soon the Brigade H.Q. was overrun and the Brigadier taken prisoner. The tanks fanned out and in two main columns began to mop up the infantry—the Regiment Botha men and the South African Irish. The Transvaal Scottish were farther north and were dealt with later. But before the battle was over the South Africans were attacked from every side and angle at once. They did not know where they were.

From among the wreckage ahead, among burning tanks and trucks and silent guns, enemy troops now appeared with their hands up in the air. Others were cursing over piles of spent shells, their ammunition exhausted. Their ambulance men were tending their numerous wounded.

I called for doctors and medical orderlies to assist them. Quite a number of our own people came forward. A South African officer complained that there were insufficient bandages for the wounded. I pointed silently to my own ignominous injury. The blood had flowed freely down my leg and clotted on my uniform. I looked curiously at the voluminous cape I had been wearing when I went into action. It had been rucked up above my bottom as I lay in the slit-trench. In it now were twenty-four holes—some of them neat round punctures, others jagged tears. We, too, had insufficient stocks of field-dressings or banadges for that day's work.

At dusk I had my wound dressed, and got a cup of hot tea. I slept that night on my face, in my own truck. All round lay the dead and wounded, and the prisoners. Many South Africans made off in the darkness. Others were too spent to face a desperate venture on foot into the night and the unknown Desert battlefield.

Dawn came up on the chaos of Sidi Rezegh. Wrecks still smoked. Men lay with glazed eyes staring at a sun that did not rise for them.

Lines of prisoners were formed up and marched off, escorted by a few vehicles and detachments of our troops. I drove beside one column for the first six miles of their northward march. An irrepressible German sergeant-major named Taudt began to sing in derision, 'We'll hang out our washing on the Siegfried Line . . .' Some of the leading prisoners in a passing column glared at him. But the men behind grinned ironically, undaunted. Somebody took up the refrain. In a few seconds the whole column was singing lustily, 'We'll hang out our washing on the Siegfried Line. . . .'

What could we do?

For many of them the war was over.

For me, fresh orders. We were to strike eastward in the chaos of that wavering battle. I looked at my map-board and the red and blue marks on the talc sheet of it. This place, where the dead and the wreckage lay, was Sidi Rezegh. How often had I not passed the Marabout's Mosque there in company with Rommel! We often breakfasted or lunched within sight of that tomb. Apart from the little white-domed building, there was nothing at Sidi Rezegh to justify its having a name. We never thought it would remain in our memories for ever.

This, then, was Sidi Rezegh: it had a name now indeed.

CHAPTER TWENTY

DESERT CHAOS

After Sidi Rezegh Rommel's word went round swiftly: that in face of the relatively strong tank forces still available to Auchinleck, he refused to fritter away his weakened Panzer forces in continuous fighting, and that above all we were to avoid losses in detail.

He decided that the set-back to the Eighth Army at Sidi Rezegh, where not only had the 5th South African Brigade been overrun but the British armour heavily hit, the 7th Support Group wearied in heavy fighting, and the skilful New Zealand troops weakened, had produced the psychological moment for the creation of a *Hexenkessel*, a Witches' Cauldron towards the frontier south of his defensive positions between Halfaya and Sidi Omar.

You will remember that Rommel had inoculated the German troops around Halfaya with the belief that each strong-point was a valuable self-contained fortress which must have a field of fire in every direction: and that even if our mobile forces disappeared for days or for weeks, they must hold on at all costs in the firm belief that the Afrika Korps would return to free them.

Rommel recognized the danger that Cunningham's forces might succeed in linking-up with the Tobruk garrison. But his view was that this would not strengthen the Eighth Army unless a decision were forced, especially in armour, between Tobruk and the Sollum front.

Hence the remarkable raid eastward through the wire which he ordered von Ravenstein and the 21st Panzer Division to make. Our air reconnaissance at the time was poor; the British was excellent. We did not know of the existence of two considerable Forward Supply Depots, F.S.D. 63 and F.S.D. 65, about fifteen miles south-east of Gabr Saleh. When von Ravenstein struck along the Trigh el Abd and cut across the frontier, disorganizing Cunningham's Battle H.Q., he passed north of these camps and unknowingly missed a great chance. If he had run across them,

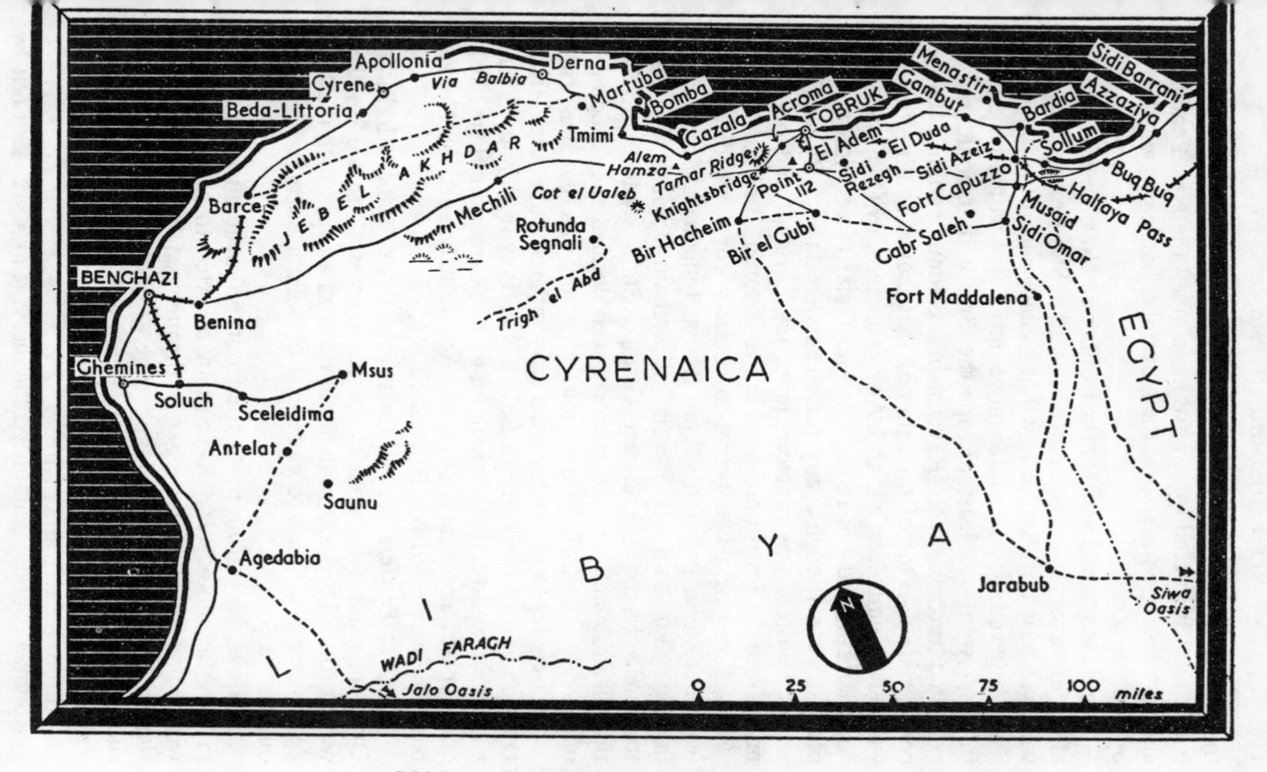

MAP 2: SIDI BARRANI TO AGEDABIA

the course of the Desert battle would probably have been different. The British could not have maintained the New Zealanders and kept them fighting—and the November battle was won largely by the New Zealanders.

Von Ravenstein struck for the frontier on November 24, the day after our victory over the South Africans at Sidi Rezegh. Rommel, who was based on Bardia now but usually out in the battle area itself, believed that a counter-move into Egypt would be successful, and would at least disrupt the British if it could not be exploited further. Von Ravenstein's column certainly caused consternation. One of his columns that moved south along the wire put Cunningham's Eighth Army Advanced H.Q. into a panic. Another attacked the Indians at Sidi Omar twice without complete success, though many prisoners were taken. By the 25th, von Ravenstein was nineteen miles inside Egypt and only fifty miles from the British rail-head in the Desert at Bir Thalata.

Von Ravenstein had petrol to continue for some distance at least, and in his position I think Rommel might have struck still farther. But back at Bardia, Lieutenant-Colonel Westphal, Rommel's I a on the Panzer Gruppe Staff, studied captured British maps and strength reports, and decided that a counter-offensive was out of the question. His view was that the British forces were far too strong, particularly with the 2nd South African Division east of the Halfaya Line still entirely fresh and waiting. He felt we could not take them on with our forces in their battle-disorganized and weakened state. Accordingly, early on November 26 he wirelessed von Ravenstein: 'Come back.'

The 21st Panzers forced their way through the 4th Indian Division, made feint attacks on Capuzzo and Musaid on their way north to Bardia, and then got through a gap, which the New Zealanders had failed to close east of Sollum Barracks, to enter our Bardia fortress.

Rommel, back from the battle-front, was snatching some sleep in his Mammoth. Von Ravenstein reported to him in person, with some pride at having got through safely. Rommel was shaken with astonishment and rage. 'Why are you here?' he shouted. 'I ordered you to be in position to attack eastward into Egypt!' Von Ravenstein told him of the signal that had recalled him through the frontier wire.

Rommel roundly denounced the message as a fake sent out by

the British with the aid of a captured Afrika Korps code-book. He took some convincing that von Westphal had sent the message. Later Rommel conceded that his I a had acted correctly in the light of the information at his disposal—information which Rommel, away among the mobile columns, had not received.

2

Also in pursuance of Rommel's plan, a combat group, including myself, of the 15th Panzer Division moved rapidly from the Sidi Rezegh area and then from south of Gambut eastward towards Bardia.

I remember how my company at Sidi Azeiz, where we clashed heavily with the New Zealanders on the 27th and captured their 5th Brigade H.Q., spotted a large British tank-recovery wagon elaborately fitted with cranes and pulleys, escorted by a few other vehicles. It looked to be valuable booty. We gave chase with a small mobile detachment, accompanied by a light gun mounted on caterpillars. The drivers of the tank-recovery tender abandoned their vehicle when we were hard upon them, took to the broken ground near by, and sniped at us. We made good our capture and returned to the main body of our column.

We halted briefly at Bardia an hour later in order to re-form. I snatched the opportunity of making a quick visit to the field-hospital there to have my wound cleansed and bandaged, and to have an anti-tetanus injection.

Two hours later I rejoined my unit. Oberleutnant Weichsel, who had taken over when the Battalion Commander had been wounded and knocked out at Sidi Rezegh, ordered me to fall my company in at the tail-end of the column. We sped on, and headed south on the Libyan side of the frontier wire, past Capuzzo (against which a diversionary attack was made) and the Omars towards Maddalena. Frequently we were fired at, sometimes from the left, sometimes from the right. Once an urgent report was shouted to me: 'Tanks in our rear!' I raced up the column to report to Weichsel. He heard me, and answered with Rommelian brevity: 'Shoot them down!'

Back with my men I ordered the subaltern next in seniority to me to take over command of the company, and I ordered a troop of three anti-tank guns to pull out of the column.

The column swept on. Within minutes it was merely a dust-cloud in the distance. We set up our guns. True enough, British Mark II's were on our trail—twelve of them. They rolled within range. We had kept our sights on them as they advanced. Simultaneously, on my fire order, three shells screeched out to greet them. The leading tank burst into flames and stopped. The rest slowed down and fanned out.

We were spotted. They turned their machine-guns on us. The stuff just belted past us as we lay flat behind our guns. A bullet grazed my shoulder. Still they fanned out. The tanks on the flanks seemed to be moving in on us, like the horns of a Zulu impi. The situation was, I thought, none too comfortable. I glanced back with a vague idea of withdrawal if that were possible amid this fire. To my horror I saw two more British Mark II's moving towards us.

Then to my gasping relief I recognized swastika markings on them: they were two of the British tanks that had been captured at Halfaya during 'Battleaxe' months before. The tanks growled right up alongside me. I exchanged a few swift words with the sergeant-major commanding them. 'Get cracking back to the column with your guns, Herr Leutnant,' he shouted. 'I will keep you covered.'

The British tanks had ceased firing. I guessed they had been confused by the appearance of the tanks in our rear and thought that we had been taken prisoner. Before they could analyse the situation I had my guns moving, and we hared off in pursuit of our column, with the sergeant-major and the two tanks lurking behind to cover our retreat.

It took an hour to catch up with the column. By then darkness had fallen.

3

Our combat group was called off the task of raiding Maddalena and attempting to capture Eighth Army Headquarters. I never really learned quite why, for it is obvious now that we should have had no difficulty in overrunning Cunningham's almost undefended H.Q. But it seems that Rommel had now decided he must retrieve the position round Sidi Rezegh.

Meanwhile, because our Panzers were not between Sidi Rezegh and Bardia to oppose them, the New Zealanders, leaving a brigade behind at Sidi Azeiz, had fought their way eastward to

Sidi Rezegh and Bel Hamed. They took Sidi Rezegh on the night of the 25th. Next day the Tobruk garrison made a successful sortie through the Italians, and on the 27th they linked up with the New Zealanders. Pienaar's 1st South African Brigade during this period had sat steadily behind a screen of 25-pounders at Taib el Essem and held off the Ariete Division and some of our Panzers.

From Bardia on the 27th Rommel wirelessed for all units to return from their frontier tasks. He planned to use every Panzer he could to strike at the British 13th Corps between Bardia and Tobruk. The British 7th Armoured Division had been gathered together again and now had 120 tanks running. Several times during the afternoon they tried to hold off Ravenstein's division, but they lost more tanks in these battles than we did.

The British, however, had one big success when von Ravenstein accidentally ran right into Freyberg's New Zealanders and was captured—the first German general to be taken prisoner in the war. Major Wustefeld, of the Afrika Korps Staff, was also captured that day, and we lost 600 other men as well.

I had seen and spoken with von Ravenstein near Sidi Azeiz only two hours before he was captured. Perhaps that was why, when he fell into the hands of the enemy, he decided to call himself 'Colonel Schmidt' and hoped they would not identify his badges of rank. But when he was taken up to General Freyberg, he automatically introduced himself, 'Von Ravenstein, General!'

Von Ravenstein had with him a map showing our complete dispositions, and this fell into the hands of the enemy. He was not repatriated to Germany from Canada, where he was imprisoned, until 1948, and now lives at Iserlohn, where I had first met him when doing my pre-war military service.

4

I was detailed to command a rearguard of two companies during this day. We were continually pestered by tanks and reconnaissance cars that followed up behind our Panzer columns wherever we moved. The Desert battle for me was a strange action fought in reverse. We would be fighting our way forward one way, but I was always looking backward, stopping to fight, and then moving backward again.

As often as not we would have to face sharply right, for the enemy would be skirting round to the south as well. My companies took it in turns to leap-frog each other. One would halt and fight, the other move back, then pause to shoot while the first passed through. The Desert was alive with small mobile columns of the enemy—'Jock Columns' they were called—which were a nuisance, as mosquitoes are, but in the end no more violent in their sting. They were never really strong enough to do irreparable damage.

Rommel still believed that the enemy had suffered more than we had, and when the weather broke on December 2 he started to regroup, gathering us up towards the Sidi Rezegh area.

The days that followed are hazy, but one recalls frequent local actions. I remember particularly my own rearguard action from Bardia to El Duda. We were assaulted by a strong force of tanks which followed so hard on our heels that we had scarcely time to take up our routine defensive positions. I was most relieved when we received unexpected artillery support from one of our own defensive positions south of El Duda. We were heavily bombed that day.

The day after that we tried in vain to overcome the stubborn resistance of the British at El Duda itself. The enemy's tanks made several spirited counter-attacks from El Duda, and achieved considerable success. From then on Rommel finally decided that he could do nothing to thrust the Eighth Army back in force, and our front line ran from just south of El Adem away down towards Bir el Gubi.

I made time to visit our field-hospital at El Adem and receive another anti-tetanus injection, for my wound had not entirely cleared up. Outside the hospital I ran into Freiherr von Neurath, son of Baron von Neurath, the former German Foreign Minister. Von Neurath had been in Tripoli as a consular representative, and here in the Desert he held the quasi-military rank of Sonderfüher. I am not certain what his functions were, but presumably he was available for duty as a civil affairs officer if and when we captured any enemy-held cities.

Now the 2nd South African Division, which had not been in battle before, was advancing westward. The dog-fight round Sidi Rezegh, too complicated to deal with in detail here, ended with the Eighth Army on top.

Rommel ordered a general withdrawal.

CHAPTER TWENTY-ONE

REARGUARD

'By December 12, under cover of costly rearguard actions, Rommel had reached a line stretching south-west from Gazala,' said a British official report afterwards.

I certainly received a specialized training in rearguard work in those few days. Near the Gazala Heights I got orders to establish a wide defensive line facing east, with two companies and two long-range 210-mm. guns. I reconnoitred the position hurriedly, sited the various support-points, and established my own headquarters on the southern flank, where I thought attack most likely.

The first tanks approached towards midday. They were moving far to the south of us, at the foot of the Tamar Ridge. Our long-range guns opened fire, but the tanks turned north undeterred, and rolled on towards our flank. Meanwhile between thirty and forty tanks, spread out, advanced towards us from the front. We lay flat behind our well dug-in and camouflaged anti-tank guns.

We held our fire and then opened up at relatively short range. Two tanks burst into flames at once. The rest hesitated. With our long-range guns also blazing away, the British turned and withdrew to beyond effective range.

Far off we could see many hundreds of the Eighth Army's vehicles advancing westward with tanks among them.

At nightfall I received orders to send the long-range guns back to rejoin the main body. For the rest, our position was on no account to be abandoned until instructions were received.

I waited for orders through the long winter night, but in vain. It was clear that we should not be able to withdraw in daylight. As I resigned myself to a last stand, orders to withdraw came through by wireless just before dawn. I passed on the instructions by our portable wireless set to my northern company, under command of Lieutenant Klenk, but got no confirmation of receipt. So I hustled out a dispatch-rider to make contact with him. The man was not seen again. My last resort was to fire

Very lights in the hope that Klenk would grasp their significance, and we pulled out quietly towards the west. Klenk guessed the meaning of my flares, and eight days later his company was able to rejoin us after diverse adventures, trekking through the Jebel Akhdar while we went through the Desert.

Dawn broke with us driving in wild haste. We made good progress in the bleak winter sunshine, but for the rest of that day our column was the only sign of life we saw on the Desert floor.

Once a swarm of R.A.F. aircraft flew towards us. There were some sixty machines in all, and I thought that we were in for a bad time. In desperation I ordered the column to fire with everything that would bear. The aircraft surprisingly replied by sending down recognition flares. We accepted them gratefully and ceased firing. This extraordinary incident could be explained only in one way—the airmen must have believed that because of the large number of captured sand-coloured British vehicles in our column, we must be the spearhead of the Eighth Army racing westward.

We caught up with our main body next day—a little too early, in fact, for we ran slap into an air attack. A strong formation of R.A.F. planes carpeted us with bombs. I plunged from my car into a funk-hole. When the raid was over I found the upholstery of the car ripped to shreds. I called out to my driver, Lance-Corporal Schmidt, but got no reply. A soldier touched me on the arm and pointed under the car. The driver's torn body lay there. A few minutes before we had been talking of his wife and family, and of the leave he was looking forward to. There would be no reunion for him now.

Several of my men were screaming with pain. Close by another was writhing, minus both hands and both feet. A doctor was soon at his side and bent over him. His ashen face twisted into an attempt at a smile as he asked: 'Will I be able to continue with my career as an actor, Doctor?' The doctor said: 'Yes, of course, old chap,' and was giving him a shot of morphia when, mercifully, he died.

The war was going on, and we had to go on. We had scarcely time to bury our dead, for the tanks were hard at our heels. Rommel's army headed west again into the setting sun.

CHAPTER TWENTY-TWO

BACK TO EL AGHEILA

WE were back in Benghazi. There our supply depots were burning. A few of my trucks stopped while the men rescued what they could carry in the way of stores for the company. We came on one truck-load of undreamed-of delicacies—Italian tinned fruit, Spreewald[1] cucumbers, beer, cigarettes, chocolate. We had not set eyes on such stuff for months.

All the way back to Benghazi the Afrika Korps was sniped at by parties of Arabs. We ourselves on the day before Christmas got into a skirmish with South African and British armoured cars.

We managed to capture a young British officer and three other ranks who had ventured too far forward. The officer seemed a pleasant type but was most reserved, which was perhaps not unnatural in the circumstances. I did not question him beyond the bare minimum to establish his identity.

That night, since it was Christmas Eve, I saw to it that the Englishmen were each given a bottle of beer, chocolates, and cigarettes. 'You have pretty generous Christmas fare,' he remarked. I did not tell him that we only had these luxuries because we had salvaged them from a dump which was being burned because the enemy was on our heels.

The young British officer asked me for permission to sleep in the open with his men, and added: 'I will give you my word not to attempt to escape.'

I replied: 'I fully believe you would keep your word and I would grant your parole, but our regulations demand that you should be handed over to Division without delay.'

He insisted again that he had offered his word as an officer and a gentleman. My superiors did not know that we had taken any prisoners. Feeling slightly festive but a little guilty, I granted him his wish.

On Christmas morning I rolled sleepily out of my blankets in

[1] West of Berlin.

my truck. The three British other ranks were drawn up smartly in a line, paraded by their officer. He saluted briskly and reported: 'All present and correct.' I was sorry to part from this gallant and honourable soldier when we had to turn our prisoners over to Division.

The British entered Benghazi—for the second time—that Christmas Day.

We trailed on southward on the way back to the defile between the El Agheila marshes and the sea. The Afrika Korps for the moment was a beaten force, but not dispirited. I saw no signs of wilting morale among our rearguard troops. We stood and fought wherever there was high ground. Light forces of British tanks, apparently of the 22nd Armoured Brigade, probed at our positions and forced us to shift our ground several times.

The Afrika Korps Command issued orders that ammunition was to be conserved and no action taken during the festive season if it could be avoided—not because they wished no fighting for sentimental reasons, but simply because we were short of ammunition. But officers and men in the front line felt that something must be done to celebrate the beginning of the New Year. Plans were made in secret, with not a word reaching senior ears.

On the stroke of midnight on New Year's Eve every position as far as the eye could see contributed its share to a first-class exhibition of fireworks. Light 'flak' and machine-guns fired tracer. Every available Very pistol pumped up red, green, and white flares. Hand-grenades, which we had so far used but little, went off with a most satisfactory bang. Even some big guns belched forth into the heavens, or into the distant Desert. The din was terrific, and the desolate countryside was lit up for miles. The display lasted for precisely three minutes and then darkness and silence descended on the Desert once more.

We were as pleased as truant schoolboys when, from the dark distance where we knew the screen of British tanks lay, a counter-display of yellow Very flares also went up to greet the New Year.

Not a word of reproof came down the line from Rommel or his generals.

A few days later one phase of the Desert battle was over. We were back at El Agheila, from which we had sallied out, almost unexpectedly, about eight months before. Meanwhile there had been hard fighting, much of it crammed into a spell of continuous and relentless action. All our formations had suffered heavy losses, and both men and equipment were worn out. But the British were in little better shape. They could not hammer through us and continue the advance on Tripoli.

The issue had been in doubt during the first weeks of 'Crusader.' Rommel might have won the upper hand, I think, if he had had the benefit of stronger air support and more intensive air reconnaissance. But meanwhile Auchinleck had gained at least a moral and material victory. It had been greatly to his credit that, after the set-backs at Sidi Rezegh, Auchinleck had pressed on boldly. He had given command to Major-General Ritchie and ordered him to resume the offensive in full force.

But Rommel's Sollum front still held. And Rommel had not, he assured us, abandoned the idea of staging a counter-offensive at the first favourable opportunity. He did everything in his power swiftly to restore the full strength of his formations from the reinforcements of men, supplies, and equipment that had recently been rushed across to Tripoli.

Auchinleck, too, wished to settle the issue on the frontier. He turned his attention to Bardia, Sollum, and Halfaya.

Major-General I. P. de Villiers's 2nd South African Infantry Division, whose task at the beginning of the 'Crusader' offensive had been to protect the rear of the Eighth Army against a possible wide encircling movement by Rommel, was lying in front of Bardia, in the Capuzzo area and around Sidi Omar. On the morning of December 31, after heavy artillery preparation, de Villiers launched an attack on Bardia which ended after two days of heavy fighting in the surrender of Major-General Schmidt, who was in command there.

We had not much time left, obviously, if we were to rescue our beleaguered garrisons at Halfaya. It soon became clear that no counter-offensive could be launched in time to recover Cyrenaica and reach them. After an attack by a battalion of the Transvaal Scottish and some South African Police, Sollum fell to de Villiers on January 12. An attack which the South Africans were preparing against the Halfaya positions became unnecessary when the defenders—Italians and a strong detachment of Germans under our old friend Major the Reverend Bach, who were without water and rations—were forced to capitulate on January 17.

The Afrika Korps was still 300 miles to the west. But the

'Desert Fox' was ready to strike. Rommel himself showed no signs of being shaken by our headlong retreat. His optimism, which was infectious, and by now on the way to becoming legendary, was increased by the arrival of fresh equipment from Tripoli.

Our Intelligence learned that Auchinleck's experienced 7th Support Group, who had fought so well in 'Crusader,' were to be relieved by a fresh support group, the 1st, who were without experience of Desert warfare. Rommel's determination to strike a counter-blow at the earliest possible moment was strengthened. We got ready. And on January 21 Rommel gave the word 'Go.'

The British apparently thought we were making only a reconnaissance in strength, for their official communiqués described our advance in those terms. But our air reconnaissance had disclosed that the British had a concentration of tanks in the Msus area, which we assumed were being overhauled and repaired. We were to strike at them.

CHAPTER TWENTY-THREE

ROMMEL STRIKES AGAIN

My company had been lying above the Wadi Faragh on the extreme right flank of the Afrika Korps. From the steep slopes of this, the largest wadi in the Sirte region, we had impressive views to the south of the massive, barren cliffs of a prehistoric seashore.

Major-General von Vaerst had taken over command after the death of Neumann-Silkow early in 'Crusader.' From this commander, who had rapidly won our confidence, now came the order to march north-east.

On the extreme south as we were, my own vehicle was on the edge of the steep slopes of the wadi on my right hand. Now and again I sighted British vehicles moving rapidly eastward over the escarpment-crossed terrain of this barren country. Now and again we made a pounce forward with a light gun mounted on caterpillars. Once we surprised a stationary reconnaissance car. Next to it were its crew—three men who were sitting unalarmed on camp chairs round a little fire, brewing tea. We drank the tea, claimed the vehicle as booty, and left the three enemy soldiers with polite hopes that they would get a lift home.

We had our first skirmish with British tanks on the second day of the march (January 22), in the Antelat area, after pushing through a light screen of the 200th Guards Brigade. We sighted about thirty tanks stationary at the foot of a rise in hilly ground. When we received the order to attack, we were certain we had not yet been observed. We brought our 50-mm. anti-tank guns into position in a hollow.

The enemy was totally surprised when we opened fire, and a dozen Panzers raced down against the tanks. He decided his position was untenable and pulled out hurriedly with the loss of a few tanks.

We had now developed a new method of attack. With our twelve anti-tank guns we leap-frogged from one vantage-point to another, while our Panzers, stationary and hull-down, if possible, provided protective fire. Then we would establish ourselves to give them protective fire while they swept on again. The tactics worked well and, despite the liveliness of his fire, the enemy's tanks were not able to hold up our advance. He steadily sustained losses and had to give ground constantly. We could not help feeling that we were not then up against the tough and experienced opponents who had harried us so hard on the Trigh Capuzzo. We had taken both Antelat and Saunu by the 22nd.

The 2nd Armoured Brigade, the 9th Lancers, and the 10th Royal Hussars all tried to stop us. But they could not cope with the Rommel attack. Under the General's personal direction, his troops had now developed one definite ability, and that was to adapt themselves quickly to circumstances as these developed. They had learned how to apply his precept—'Small successes are likely preludes to bigger successes.'

With this cultivated instinct to exploit any success, and to go on hitting whenever the enemy seemed to reel at all—and with three days' rations—the Afrika Korps Panzers pushed on. But they would never have been able to do so, or to dare it, if they had not had implicit confidence in the superiority of our anti-tank weapons at that time over the enemy's tanks and anti-tank guns.

The relative quietness of our friends, the R.A.F., at this time was also conducive to heightened morale. The trouble, we gathered, was that the British had been able to get nothing like as much fuel forward to Benghazi as they had hoped; consequently they could not keep their short-range fighters in the air from the Benina airport and other landing-grounds forward of Tobruk.

Our air reconnaissance had reported correctly upon the existence of the British tank-repair camp. We drove in upon it virtually without resistance, and in one field-workshop alone found valuable booty—a number of tanks capable of being put into running order again.

We were not entirely happy about our petrol position. Yet one young officer who said to Rommel, 'Herr General, we need more fuel,' received the brisk answer: 'Well, go and get it from the British.'

Our advance continued over the wide plains round Msus, an ideal jousting-ground for a fight to a finish between armoured forces, clear of all signs of civilization, with nothing to distract men from the extraordinary duty of destroying each other. The 1st British Armoured Division, inexperienced in the Desert, came down against us, and the 4th Indian Division came out from Benghazi to give battle. We cut the Indian Division in two and bottled up their 7th Brigade in Benghazi. The British tanks were not strong enough for our Panzers, and they were short of fuel. Everywhere we came across isolated groups and supply columns of the armoured division stranded for lack of juice.

We stood with our anti-tank guns on a defensive line near Msus for a couple of days, but the whole trend of the battle was eastward. Auchinleck, taken aback by the turn of events, flew up from Cairo to Major-General Ritchie's headquarters at Tmimi and cancelled the orders given to the 13th Corps to continue withdrawing. He hoped to counter-attack. But by February 4 the Eighth Army was in a new defensive line at Gazala, with Pienaar's South Africans barring Rommel's way east.

Rommel, however, had gone as far as he could—farther, indeed, than he had hoped to get in this one particular phase of his counter-offensive. He could not risk a further advance against the bulk of the Eighth Army until he had received reinforcements—notably new Panzers then being unloaded at Tripoli. So he settled briefly on the Tmimi–Mechili line.

CHAPTER TWENTY-FOUR

THE TOBRUK PLAN

AUCHINLECK and Ritchie swiftly built up a strong line at Gazala. We, on our side, gained the impression that Auchinleck was offensively minded and had no intention of allowing Tobruk to be besieged again, but instead looked on possession of the port as vital to supplying the Eighth Army for a fresh drive against the Afrika Korps.

The British line—or rather, a series of strong, defended localities linked by a vast minefield that stretched from the sea southward to Bir Hacheim—grew steadily in strength, under the watchful eye of our reconnaissance. Rommel made it clear that he intended to launch a counter-offensive before the British did, and this information cheered every soldier in the Afrika Korps. But there was a long lull, on which I will not dwell at length.

From mid-February until late March there was nothing beyond patrol activity. Then Ritchie staged a diversion to distract Axis attention from a powerful convoy which was being passed through from Alexandria to Malta. This island was, as Rommel said frequently, the sharpest thorn in his side. He felt that had the island been taken shortly after his expeditionary force landed in North Africa, he would have succeeded in invading Egypt in 1941 and even forcing his way through to the Nile Delta, because he would not constantly have been denuded of regular supplies and reinforcements.

Indeed, I remember his refusing reinforcements in 1941 with the remark: 'The supply routes to Africa must first be secure before I agree to the transportation of further divisions.'

At one time we believed that the High Command in Berlin had decided that Malta should be taken. The Luftwaffe made continuous attacks from Sicily against the bravely defended island. It is true that the result of these heavy attacks materially improved the supply position in Africa, but the island should have been neutralized if we were to be put in a position to guarantee victory.

MAJOR-GENERAL VON RAVENSTEIN

Imperial War Museum

ROMMEL, WITH THE AUTHOR, EXAMINING A BIG GUN NEAR HALFAYA

We had little fighting in the Panzer divisions during those months of lull. I remember that our tanks were being rested in the Derna area during March, and my company were enjoying a period of relaxation in the Martuba wadis with leisure to appreciate the colourful Desert skies of early spring, when we had one unexpected attack—by rain. A terrific thunderstorm broke during the night, and taught us the lesson that a languid life in an attractive wadi had its disadvantages and, indeed, dangers. Quite a number of valuable vehicles and weapons were damaged and swept away down the wadis.

2

April passed, and most of May, with the force preparing to strike for Tobruk once more.

Rommel now decided to put into force a duplicate of his operational scheme for the reduction of Tobruk the previous November—when we had been forestalled by five days by the Eighth Army's 'Crusader' attack.

Under cover of darkness on the night of May 26 the Afrika Korps was to strike round the southern flank of the Gazala line at Bir Hacheim, and then to thrust northward in rear of the enemy. An attempt was to be made the same night to take Bir Hacheim with the Italian Ariete Armoured Division, and at the same time the Trieste Division was to attempt to force a gap through the British minefields on the Trigh el Abd heights—that is, below the section of the line held by the 1st South African Division.

The Italian formations facing the Gazala Line were to contain the South Africans and the British 50th Division on the left, preventing them from any adventure forward along the coast road.

On the second day part of our armour—from the 21st Panzer Division—was to strike at the rear of the Gazala Line, while the Italians attacked from the front. While it was hoped that this attack might succeed, and at least keep the South Africans and the 50th Division from intervening farther east, in their own rear, our main objective was a direct attack on Tobruk. We were to go for the port with the 15th Panzer Division, and Rommel's timetable provided that we should take it on the third day.

Major-General von Bayerlein had now arrived to become Cruwell's Chief of Staff in the Afrika Korps under Rommel's Panzer Gruppe Afrika, of which Gause was still Chief of Staff. Major-General von Bismarck was appointed to lead the 21st Panzer Division. The 15th was still commanded by Major-General Vaerst.

The battle was a gamble. Gause and von Bayerlein both pointed out to Rommel and Cruwell that a critical situation would very likely develop during the battle between the opposing armoured forces, if our lines of communication were not secured by the capture of Bir Hacheim or by the creation of a definite gap through the minefields.

Rommel had seen this clearly enough for himself. But he said: 'That chance has to be taken. And it must and will cease to be a gamble by virtue of skilled and determined attack on the lines of the plan formulated. Let it not be forgotten that the British are not without strategical training. They must have considered the possibility of our striking up behind the Gazala Line. We are not likely to paralyse them by complete surprise. Therefore we must beat them by carrying out effectively what we perceive to be the essentials for success in employing this particular plan. Our tanks will be behind the enemy's line, and in battle—well, lines of communication must be driven through to serve them.'

3

We lay in readiness in the Rotunda Segnali area, and during the night of May 26–27 we advanced round the southern flank of Bir Hacheim. At the same time the Italians went for Bir Hacheim and for the minefield between Gazala and Alem Hamza on the Trigh el Abd heights.

We swept up towards the coast in the morning. We met with heavy air attacks and strong artillery fire from our flanks, and the 3rd Indian Motor Brigade did its best to hold us back. We smashed a way through the Indians, but not without losing a number of tanks. The 21st Panzers were on the left flank of our advance, and they headed west of Acroma, menacing the rear of the Gazala Line; but the British 1st Armoured Division gave them battle at what was afterwards the Hexenkessel ('Cauldron') at

Knightsbridge. In the 15th Division we headed for Acroma, with battle groups hiving off to attempt to reach El Adem, Sidi Rezegh, and El Duda again.

Our elation at our swift advance in the early stages was short-lived, for we ran into two British Armoured Brigades, which afterwards turned out to be the 4th and 22nd. For the first time now we began to experience doubts about the superiority of our own weapons.

The clash took place on the escarpment some miles south of Acroma.

I was still commanding my company in the reinforced 2nd Battalion of the 115th Rifle Regiment, with orders to reach and take Acroma. It was no light task, particularly since we could not forget that we were in rear of the enemy's Gazala Line and we knew that powerful enemy tank forces were lying in wait for us.

CHAPTER TWENTY-FIVE

MY BATTALION IS OVERRUN

We reached the edge of the escarpment. The Panzers that had supported us while we broke through the Indians now lay back. Though the country to east and west was relatively flat, we saw neither troops nor artillery, but guns laid down fire upon us from both flanks. Shells ploughed among us as, with myself on the extreme left flank, we reached the edge of the declivity. Once or twice now I spotted high, stubby, self-contained tractors speedily towing British guns in the distance.

Now an occasional tank appeared in the distance, fired a few rounds at us, and disappeared again. Even more uncomfortable was the strafing we now received from Hurricanes. We called them, in the rough slang of soldiers, '*Huren-Kähne*,' which I leave you to translate for yourself. They attacked us repeatedly. They set light to two of my best and newest caterpillars, and the columns of smoke that rose from these pin-pointed our position.

I stood high in my car on the summit of the ridge, with the sun at my back, and through my glasses I saw, away towards Acroma, thick clouds of dust—caused, I guessed, by tanks. Now we were against the sunlit skyline. We dropped down over the lip and swept forward unchecked and unshelled.

Almost all our vehicles were down on the plain, spread out in a wide fan and racing towards Acroma, and we could see only a few tanks ahead of us when the first enemy shells began to fall. We halted, got our guns into action, and replied to the enemy's artillery. He held his fire. We limbered up again and sped on. Ahead of us we saw those old familiar landmarks, the telephone poles linking Acroma and our old headquarters at the 'White House.'

Now the enemy let loose heavy artillery fire from the stone battlements near the little Desert fort at Acroma. We were forced to halt before we reached the British sangars, and we swung our own guns into action again. Once more there was to be a meeting between our anti-tank weapons and their old deadly foes—the British tanks.

We tucked our vehicles away in a small wadi slightly to the west. Feverishly the men tried to dig in their weapons and themselves. But the ground was stony, and it took a Herculean effort to scrabble out any protection whatever. Some of the infantry detachments, however, were lucky in finding old slit-trenches that had been dug in an earlier clash. We awaited battle.

I had just given instructions to the N.C.O. in charge of the gun sited behind me, when two gazelle leaped up from among the rocks fifty yards ahead of me. I snatched up a rifle belonging to one of the gun crew near at hand. As a recruit in the army I had always been a poor shot. But now I seemed to be given a charmed touch. I dropped one gazelle with a single shot as he crossed our front. We brought the dead buck in at once and cut it up. Then we lit a fire with petrol and cleaning-rags in the wadi, where the vehicles lay, and roasted it forthwith.

All was still quiet in my sector on the left. But the company on my right came under machine-gun fire, and I heard them replying. I investigated the slit-trench that Lance-Corporal Muller had dug for me and himself. Formerly my batman, Muller was now my company runner, as all officers under the rank of colonel had been deprived of batmen in order to conserve front-line manpower.

I looked out through the glasses, which Muller had laid conveniently for me on the edge of the trench, and saw that we were almost on top of the British outposts: not a mile away runners were moving among the rocks. To the right of me stood my company sergeant-major, Taudt, exposed from the waist upward in his trench, calmly firing at the enemy.

I thought again about our venison, and called out to Muller to run back to the wadi and see that our share was not 'swiped' by the hungry gunners behind us. But I got no answer. Instead, at that moment there came a cry from many throats—an old familiar war-cry of the Desert: 'Tanks on the right!'

At that moment I saw Taudt fall, hit in the head. He dropped dead.

A dozen tanks emerged from dead ground ahead of the companies on my right. They were of types we did not know, heavier than the tanks we had met hitherto. As we knew to our cost later, they were American General Grants, which had arrived in quantity in the Middle East, though not in the numbers that Auchinleck had hoped for. They were nearer to being a match for our Mark III and Mark IV Panzers than anything the British had sent into the Desert before. The previous tanks supplied by the Americans—the General Stuarts or 'Honeys'—were fast but not really more effectual than armoured cars. Certainly they were not fit to meet heavy Panzers.

I held my fire, but the companies on the right let rip with the 50-mm. 'pak' guns. I saw some of their shells bounce harmlessly off the Grants. On the other hand the enemy's replying fire was grim. His shell-bursts among our infantry were particularly deadly.

Now a shiver went through me. From out of the dip emerged rank after rank of the new tanks—a good sixty in all. They came at us with every muzzle blazing.

I got my right gun into action. It stopped one tank. Several others were burning. But the bulk of them came on relentlessly. What was wrong with my left gun, I wondered? It was silent, its muzzle still drooping to the ground. I leaped from my trench despite the stuff whistling all round and raced to the gun.

Two of the crew were sprawled on the ground. The breech of the gun was shattered. The loader lay beside a wheel, bleeding from a machine-gun bullet in the chest. 'Water, water,' he gasped.

A fresh salvo burst beside the gun. Tanks were obviously attacking it at almost point-blank range. To stop there meant death.

I dropped prone, and tried to cradle the head of the wounded man in my arms.

He shook his head at me.

'I'll carry you to my trench—there's water there,' I shouted in his ear. He shook his head again. To my consternation, he heaved himself to his feet and half stumbled, half ran towards my slit-trench.

Now the tanks were right on top of the front lines in the sector to my right. I scrambled back towards my trench. Muller was not there. I dragged the wounded gun-number halfway into the hole with me. My Italian water-bottle, half-full of coffee, lay there, and I thrust it into the man's shaking hand. He drank greedily, and then sagged back, dead. His legs dangled in the hole; his torso lay twisted on the rim of it.

Shell-bursts were now erupting all round. Was I alone out

here now? As I wondered this, there came a reply from behind, where Sergeant Weber was firing my third gun. He pumped out shell after shell. But there was little help in his valour.

Twelve tanks swung at us to neutralize this menace. Their guns blazed insistently at us, and they came straight on.

I dropped my glasses and rolled to the bottom of my trench, where Muller had spread a blanket. I dragged it over myself in ineffectual protection. The toes of the dead man's boots dangled six inches from my eyes.

The earth trembled. My throat was like sandpaper. This, then, was the end. I had escaped at Sidi Rezegh. But now this was it. My fiancée would be told: 'With deep regret we have to inform you that . . .' She would read that I had died a hero's death for the Fatherland. And what would it mean? That I was just a bloody mess in the sand at an unidentified spot near an unimportant point in the Desert called Acroma.

A tank crunched by at the edge of my trench. I heard an English voice calling. Was it a man in the tank, or an infantryman following up with bayonet fixed?

A blanket is not much good against a bayonet. But perhaps they would not see me. Perhaps I should just lie here and go mad. Perhaps I should be killed by a shell. Perhaps another tank would crush me.

The minutes crawled by. I now heard German voices. Apparently the British were rounding up prisoners in my own sector. And here was I in the trench.

Firing had ceased. After perhaps a quarter of an hour I heard the tanks rolling off towards the south. Silence descended on the battlefield. But I still lay there like a sleeping man.

When I lifted my head the sky had dimmed from its brassy afternoon glare. Evening was coming. I saw no sign of life all round. Then I was startled by a figure that burst like a jack-in-the-box from a slit-trench some way back. It was my man Muller.

He had an anguished expression on his face. 'Are you well, Herr Oberleutnant?' he called to me. And he added oddly, 'I am not.'

'Get down here,' I ordered Muller. 'We shall wait until it is dark before we move.'

'Herr Oberleutnant,' said Muller, 'that venison was just ready when the Tommies came.'

As soon as darkness had fallen on the battlefield Muller led me back to the wadi, where the gazelle had been roasted. A haunch, still warm, lay on a sheet of iron there. Muller's flask still held coffee. We tore off hunks of the tasty but exceedingly tough meat and swallowed it.

I can still remember the feeling of the juice running down from the corners of my mouth. It was good to be alive. That sense of futility and the inevitability of death that had overwhelmed me in the slit-trench had gone. The will to live is strong in us.

Not all of us, though, had lived on. I looked at Sergeant Weber's gun. A British tank had driven straight at it, and over it. It was mangled. Weber himself had got away. We met him a hundred yards up a wadi, with eight other survivors.

There was little left of the battalion. Some of our vehicles lay round destroyed. Many had been carried off as booty. A few had escaped.

I took command of the party, and we set off south. About ten o'clock we ran into another little knot of survivors from the battalion. We plodded on.

Very lights flared up in the sky: from their bright magnesium tint I guessed they were German. One of my men sent up a green over white over red flare, and we walked on, periodically exchanging these recognition signals. An hour later we walked in upon a squadron of armoured cars. They were a special formation under Rittmeister Hohmeyer, Rommel's own personal reconnaissance unit.

Next morning the trucks attached to the armoured car squadron ran us over to headquarters of the 115th Regiment, which had now dropped back southward. We learned that the battalion had been virtually destroyed. The battalion commander, Lieutenant-Colonel Roske, who had joined us only in March, was a prisoner. I was the only surviving company commander, and indeed only one other officer had escaped. About thirty men remained of perhaps 350 who had gone into action.

These remnants were split up among the other two battalions in the Regiment pending regrouping. The battalion, reborn, was to fight in the end at El Alamein.

I was now regarded as being qualified for appointment as a Battalion Commander, and went into the Divisional Reserve. I was attached to Regimental Headquarters and went in with the troops when we attacked and took Tobruk; after that victory I had a chance of flying back to Germany on leave. My original spell of leave was to have been three weeks, but it was extended to eight; and the young officer from the Desert certainly had tales —among them the story of Tobruk—with which to regale the stay-at-homes.

CHAPTER TWENTY-SIX

IN THE BALANCE

THAT day my battalion was overrun had been a crazy day of battle. Rommel's objective was still Tobruk; but we were not in the happiest plight. For long it seemed as if we should be the vanquished and not the victors in this relentless Desert encounter.

One of our battle groups from the 90th Light had overrun the headquarters of Major-General Messervy, the commander of the British 7th Armoured Division, and made him prisoner with all his staff. The General was wearing shirt and shorts, and wore no badges of rank. He was not identified. He escaped in the confusion of a counter-attack, and we never knew we had him in our hands until much later.

We were up against it. Unnoticed, Cruwell, commanding the Afrika Korps, had been shot down in his Fieseler Storch over the 50th Division positions in the Gazala Line, and had been taken prisoner. Rommel and his staff were, as usual, forward with us. The Commander bore a charmed life, but Gause was wounded. Bayerlein took over the post of Chief of Staff to Rommel. Nehring was flown swiftly across the Mediterranean to replace Cruwell.

We were badly stuck at Got el Ualeb. There the British 150th Brigade occupied a strong position, and our early efforts to breach the minefield had failed. We had to depend for supplies on the long, exposed route around Bir Hacheim. The bulk of our force moved south under Rommel's orders to make contact with a supply convoy, which the R.A.F. in any case bombed intensively.

The British armour closed with us on May 29, and there was a desperate tank battle. We had a full armoured division[1] against us, plus two other brigades, but in the afternoon a sandstorm blew up and ended the battle. One could see neither foe nor friend. That battle might have gone ill for us, and it might have saved Tobruk for the British.

At dawn next day the British came at us again where we lay, but

[1] The 1st Armoured Division.

we gradually moved westward without being forced into any precipitate withdrawal. The Italians during the battle on the day before had at last managed to force a gap through the minefield at the Trigh el Abd and the Trigh Capuzzo, and we had a channel by which we could either retire west of the Gazala Line again or else be more easily supplied. The gap was heavily shelled from both sides by the French and the British, but at least it was passable.

Rommel decided to pull his tanks back through the gap. We used our proven method of covering the withdrawal, and set up a screen of anti-tank guns in a wide arc astride the Trigh Capuzzo. The right flank of the screen rested on the British minefield.

British tanks came up from the south to try to outflank our screen on the north, but they were too far off; and, besides this, it seemed that General Ritchie was now debating whether it was not time for him to move over to the offensive and send his tanks away around Bir Hacheim in the south to take us in turn in the flank and rear.

That day, indeed, as we learned afterwards, he planned to launch the South Africans and the British 50th Division up the coast road, as a diversion to distract our forces from his tank move in the south. But his formations were not ready for the projected attack.

And on the following day Ritchie realized that Rommel was not beaten and had no intention of withdrawing, but was just regrouping west of the minefield gap. He was already planning to attack again the moment he could.

2

The day scheduled for the capture of Tobruk had passed, and we in the salient at the minefield gap were not entirely happy. Ammunition was short, and supplies were scarcely trickling through. Every single supply-column that came forward was heavily attacked by the R.A.F. The Free French at Bir Hacheim were still fighting heroically and had taken prisoners in counterattacks. The advancing mobile reserves of the Eighth Army, so we thought, looked as though they might be able to hem us in.

We were sitting as though in a cage between the minefield and the enemy, with little ammunition, short rations, and less water. We could spare little for our prisoners, who were mostly men of the 3rd Indian Motor Brigade. Even our own troops surreptitiously tapped water from radiators to drink.

The fate of the Afrika Korps depended on whether communications could be effectively established through that minefield.

Rommel gambled again on the afternoon of May 31. He threw everything he had into an attack on the 150th Brigade. British tanks came to the aid of the infantry, but by noon on the next day they were overwhelmed. We wiped out most of a brigade of the enemy's tanks.[1] Ritchie also counter-attacked with another British brigade from the north and an Indian brigade from the east.[2] These attacks failed.

Ritchie's aim had been to fight a way through the minefield and send his tanks westward to close our own gaps and stage another tank battle, while the South Africans in the north tried to advance along the coast road.

The British effort was a fiasco. Briefly, the upshot was that Ritchie lost four regiments of field artillery, an Indian brigade,[3] the motor battalion of an armoured brigade;[4] and we knocked out a large number of tanks, besides inflicting numerous casualties on other units. The enemy was badly disorganized, because we overran the tactical headquarters of one division and smashed up his communications through destroying a number of Signals units.

Rommel was on top then. By the evening of June 5 he reckoned, I think, that he had Tobruk in the bag after all.

[1] The 1st Army Tank Brigade.

[2] Ritchie's main counter-attack was launched on June 5 with the 9th and 10th Indian Brigades, supported by the 22nd Armoured Brigade, from the east. The 69th Brigade, supported by the 32nd Army Tank Brigade, attacked from the north.

[3] The 10th Indian Brigade, commanded by Brigadier C. H. Boucher.

[4] The 22nd Armoured Brigade, under Brigadier W. G. Carr.

CHAPTER TWENTY-SEVEN

AT THE GATES

AGAINST Bir Hacheim Rommel now launched Special Group 288, a highly mobile formation originally trained for special operations in the Middle East. (I was later to command a battalion of this formation.) But, despite strong Stuka attacks and intensive artillery preparation, Koenig's Frenchmen continued to defend themselves tenaciously.

They held out until the night of June 10, supplied by air. Then it was no longer possible for the British to supply them, and they were ordered to withdraw. A large part of the garrison succeeded in breaking out and rejoining the Eighth Army farther east. Theirs was the first sign of a revival of French fighting vitality since the *débâcle* of France in 1940. This time they had held out against the great Rommel of the 'Ghost Division.'

The Gazala front had now been pierced in two places, although Pienaar's South Africans were still intact at the northern end of the line. Rommel decided to risk a thrust at El Adem. The 90th Light Division pushed forward, followed by the weakened Panzer divisions, and won the ground south of the aerodrome.

In these days was fought the terrible tank-to-tank battle of the 'Cauldron' at Knightsbridge. The story of that victory lies simply in the superior hitting power of our Panzer and anti-tank guns. The British armour was beaten, and when the tank battle was lost Tobruk was really lost.

When Ritchie's tanks had been worsted, he realized that the South Africans and the 50th Division at the seaward end of the Gazala Line were imperilled, and he pulled them out. The 50th Division broke out through the Desert and fought a way through our formations to get to Tobruk and, though it suffered heavy losses, did not seem damaged in morale.

The South Africans came out nearly intact between the evening of June 14 and the afternoon of the 15th, using three roads down the escarpment to the coast road. We got troops and Panzers down the escarpment, and cut the coast road, but many of the enemy struggled back to Tobruk over the rough tracks nearer the sea.

Auchinleck, as Rommel pieced it together afterwards, had planned earlier to avoid a second siege of Tobruk. His plan was to occupy the stronghold, and to keep back Rommel's forces by holding tactically sound positions some distance south and south-west of the Tobruk perimeter with static troops and with mobile columns based on his defended localities.

After our capture of the Gazala positions Auchinleck apparently gave orders that we were to be halted on a line from Acroma to El Adem and southward, and that encirclement of the fortress was to be avoided at all costs. Auchinleck had not abandoned his plan for a counter-blow with reorganized formations as soon as he had received reinforcements from Syria[1]—Rommel regretted he could do nothing to stop these arriving—but at the same time Auchinleck got ready defensive positions on the Egyptian frontier.

The Tobruk garrison was strengthened to include four to five infantry brigades plus slow 'I' tanks and artillery—but not enough artillery, as we found.

General Klopper, of the South African 2nd Division, took over command of the fortress. His own 4th and 6th Brigades and a composite brigade from Pienaar's 1st Division took over the sector in the west of Tobruk from the sea to the El Adem road. The 6th Brigade was in the extreme west, the 4th more on the southern flank. They covered the sector which Rommel had attacked assiduously in 1941, when the Australians held Tobruk.

East of the South Africans now was the 11th Indian Brigade,[2] holding the sector in which I was particularly interested—for we were going to assault the fortress this time from El Duda, where, in November, the British had broken out, and Rommel had also planned to attack.

The day Klopper took over command, June 15, the Panzer Reconnaissance Group commanded by Rittmeister von Hohmeyer, under Rommel's personal control, reached Sidi Rezegh. The Desert Fox at once put the final touches to his plans for the assault.

Tobruk had become an obsession with him. For over a year its capture had been the dominant desire in his mind, even though he

[1] The 10th Corps Headquarters and the New Zealand Division.
[2] Brigadier A. Anderson.

engaged in other operations. He said he could not take Egypt if he left Tobruk behind. His meticulously thought-out plan for the November attack had been thwarted by 'Crusader.' But now he had the upper hand again, and he intended to apply his old plan as chronologically and exactly as possible, and to use every available ounce of force.

Once more I found myself on the familiar ground south of El Adem, with Rommel all the time moving round among us, stocky, determined, behaving just as he had done in the months when I was at his side.

Enemy artillery fire and aircraft made our lives a misery. A distraction was an attack by a combat group of our 15th Panzer Division. The British, backed up by tanks, held firm. Our friends of the 21st sent a battle group to attack the Indians at Sidi Rezegh, but were held off by guns and bombing. While the 90th Light made a feint towards El Adem, the greater part of the 21st moved down the valley towards Sidi Rezegh again, and next day they took it.

During the night the El Adem defenders[1] were withdrawn, to the great disappointment, I believe, of Auchinleck, who wanted them to be reinforced and to hold on. Now the fate of the garrison in Tobruk itself was more than ever sealed.

So, on the 17th, I set eyes again on the mosque at Sidi Rezegh, where I had been wounded and where the South Africans had suffered so heavily seven months before. There was another fierce fight that afternoon. Rommel threw about a hundred of our Panzers against the British 4th Armoured Brigade and smashed up all but twenty of their tanks. The British armour fell back almost to Gambut, leaving Tobruk unprotected.

Now I saw that familiar, upstanding, angular Command Vehicle—the Mammoth—roll down the El Adem slope again, with Rommel sitting in his customary position in the roof aperture. He said:

'The shield that should have protected the weak side of the fortress east of here has been smashed. We have won the first round before the battle for the immediate protective belt of Tobruk. We must take advantage of this situation immediately. All formations will assault the fortress with all the power at their command.'

[1] The 29th Indian Brigade (Brigadier D. W. Reid).

CHAPTER TWENTY-EIGHT

WE SMASH TOBRUK

THOSE June days in the Desert in 1942 were hot, but the nights and early mornings cold. None was colder, I thought, than the night of June 19–20. Or was it perhaps suppressed excitement that made me shudder so often? The night was calm except for occasional explosions. But in a few hours there was to be bedlam.

Groups of crouching figures huddled in woollen blankets in a little wadi at El Duda. There was almost no conversation, and that in whispers, as though the enemy, who was, perhaps, miles away, might hear us. What chatter there was seemed flippant and irrelevant: it was characteristic of talk before a battle.

Next to each group—combat engineers and infantry storm-troops—lay the arms and other paraphernalia gathered during the day: explosives, grenades, mine-detectors, wire-cutters, flame-throwers, smoke-screen candles, machine-guns, ammunition.

A few minutes to zero hour.

A few minutes for thought—especially for those of us who had taken part, during April and May of the year before, in the futile assaults on this almost hated fortress.

I felt more optimistic now than when we had been in the Pilastrino–Medawwa sector the previous year. Was this because we seemed to be riding on a wave of success? Or was it because we sensed—in fact, were certain—that Tobruk could not be as well prepared as it had been in 1941? Or was it because ever since I had got to know the Tobruk front well, I had regarded El Duda as the best spring-board for an attack?

My thoughts went back to the beginning of April 1941, when Rommel, during a tour of this sector, ordered me to lead a night reconnaissance patrol. Hundt, an experienced officer of the 5th Light Division, and I (each with three men operating the mine-detectors) had silently explored the position we were now occupy-ing, and the ground ahead. After several hours we had worked

KESSELRING AND ROMMEL IN CONFERENCE
Imperial War Museum

THE AUTHOR IN HIS CAR IN THE DESERT

The Afrika Korps insignia is painted on the door.

our way right forward to the foremost trench positions. To our surprise we had found them unoccupied.

Before daybreak we had crawled back in a more northerly direction, parallel to the Bardia road. Rommel had been most interested in my report, but was not prepared then to mount an operation of any kind on that part of the perimeter. But the value of the patrol to me was that now I knew the lie of the land.

2

'Get ready!' The call passed down the line. Midnight had just passed. Cigarettes were stubbed out, weapons and equipment clattered, dark shapes rose up everywhere. We boarded our vehicles and drove cautiously some distance nearer our objective. We debused, and stalked forward on foot over the last few miles, with straining eyes and quickened ears. Half-right in the firmament was the bright North Star, which helped me to orientate myself.

We brought the mine-detectors into action, but no mines interrupted our progress. Sea-shells—relics of a bygone age when the Mediterranean had washed over this Desert plateau—crunched treacherously under our boots.

Then barbed-wire loomed up in the grey night. The hands of the mine-detectors began to move, and the instruments sang out a muffled warning. All was quiet in the enemy lines. Only an occasional shell swished high overhead.

The infantrymen crept silently into position. Under cover of our weapons a few combat engineers worked silently forward to the barbed-wire. In dead silence they nipped the barrier, strand by strand. They lifted a number of mines. They crawled back to us. We lay on our bellies and waited for instant action at dawn.

To one side we heard a rat-tat of a Vickers gun, followed by a shorter but quicker burst from a German machine-gun. Assault troops on our flank must have come in contact with the enemy or perhaps run into a patrol. Then all was quiet again, and we settled down to await the signal to attack.

The false dawn gleamed in the sky. Then day broke. Our guns opened up. First singly, then with growing intensity, they plunged down on the enemy perimeter. The first shells burst only a few yards ahead of us. I began to fear we should have to fire a Very light as a warning, and that would betray our positions. But the barrage crept forward.

Then a full-throated roar: our Stukas were approaching. Carefully we laid out the identification strips we had brought with us. Before now we had been given a taste of our own Stuka bombs (which was to happen again at El Alamein).

The battle was on. Away to the flank that had been jittery before, heavy machine-gun and mortar fire broke out. The Stukas dropped their noses and swooped down over our heads. They plunged at the enemy perimeter. Bombs screamed down and crashed into the minefield. Rommel had thought up a new trick in the Desert. He was not bombing the defenders, but blasting a way through the minefield. One crash would be followed by another and another and a whole series: one bomb would detonate a chain of mines, like some atomic fission continuing on beyond the first explosive shock. The Stukas, their bomb-bays empty, their motors roaring, swung back low over our heads. They flew without interference, for the R.A.F. had been driven off Gambut airfield, and the Luftwaffe had no *Huren-kähne* to harass them.

When the first bomb fell we saw a few figures ahead darting back towards shelter. Enemy outposts. But we were lying in a shallow wadi and seemed not to have been spotted. Now was the moment. We emptied our machine-gun belts in swift succession towards the ground where the enemy had disappeared, and hammered away at a barely perceptible structure that suggested the existence of a strong-point.

Our combat engineers jumped up and advanced. They carried explosives with which to destroy further wire entanglements. Then hell was let loose.

Heavy fire from the defending 11th Indian Brigade[1] met us. From the flank one machine-gun was steadily raking us with long bursts, but the combat engineers pressed on relentlessly. They sent up Very lights as signals to the artillery. The barrage crept farther. Then they lit their smoke candles.

This was our signal. Under cover of the smoke screen we swept forward. A few men fell. But rapid strides soon took us to the first trench. It was empty. We had cover now, and a good field of

[1] The 2nd Queen's Own Cameron Highlanders, 2/5 Mahrattas, 2/7 Gurkhas,

fire. Through the shell-fire from Tobruk, which was now falling behind us, our motorized infantry with anti-tank guns and Panzer support was rolling on towards the gap.

The combat engineers tackled the anti-tank ditch. It had silted up in parts. They bridged it and filled it in. The Panzers rumbled forward. Our reinforced infantry now scrambled from trench to trench. I spared a moment to look away towards our right. We had made good progress there. Our troops had swept on ahead, and were already laying flanking fire on the positions ahead of us.

Good—a great help!

We were not being heavily hammered by the Tobruk artillery, for the main weight of the enemy's shelling was being flung against the Panzers and the motorized infantry of the 15th Division. And we were almost through the stronghold line.

For a moment an unexpected minefield delayed our advance. Then the Panzers broke through, with the infantry and the anti-tank guns behind them. The Indians, particularly the 2/5 Mahrattas, hit back as best they could. But they seemed to have been stunned by the suddenness of the attack and the shock of the Stuka bombing. The 2/7 Gurkhas came racing up in Bren-carriers to counter-attack. But they were swept down, swept aside, swept back by the concentrated fire of machine-guns, anti-tank guns, and mortars.

It was half-past seven or later before the Tobruk artillery really began to lay down concentrated fire on us—and then it was too late. The enemy gunners had followed the Panzers in among us. But by now we had good cover, and were glad of it.

The attack had gone according to plan, except that it had succeeded sooner than expected. We had lost a few dead and wounded, but the casualties were relatively light. Now we passed our first prisoners back, and went forward. My men linked up with some advancing troop-carriers of the 115th Rifle Regiment.

During that forenoon Rommel's Panzers, screened by a line of mobile anti-tank guns from the 1st Motorized Infantry, ploughed steadily along towards their first objective—the fork of the Tobruk–El Adem and Bardia roads, which the Tobruk defenders called King's Cross.

As early as 1941 we had known that the enemy had sited his most effective batteries in this area. We were held up by a number of batteries, at first of Royal Artillery and later, I think, of South

African Artillery, but gun after gun was knocked out or overrun by our Panzers and infantry.

Other Panzers met the 4th Royal Tank Regiment near King's Cross and smashed them up. The British tanks were a scratch formation and had been hurriedly rushed forward as a counter-attack force; they seemed disorganized and were not co-ordinated with infantry support. They were no match for our Mark III's and Mark IV's, and by the middle of the morning only half a dozen of them were still runners. They struggled away from the scene of the action.

A few other tanks, a squadron or so, tried to attack us from where the Cameron Highlanders of the Indian Brigade were still fighting as best they could. But they, too, were smashed up by the 90th Light's anti-tank guns on the Bardia side of King's Cross. Only four of the tanks, our men said afterwards, got away from that fight.

But our Panzers were not interested in a few surviving tanks. The plan was for them to cut the fortress in two by pressing on north to the harbour.

We knew that the South Africans had not yet been engaged. They had been waiting in vain for us to attack them frontally on their sector. Now we were inside the fortress behind them. One group of our Panzers turned to the west, with portions of the 90th Light, to complete the consolidation of a west flank facing these infantry reserves of the enemy's, and to deal with the 201st Guards' Brigade.

Fourteen other Panzers, accompanied by motorized infantry from our 15th Division, raced down the road towards the harbour, despite defensive gunfire and the vain firing of infantry in trucks. Our Panzers, supported by our 115th Regiment, overran more British batteries. Soon we could see the harbour clearly. Two small ships, steaming furiously, were fleeing; we turned 88-mm. 'flak' guns on to them, but they reached the open sea.

And then we were racing past a mass of immobile trucks—the vehicles the enemy would have needed if he were ever to attempt a break-out from the fortress with his beaten garrison. We were at the harbour, according to plan, before dark. We had disorganized and disrupted Tobruk, and not even needed to exchange fire with the greater part of the garrison—Klopper's South Africans.

Rommel himself had been inside the Tobruk fortress since midday. Prisoners marched past his Mammoth at the King's Cross intersection, but few seemed to guess that the short, sturdy, figure, standing with legs straddled on the roof, watching, through his field-glasses, the advance of his Panzers, was the Desert Fox himself. Rommel knew now that his ambition, his aim for fourteen months, had been achieved.

General Klopper, as far as we could make out, was not far away at the time. By four o'clock in the afternoon tanks were within half a mile of him, and he seems to have shifted his headquarters then, through *force majeure*. There was little more he could do.

Thick columns of smoke mounted vertically to the heavens. Burning ammunition was exploding in dumps near the port. When the sun went down, the harbour was entirely in Rommel's hands. The Guards' Brigade—Klopper's fortress reserve—had been overrun and their headquarters destroyed. But the South Africans were still virtually intact.

During the night, Rommel planned to attack them from the rear, and drafted a special scheme for an assault, on a compass bearing between the port and Pilastrino.

Meanwhile Klopper was holding a midnight conference with his officers as to whether he should attempt a break-out—which was impossible for lack of transport—or fight to the end. He was in wireless touch with the Eighth Army. Ritchie, however, was not there, and so his only orders came from subordinates. The Eighth Army wanted to hang on for twenty-four hours. But at the same time the Eighth Army failed to get a tank force back from the Gambut region to the Tobruk perimeter to help Klopper.

The hasty plans considered by the South Africans throughout the night for a last stand were futile. In the rocky ground of the Tobruk perimeter it would have been impossible by dawn to throw up hasty new defences to face the rear of the old line. Nothing could have been improvised to stave off Rommel's attack, particularly since there was no sign of any diversion or intervention by the British armoured forces.

At a quarter to eight in the morning Klopper surrendered.

3

Twenty-five thousand men and enormous quantities of supplies fell into Rommel's hands. Before the day ended, Hitler had promoted him Field-Marshal. We all celebrated—with captured tinned fruit, Irish potatoes, cigarettes, and canned beer.

For a day or so we rejoiced in the blessings of the British Naafi. It was a pleasure to snuffle round the field-kitchens, where pork sausages and potatoes, so long a rarity, were being fried. There was British beer to drink, and tinned South African pineapples for dessert.

We spurned our own rations, especially 'Alte Mann,' with distaste and contempt. Instead we gloried in Australian bully beef, of which the Australians were as sick as we were of 'Alte Mann.' It was some time, however, before we could find ourselves agreeing with the sentiments expressed in captured enemy letters, which were far from extolling the deliciousness of bully. When conditions permitted, we used to send home parcels of Australian bully. It was regarded in Germany as a luxury.

CHAPTER TWENTY-NINE

POST MORTEM: WHY TOBRUK FELL

THERE was little time then for a post-mortem on Tobruk. But the military question posed was clear to see. Could it be fairly held that Tobruk had held out through a seven months' siege and had now failed to resist one day of similar assault?

I think not. In the early part of 1941, when he first bumped against the Australian perimeter at Tobruk, Rommel had not even one complete German division at his disposal. He employed a great part of his available strength in preparing a practically fool-proof investment of the position. He certainly did not attack the fortress for seven months on end. The only sustained assaults he made were those in April and early May of 1941. Thereafter he concentrated his attention on the frontier, while perfecting his plans for an all-out assault in November. That assault might have succeeded; but it would have been launched against a tougher fortress than the Tobruk of June 1942.

Through the months of the Australians' tenure of Tobruk, they had steadily and skilfully strengthened the defences until Tobruk could in no way be compared with the place that Wavell took. Rommel's early attacks were directed against two particularly strong sectors in the south-west of the fortress, and as he repeated his tactics the defenders were successful in concentrating their reserves, and especially their tanks, where the threat developed. And when the offensive died down they were able to build up strength all round the perimeter.

When Rommel attacked in June the defenders were not nearly so well prepared physically or psychologically. There was nothing wrong with the morale of the South Africans, though the greater part of the Division here was relatively inexperienced; they had not been hardened by constant battle as most of their comrades and most of the Afrika Korps had been. The garrison as a whole probably did not envisage defeat, but nevertheless the Eighth Army had been forced out of the strong Gazala Line, the terrible tank battles of Knightsbridge had been lost, and those in the fortress knew that the mass of the rest of the Eighth Army had fallen far back to the frontier.

Though not depressed, the garrison was not obviously in a victorious mood. Rommel was flushed with success, and so were the men of the Afrika Korps.

Physically, the Tobruk fortress had been allowed to deteriorate because no renewed siege had been visualized. In November the Eighth Army had been confident of relieving it almost at a swoop. After a fluctuating battle it had been relieved in early December. Rommel had been thrust back to El Agheila, though he could not be pushed beyond there; and Tobruk seemed psychologically to be looked on by the British just as a convenient forward supply base.

Even when the Eighth Army fell back to Gazala, Tobruk was not intensively prepared to resist an enemy attack: would not outlying strong-points and mobile columns hold the enemy at a distance? The minefields were, in fact, weakened, and many thousands of mines shifted forward to strengthen the Gazala Line. The anti-tank ditch was even allowed to silt up.

And finally, for some reason, when Tobruk was really menaced, it seemed to be expected that Rommel would once again attack in the Medawwa sector. This, despite the capture of some of our secret documents, which revealed Rommel's early plan for outflanking Bir Hacheim and the Gazala Line and striking up at the El Adem and Sidi Rezegh areas! That early plan provided for an attack on the fortress from El Duda if we got so far; and now Rommel had put the early plan into precise operation, still achieving, as results showed, more than an element of surprise.

Rommel must be conceded an advantage now that he had lacked fourteen months before. At that time his knowledge of the defences was almost nil, and even later it was negligible. The first map which contained any accurate detailed information was available only after the first attacks, and the number and formidable nature of the strong-points came as a surprise. But the defences had been studied closely in the following months, and the strength and weakness of each sector had been accurately assessed by the time plans were made for the projected attack in November.

Now, in June, every part of the defences was weaker than in

November. Tobruk had a sea frontage of twenty-five miles and a land frontage of thirty-three miles. Yet to protect this considerable front the Eighth Army had provided only sixty-one anti-tank guns, of which, as we later learned, only eighteen were 6-pounders. That did not permit the garrison commander to concentrate a sufficient force in reserve to provide an anti-tank screen that could beat off a weighty thrust of Panzers, or to hold them up long enough to enable his own defending tanks to concentrate for an effective counter-attack.

Tobruk fell because no proper plan had been formed to meet the contingency that it might be attacked headlong, and because the armour that was supposed to keep Rommel from getting within striking distance of it had been shattered in the field.

CHAPTER THIRTY

ON LEAVE

ROMMEL had taken Tobruk, but he was not content. He was not going to linger there in triumph. Not two days after he had swept in, his forces had been reorganized for a further advance.

On June 22 light forces had dashed along the coast road and entered Bardia, which Rommel had regarded as such a prize when von Wegmar reached it the year before. That night the 1st South African Division, who had been holding rearguard positions on the coastal end of the Halfaya escarpment, were withdrawn; and in the morning Rommel was getting ready to push across into Egypt south of Sidi Omar.

At dawn on the 24th he threw his mobile forces forward from Halfaya, through the Desert, and along the road. By nightfall we were level with Sidi Barrani, only forty miles or so from Mersa Matruh, and some of our armoured cars were actually twenty miles still farther forward.

Rommel had conferred with his nominal superior, Bastico, the Italian, when his vanguard reached Bardia. Bastico held that we should halt at and occupy the Sollum front again, and not attempt an advance into Egypt. But Rommel assured Bastico that Kesselring had promised all supply problems would be solved, and that therefore the logistics of an advance into Egypt were safe. On that, Bastico left the final decision to Rommel. And Rommel decided to go on.

My own unit crossed the frontier away in the south at Maddalena and marched rapidly eastward. We reached the railway-line east of Sidi Barrani on the evening of the 25th. That was the day Auchinleck relieved Ritchie of command of the Eighth Army and took over leadership in person. Rommel had now knocked out two Eighth Army Commanders (Cunningham and Ritchie) and had faced two Commanders-in-Chief (Wavell and Auchinleck). He was to see Auchinleck go, too; and then to meet Alexander and Montgomery.

These two famous British generals were in the Desert before I saw action again, and that was at El Alamein in August, for I enjoyed the unexpected fortune of home leave.

2

I now made a mistake in my assessment of the strategical situation. I thought that Rommel would not advance deep into Egypt; or that if he planned to do so, the Eighth Army would still be strong enough to hold him on the Sollum front.

I should have known better, if only because I knew Rommel's daring cast of mind. He had just brought off the seemingly impossible, and reduced Tobruk in a trice. He had become a world figure and the hero of his country. Hitler had at once promoted him Field-Marshal: his meteoric climb had advanced him from Colonel to Field-Marshal in three years.

Proud though I was of my minor association with the popular hero of the moment, I regarded myself entirely as a front-line soldier; and, when my Regiment was bivouacked some distance east of Tobruk two days after the capture of the fortress, I went to the II a of the 15th Panzer Division and asked pressingly, though respectfully, for a new fighting job. My own battalion might have been destroyed, but there was room in others for a fit young officer.

'True, Schmidt, you want men to command again,' the Staff officer nodded. 'But don't we all? What we lack is troops.' Then he said half jokingly, 'If we can't give you a command, why don't you go on leave?'

I reckoned that there was little chance of dramatic action on the Egyptian front for the next few weeks, and made a snap decision. I surprised the Major by saying, 'Yes, indeed. I should be delighted. After all, although I am only twenty-six, I am the "oldest" member of the German forces in Africa....'

Before I knew where I was, I had been hustled to Derna. An ideal opportunity for sending me home had been available to the II a. An urgent top-secret dispatch by hand of an officer had to go to Rome. I was told to fly there with it.

And so, within days of being in a bloody and historic action, I found myself walking the peaceful streets of the Eternal City, with elegant women and debonair men frequenting restaurants where life was suave and luxurious.

How sensible and sensuous at the same time the joy of a fawning barber—to have a haircut, a shampoo, a shave, a face massage, and a manicure from a glittering blonde! I ate ice-cream in a café and looked at the beautiful women who passed.

How glad I suddenly was that I should so soon see Herta, my sweetheart. And to think that, only a few days before, my greatest joy would have lain in seeing a successful Panzer battle reach its climax. Now war seemed unimportant, after all these months when it had been paramount; now personal relationships took their true place in life again.

After a bath I luxuriated in a crisp new shirt. The wife of a German-speaking Italian antique-dealer, from whom I had bought some trifle, offered to show me the ropes and to buy me items of clothing without worrying about coupons. So I gathered up silk stockings, an afternoon frock, a sports costume, a Borsalino felt hat, a handbag, gloves, a coat . . . I was relatively well-off, for I had received special pay from the Italians in Eritrea apart from my standard German army pay, and in North Africa there had been nothing on which one could spend money. Even the sunsets were free.

When we had done with shopping, I bought a pair of shoes for my obliging guide. She seemed to be more enthusiastic about this gift than about the victory of Tobruk.

I walked idly round the Palazzio Venezia. An exquisitely groomed young man in a black suit and black hat addressed me. His companion was a girl dressed in the full fig of Roman fashion, wearing fox furs despite the summer's day. She glanced idly at a shop window, while her escort spoke to me. He was my acquaintance of the Desert, the young Count who had helped me mend the tyre of the Mammoth when Rommel was stranded east of the frontier wire in Egypt.

'My dear fellow,' he said, 'pray let me introduce you. . . .' He effected the introduction. Then he went on with the affability of the well-bred: 'You simply must come and see me some time.'

I accepted the casual invitation with the enthusiasm of convention, but knew as well as he did that the whole business was purely one of form.

My mission in Rome was completed anyway. I had delivered

my dispatches to the Military Attaché. A leave train whirled me through Verona to the Brenner Pass, where I bought a bottle of Marsala which, when opened, smelled singularly of scented face-powder.

Then through the Alps to Munich. Civilian life here was far more straitened than it was in Italy. There was none of the elegance of the Roman promenade. Men and women were all working, all in a hurry, all in uniform or in factory clothes. In Rome swarms of porters had almost fought to carry my bags. Here in Munich I had to carry my own and like it. A captain and I, indeed, together wheeled a barrow with our luggage on it to the platform where the Cologne train was waiting.

At Hagen I left the train and walked to my parents' house. (There were no taxis.) My father walked down to my fiancée's home to tell her of my arrival, breaking the news gently to her that I was not lying dead in Africa. I changed out of military uniform into my old student's clothes, shedding my feeling of responsibility as I dropped on the bathroom floor the clothing that had taken me through the African campaign so far.

3

Herta and I went for walks in the quiet woods and planned for the day when we would marry. This was not entirely simple: an officer wanting to marry had first to receive special permission from the Adjutant-General of the Wehrmacht High Command. Permission was granted only on production of proof of the Aryan descent of the bride, a satisfactory medical certificate, and three testimonials of character from persons of repute. Finally, one's divisional commander also had to approve.

Herta sought, with womanly guile and all the instinctive shrewdness of the daughters of Eve through the centuries, to discover my sins of omission and commission during my long absence in Africa. She discovered them all right.

'What on earth did you do all that time in Asmara,' she asked, 'when your volunteer company had been disbanded and you were living in that posh hotel? Are you going to tell me you lived there all the time with Sergeant-Major Pohl?'

I did my best to give an account of all my doings, perhaps

slightly expurgated, but soon she knew more than I intended. Dear, dear, how scarlet my innocent little actions seemed to become! Under her subtle questioning I began to wonder whether the Desert was not relatively safer than home.

What could I do but admit, under smiling cross-examination, that, yes, there had been beautiful women living in the hotel. Yes, that their husbands were away with the forces. Who was the nicest of them? Oh, well, the wife of an Italian major....

What good after that to protest that the charming lady was the mother of three noisy children? Of course, I did not say that the eldest of the children was a beautiful girl of seventeen. She was always surrounded by a crowd of dashing young Italian subalterns. But I noticed in the hotel lounge that she was trying to learn German, and that her accent was not perfect. What else could I do but offer to assist?

The Italian opposition appeared to withdraw from the field. The language lesson proceeded with affability and success. That evening the signorina's mother sent across to my table, with her compliments and thanks, a bottle of Italian wine. Pohl, who shared my table, said sourly, 'From your mother-in-law, huh?'

Not to be outdone in courtesy, the following day I sent the signora a bottle of German export beer, which was part of the cargo the *Coburg* had loaded for the Far East many months before.

Next day our tables were moved closer together. Pohl, who had been married five years and therefore might be presumed to have lost his taste for mothers-in-law, ascribed this to the machinations of 'that mother-in-law of yours.'

Some days afterwards I asked the signora whether she would permit her daughter to come out for a day's hunting with me. Only later did my Italian friends explain the significance of my invitation: among Italians it would be interpreted as tantamount to an offer of marriage, and the grant of permission would be regarded as approval of the suit. The signora gave her consent to the excursion.

On the Sunday morning of the hunt I had planned, the signorina sent a message regretting that she felt unwell and could not come. So I had to put up with Pohl as a not entirely satisfactory substitute.

We were nearing the outskirts of the town when the paymaster of my now-disbanded company hailed me: 'Herr Leutnant, the Italian High Command has word that the aircraft in which you are to leave will be ready to go in half an hour. . . .' That was why I flew away from Asmara without saying good-bye to the ladies, and without kit, to meet Rommel.

Well, that was the story Herta wheedled out of me. All perfectly innocent. Would you think it could possibly get the narrator into trouble?

4

There I was, then, an Afrika Korps soldier on leave in Germany, hoping in vain for permission to get married. Four pleasant weeks of leave, and that was all. I remember walks with Herta along the Rhine, idle days in motor-boats, the time we climbed the Dragon Rocks and the Seven Mountains, the evenings when we drifted into the Café Dresden in Godesberg, where Hitler always kept a private room. . . . Ices and cakes; but the ices and cakes in Italy were better, sweeter. Only romance made those tasteless delicacies sweet to me then.

The girl had to go back to work, but for lack of transport facilities I got an extension of leave. There was no temptation to hang on in Germany doing nothing. But anybody who has known an army knows what a demand for transport and a movement order means. I was small fry. No use to say I was, or had been, Rommel's A.D.C.—and this though Rommel was Germany's hero at the moment. I was officially just a junior combatant officer without a specific unit to which to return. And Africa? Small stuff, again. The Eastern Front was the terrible, terrifying one now.

I fixed it so that I could spend my spare time at Bonn University, trying to catch up on the years of agricultural studies I had missed while in uniform. It was a distracted undertaking: with one ear I was listening to a lecture, and with the other straining for word of Africa. Only at week-ends could I slip home and see my sweetheart. And then again, waiting for word of a passage back to Africa, days spent at Bonn.

At the university, as everywhere else, girls outnumbered men. The girls were mostly trying to avoid work in factories. The men were mostly those unfit for war, plus a few on leave and snatching a chance of lectures. The girls were not interested in the war, or in the soldiers. A curious apathy seemed to lie over every one. Few doubted ultimate victory, but all they wanted was a swift end to the war and their present difficulties. At Bonn one saw relatively few in army uniform. Those who were in uniform were usually in the grey of the East Front soldier—the man who was fighting Russia. A number wore the light blue of the 'Anti-Flak' chaps from Sicily. The khaki of the Afrika Korps was a rarity. Wearing civilian clothes, I several times received a white feather.

My father, a man of the world, was a pessimist. He listened to what I had to say about the course of the war in Africa. And then he would shake his head. He listened, against orders, to the Allied radio.

'Rommel?' he would say. 'Perhaps. But let us be realists, my boy. . . .'

The heavy attacks had not yet begun on the Ruhr. But Cologne was hit. I went for a week-end to Cologne, and stayed at an hotel near the cathedral. The next week-end I went again. Only the spires and the wreckage stood now.

5

I reflected:

'Well, now, what has happened in Africa since I left? I was wrong when I thought we would not advance. We have swept forward to El Alamein. Rommel's forces lie at the gates of Alexandria and the Delta of the Nile. Sooner than we hoped, we broke through the minefield south of Matruh. We had a few fights with the 1st Armoured Division, but we were soon on the coast twenty miles east of that British stronghold. We had taken many prisoners. The possibility of a second Tobruk had gone. For the second time in a brief period, as time in the Desert goes—a bare fortnight—the 50th Division and the New Zealanders broke through Rommel's advancing formations, and got back to the Nile Delta. And then our men reached El Alamein. There we had only a few Panzers accompanying the mass of our transport vehicles. I hear we had scarcely more than twelve runners when we got there. And we were stopped not far short of Alexandria, by the South Africans. . . .'

Poor little Herta. She looked so pale when we waited in silence for the train. She could not restrain her tears. It was hard enough for me, but uniform and ribbons are disciplinary. Even so, as the train moved and she raced alongside it on the platform to prolong the last wave of farewell, I felt my eyes smart. If only—ah, well, to Africa again.

I took the train through Germany and down Italy to Brindisi. From there I was flown by way of Athens and Crete to the Tobruk airfield at El Adem, that place of poignant memory. I drove a car through the Desert, by the old coastal road, to the front, at El Alamein.

Now, truly, my leave was over: we were dive-bombed on the way forward. How far away lay the suave idleness of Rome, the tense gravity of home. This was the front again.

CHAPTER THIRTY-ONE

A STRANGER AT EL ALAMEIN

A NEW appointment awaited me at El Alamein. I took over command of a battalion of Special Group 288, a battle formation that, although originally trained for intended operations in Persia, had hitherto fought usually in co-operation with the 90th Light Division.

I was swiftly put into the picture of what had happened since I left the Afrika Korps.

Pursuing the Eighth Army, Rommel's reconnaissance forces had struck east until they had almost reached the insignificant railway halt of El Alamein when artillery fire greeted them. Our own artillerymen found an observation post on a ridge named Tel el Eisa. An armoured reconnaissance vehicle came rushing up. In it was Rommel himself. He gave orders for the troops to attack the northern sector of what appeared to be the new enemy line, taking advantage of the sinking sun. Infantry of the 90th Light, supported by a few pieces of artillery, went forward. They were met by machine-gun fire, detrucked, and dug in under cover of their own vehicles.

The battle of El Alamein, although they did not know it, had begun.

2

The sudden interruption of the forward gallop was actually welcomed by technical troops and by some commanders who wished to reorganize their formations. But the infantrymen did not feel so happy. They began to realize, almost from the moment they got to El Alamein as June ended, that the old days of fluid warfare were over, and now they were condemned to the dreariness and deadliness of static warfare—almost to trench warfare.

Our attacks against the northern sector of the new, vague line were unsuccessful. Pienaar's South Africans stopped us. A simultaneous attack on the Deir el Shein depression resulted in our destroying or capturing almost the entire 18th Indian Brigade Group on July 1.

Rommel continued to hit at the South Africans, and on the afternoon of July 2 he began seriously to menace the flank of Pienaar's position, particularly by intense shell-fire directed against an immobilized, semi-mobile column of Pienaar's own 1st Brigade, who had been among our most troublesome opponents in East Africa.[1] We learned afterwards that Pienaar requested his Corps Commander, General Norrie, for tank support, or otherwise for permission to withdraw his threatened left. The Corps Commander refused. It appears that Pienaar then appealed to Auchinleck in person, but the British Commander-in-Chief supported the Corps Commander. Norrie then, on further consideration, told Pienaar that he would agree to the withdrawal, but the 1st Brigade would in these circumstances be sent to the rear in reserve. Pienaar took this as an insult to his troops, and threatened to resign his command. A compromise was reached, and a short withdrawal of the exposed flank took place.

A sequel, which reached Rommel's ears only much later and then in what was assumed to be apocryphal form from prisoners, was the famous wisecrack ascribed to Pienaar. It was reported that not only Rommel's shells but the misdirected fire of the New Zealand Division were falling on the South Africans. They were also fired on by British tanks and bombed by their own aircraft. Pienaar is supposed to have made a telephone call to the Corps Commander, beginning: 'Look here, Norrie, tell me whom you are fighting—me or Rommel? If it should be me I can guarantee you that my South Africans will take Alexandria in forty-eight hours.'

We were not, of course, only up against the South Africans, although there is no doubt that but for them, and particularly for their effective 25-pounder guns, Rommel would have broken through. The New Zealanders—excellent troops, stern in defence, ready in attack, and most intelligent—were also in the line, despite the repeated and costly battles in the Desert where they had been so long.

The 9th Australian Division, the 'Rats of Tobruk,' one of the

[1] They had fought their way north through Abyssinia, and took part, with the 5th Indian Division, in the assault on Amba Alagi, in May 1941.

toughest formations put into the field by Australia, whose army had won a grim reputation among our men for their terrible work with the bayonet, had returned to the Desert from Syria or Palestine.

We also had against us Indian formations and British tanks. And in the months to come we were to be up against Frenchmen, Poles, and Greeks as well. Egypt was defended by a sort of League of Nations army, but by no Egyptians.

Throughout July both sides feverishly built up strong defensive fronts. There was plenty of scope for initiative and daring on both sides in attack and counter-attack, and in local actions for tactically important points.

The Australians succeeded in taking Tel el Eisa, which provided a commanding forward position for the Eighth Army. Rommel, on the other hand, had an advantageous position on the Miteiriyeh Ridge, on the southern flank, where he placed his élite troops.

The Parachute Brigade under General Ramcke, newly arrived from Crete, supported by Special Group 288 and selected men from the gallant Italian Folgore Parachute Division, were able to force back for a considerable distance the southern flank of the Eighth Army at the Qattara Depression.

During the second half of the month Auchinleck, with his Australian reinforcements and new tanks from overseas, developed such lively infantry activity that Rommel was occupied with thoughts of a possible enforced withdrawal to the Sollum positions. I do not think that the British ever had an inkling of this. Rommel was not happy about our shortage of munitions—the guns were almost without shells—or about the tremendous increase in activity by the enemy air forces, which were seriously depleting our supplies over the now lengthy lines of communications.

But towards the end of the month Auchinleck had to slacken his aggressiveness for lack of sufficient reserves. Rommel did not need to withdraw. If he had done so, it is doubtful whether the Eighth Army would have been in a position to pursue him effectively. There would probably have followed another period of vague stalemate on the frontier, and both sides would virtually have been back to where they were a year before.

In early August we heard of important changes in the command of the Eighth Army. Churchill visited El Alamein, and to him Auchinleck reported on the situation and his future plans. Churchill also met Gott, who had been earmarked to take over command of the Eighth Army, which Auchinleck was still leading in person since his dismissal of Ritchie. But fate decided otherwise, for Gott was killed by one of our aircraft, which machine-gunned him and the transport plane in which he was flying back from the front to a landing-ground near Cairo. But for this, we might never have heard of Montgomery.

General Alexander also arrived now, and Auchinleck was told by the Prime Minister that the War Cabinet had decided to replace him by Alexander. The new enemy chief was given a simple directive by Churchill: 'Your first and foremost duty will be, at the first possible opportunity, to destroy or capture the German-Italian army commanded by Field-Marshal Rommel in Egypt, together with all supplies and equipment.'

Alexander took over from Auchinleck, we understood, on August 15. Montgomery arrived from England three days later to become commander of the Eighth Army, which Churchill at that time described as 'brave but baffled.' Montgomery at once issued an order that there were to be no further withdrawals.

Though no fighting of importance took place at El Alamein for some time after August 6, Montgomery had already won a far-reaching victory against Rommel before he actually assumed his command. The visit of the British Prime Minister was proof that the Allied Powers had decided that great efforts must be exerted in this theatre. There was no such sign on our side. In Berlin North Africa was regarded as a theatre of at most secondary importance. Russia was the big show. Yet superhuman accomplishments were expected of Rommel, despite utterly inadequate reinforcements of men and equipment.

3

My new chief, commander of Special Group 288, was Colonel Menton. I had known of old that he and Rommel had been bosom friends since the First World War. They were both Swabians, and called each other by their Christian names.

When I reported to him for the first time, we swiftly got into a discussion about our mutual acquaintance with the Field-Marshal.

'The staff,' Menton remarked, 'is located on the coast near El Daba.'

I had not seen the Desert Fox since Tobruk, before I went on leave, so on the spur of the moment I asked Menton whether I might postpone taking over my battalion for a day in order to pay a personal call on the Field-Marshal.

'Go along by all means,' said Menton in his broad Swabian accent. 'Your battalion can't take up their positions for eight days yet. We are expecting replacements, and they are still held up in Crete.'

Next day I drove along the coast road until I saw the black, white, and red command flag of the Army Group, and turned off into the dunes where Rommel's headquarters lay. The armoured command-vehicles were partly dug in as protection against the enemy's air force, and all were camouflaged with nets interlaced with camel thorn. A guard saw to it that I parked my car some distance away, pointing in a different direction, so that its tracks should not by mischance disclose the location of the H.Q.

The faces of all the officers I met were strange. The staff had changed since my day. I caught my first glimpse of Bayerlein, the Chief of Staff. 'What sort of fellow is he?' I asked the young officer who pointed him out. 'Ein ganz patenter Kerl!' he replied—the highest possible compliment in the parlance of the German soldier: 'A most excellent fellow.'

Then I caught a sight of Berndt, the only familiar man among them all. I was glad to see him, but his response struck me as a little strained. I could not help feeling that Berndt might be afraid I had some intention of seeking reappointment to Rommel's staff, and that I should be a rival. If he did, he was completely mistaken, for I was happy with the troops. But I naturally wanted to see my old Chief again, and said so.

'That's bad luck, Schmidt,' Berndt murmured. 'The O.B. [Commander-in-Chief] will not be able to grant you an interview either to-day or to-morrow.'

'Why?' I asked. Berndt assumed an air of secrecy. I did not press him further.

'How long have you been back with the staff?' I asked him, for the sake of making conversation.

'I've been with the O.B. again for some months,' he said,

preening himself a little. 'My duty-leave with the Doctor [meaning Goebbels] expired in March. I had very important work to do there, but I returned here just at the right time, when the "schemozzle" started. I've been in the midst of it all, old boy.'

'What are you doing on the staff?' I asked. 'Are you an aide again?'

'No, no,' said Berndt. 'I am now in command of the Headquarters Security Company, which is soon to be increased to battalion strength. But apart from that, I am always in contact with the Ministry of Propaganda, so I am in daily touch with the Field-Marshal.'

I wondered whether Berndt regarded himself as entirely responsible for Rommel's fame in the Fatherland.

Again Berndt told me that it was quite impossible for me to see Rommel, and in a whisper said that the Field-Marshal was lying in his truck, seriously ill with jaundice.

I went off feeling rather lonely and despondent. The headquarters personnel were strangers, and I no longer felt at home. I was denied a chance of even saying good-day to the man at whose side I had been for months. And my only old friend seemed to be anxious to chivvy me away, in case I wanted to intrigue him out of his post!

But unexpectedly I ran into a group of other ranks whom I had known before—drivers, dispatch-riders, batmen. They gave me such a warm welcome that I realized I still had some old friends.

One of the drivers remarked, 'Herr Oberleutnant, we drivers always remember you as the considerate officer who would only call us to the wheel at the last moment—sometimes even when the Chief was on his way to the car. These others! Your successors have us formed up and waiting an hour before it is time to go.'

4

I met Rommel again sooner than I expected. Some distance behind the actual front our Pioneers had built model strongpoints in accordance with Rommel's own specific plans. Commanders and other officers visited them daily to study their advantages, their manner of construction, fields of fire, weapon siting, communications systems, and so on. They also watched demonstrations by infantry of the methods which Rommel suggested were best for attacking and reducing various types of strong-points.

I was among a group of officers at one such show when Rommel arrived unexpectedly. His face was a little thinner, but I would not have guessed, had it not been for Berndt's remark, that he was ill. The senior officer present, a colonel, was 'reporting' when the Field-Marshal's eye fell on me. He thanked the colonel briefly, strode over to me, and shook my hand with a direct inquiry: 'How are you, Schmidt?' A handshake and a greeting from Rommel, the taciturn, meant more than a gush of words from many another man. He did not greet anybody else, and when he drove off I felt many curious glances rest on me. Officers senior to me were puzzled that a junior should have been singled out.

CHAPTER THIRTY-TWO

ROMMEL'S LAST TRY

We had to be wide-awake in the El Alamein area in those days. The enemy airmen were on the warpath night and day. British and South African planes gave us no peace, especially at night. The supply routes were almost continually lit by the glare of parachute flares. The never-ending crash of bombs disturbed our sleep.

Although it was against orders, we listened every night to the news and to music broadcast from Cairo. The British had a fairly objective propaganda station there. We learned from Eighth Army prisoners that they too listened to the 'enemy,' particularly to hear *Lili Marlene* played from Belgrade or Athens. The sentimental tune reminded us on both sides that there were other things than aerial bombs and Desert warfare.

2

Rommel was being reinforced, though not as heavily as he would have wished. In addition to Ramcke's parachutists, the 164th Infantry Division arrived from Crete. This division was without transport of its own, but was to be used as 'corset stays' in the Italian positions. Italian reinforcements included the parachutists of the Folgore Division, as I have mentioned. I wondered at the time why, when our advance was brought to a halt at El Alamein, parachute troops were not flown from Crete immediately, and dropped in the El Alamein area. The answer is that the plan was impracticable in the face of the British command of the skies.

Time was working against us. An Intelligence report conveyed the unwelcome news that large numbers of the new American Sherman tanks were being shipped and were expected to arrive at Egyptian ports in September. A South African army publication issued in Cairo published a printer's advertisement soliciting orders for Christmas cards. It showed quite clearly what was correctly assumed to be the new Sherman tank, and our technical Intelligence men studied with interest the rough details it conveyed of the tank's new gun.

The moment Rommel received a firm promise that sufficient supplies of petrol were on the way he decided to risk a decisive blow at Montgomery.

On my twenty-sixth birthday, the R.A.F., probably without premeditated ill-will, but nevertheless inconsiderately, dropped a bomb on a battalion supply truck which was carrying three days' rations for us. I was deploring the loss of many meals, meagre though they were, when I received news of the attack planned for the night of August 30–31.

As at Gazala, we were to crack through the minefields and the Eighth Army positions in the south, and then thrust up northward towards the coast road.

In the 90th Light Division's area, our Special Group 288, now at about regimental strength, occupied reserve positions west of the central point of the central sector of the whole front.

Rommel's battle orders clearly stated that this attack was to be the last round in the battle for Alexandria.

The attack began on the night scheduled. Mines were lifted and, after the moon had risen, the German divisions advanced through the minefield under artillery fire. By the forenoon of August 31 they had reached a point east of the minefield.

Where we lay in reserve all was calm, except for incessant air activity which compelled us to dig in our men and vehicles more deeply into the stony ground. Regular reports came back from the attacking formations. The early reports were more favourable than we could have hoped. It seemed that two or three spearheads had thrust through to within a few miles of the coast road and the railway. Rommel came sailing past. 'It goes well,' he said.

But still we had no definite situation report, or orders, and there was nothing to do but wait and endure the air attacks.

What had actually happened? Rommel's Panzers had rolled on to the Alam el Halfa Ridge—really the key position of the whole El Alamein front (as General Alexander later pointed out)—during the afternoon of the first day of the attack. But unexpectedly heavy defensive fire from artillery and from well-dug-in anti-tank guns met them; unusually heavy attacks were made by medium bombers, and low-flying fighter aircraft swooped on petrol and ammunition trucks. The free movement of the attacking divisions was cribbed and confined.

It became clear that Montgomery, with the help of the air superiority which Air Marshal Tedder had provided for him, was making the fullest use of his artillery and of his advantageously placed defence line to cut up the attackers without committing his tanks.

Rommel realized on that first day that surprise could not be achieved. The enemy was ready for him. He had not been able to seize Alam el Halfa Ridge swiftly, as he had wished. He wanted to break off the attack, but his Chief of Staff prevailed on him to continue the battle.

Alexander and Montgomery had, as it turned out, expected the attack ever since August 5. When the Afrika Korps made no attempt to by-pass the Alam el Halfa Ridge in a north-easterly direction—heading, that is, towards Alexandria—the battle developed exactly as Montgomery apparently wished. He wanted our Panzers to run up against the strongly prepared positions on the ridge held by the 44th Division and two brigades of tanks.

On the third day of the battle our own Special Group still lay inactive in the reserve area. Reports from forward became steadily more non-committal. We began to feel that the 'final shot' at Alexandria had misfired. I had been thinking regretfully that in the Nile Delta I should miss the three white tropical uniforms I had left in the hotel in Asmara when I flew out of Eritrea; now my regrets began to fade. I developed serious doubts as to whether I should ever, as a soldier, set eyes on the Pyramids.

Our Panzers came to a stop. The enemy, as emerged later, wondered whether this was a deliberate move in Rommel's game, designed to tempt the Eighth Army tanks out in a counter-attack. The truth of the matter is that our Panzers had literally lost their spirit. The fuel supplies Rommel had been promised by Kesselring and Cavallero had not arrived. The R.A.F. was not only influencing the course of events on the immediate battlefield, but had caused far-reaching tactical results by sinking three tankers in the Mediterranean and by shooting down a deplorable number of our Junkers 52 transport planes. Nehring, commanding the Afrika Korps, was wounded, and was succeeded by von Thoma.

3

During the night of September 3 Rommel gave up his attempt to break through the enemy front. In the days that followed he withdrew to his original positions. Our Special Group had not been committed at all. At the same time 500 Sherman tanks reached Suez. Rommel was not to conquer Egypt.

North of the coast road between El Alamein and El Daba, I was given fourteen days to re-form my battalion and train it intensively for further action.

We had received reinforcements from Germany, consisting partly of German veterans who had formerly served in the French Foreign Legion in North Africa, and partly of ex-seamen from the Merchant Navy who were now without ships. Both types were badly disciplined, but first-class fighting material when properly handled. When other battalions and company commanders objected to having these men, I readily took them over in exchange for some of my own trained troops.

We had recently received new anti-tank guns. They included captured Russian 76.2-mm. guns. I trained the legionaries and sailors specially in the use of this weapon.

Now agents reported that the British planned a sea-borne landing between El Daba and Mersa Matruh. Their reports resulted in a welcome change for my battalion. I was ordered to site defensive observation posts directly along the coast. It was a task that virtually amounted to leave. We built and occupied the most important points in two days. The observation posts were linked up by a series of well-camouflaged and efficient wireless stations.

While some of the men were on duty, the others were free to bathe in the Mediterranean. We had a welcome change of diet, too. My driver was able to buy dates, eggs, and fowls from the local Bedouin. But I looked askance at the Arabs as they rode past us placidly on their asses, their womenfolk trudging behind with heavy burdens. Those keen, Desert-sharpened eyes missed nothing. Here as elsewhere I was certain that many of them were spies. Two great nations were slogging it out in an almost uninhabited and uninhabitable wilderness, but still the nomads trekked round in the midst of war, seemingly regarding the struggle as no concern of theirs, but merely the madness of Infidels (which I suppose, strictly speaking, it was). They all looked alike. They did not wear Union Jacks or Swastikas on their *gallabiehs*, and there was no way of telling whether they were in our pay or the enemy's. Probably they were spying for both sides.

Our own agents meanwhile brought in news which made it plain that Montgomery was preparing for the greatest battle Africa had known. Like Rommel, he was using cunning and bluff. But there was one difference in Montgomery's application of the techniques of deception. Where Rommel disguised ordinary vehicles as tanks in order to conceal his weakness, Montgomery with laths, canvas, and sacking now transformed formidable new American tanks into innocuous looking transport vehicles to conceal his strength. There was a new Fox in the Desert.

He also deceived us by starting to lay a new pipe-line, complete with pumping stations, away in the south. Its completion was deliberately prolonged, and it began to look as though some time must pass before the Eighth Army could mount what seemed to be obviously an offensive planned in the southern sector of the El Alamein line. Air reconnaissance could not reveal that the pipe-line was a dummy constructed out of old petrol tins.

Psychologically, Montgomery was gaining the upper hand. The Eighth Army was receiving steady reinforcements in men and materials. His troops knew it: he told them so. He had a positive task ahead of him—to defeat Rommel, remove the menace to Egypt, and win renown in so doing.

Rommel's bi-national force was not being effectively strengthened: his troops knew it. He was at a dead end; he had achieved his long-planned triumph at Tobruk, but had never had the momentum to follow through to Alexandria; the Middle East was regarded as a secondary front; he felt he would not now be able to make himself master of Egypt.

And Rommel was a sick man. He looked more finely drawn each time one saw him. Apart from his earlier responsibilities in the war, he had now undergone twenty months of continuous mental and physical strain in the Desert. For over a year he had suffered from recurrent attacks of jaundice. For the moment Rommel was a spent force.

Treatment in Germany was the only course. He flew home.

Before he went into the hospital at Semmerling,[1] he had an interview with Hitler. He made no bones about the danger which must arise for us in Africa, and which was even then arising, with no Panzer reinforcements available on the El Alamein front. The problem of ensuring steady supplies for the African forces must also be tackled, he urged. Hitler promised Rommel everything. But it was not intended that he should return to us in Africa. When he became convalescent, he was to be given command of an army group in the Ukraine.

The command of his Panzer Gruppe in Africa devolved upon General Stumme.

[1] In Lower Austria, south-west of Vienna.

CHAPTER THIRTY-THREE

DEFEAT AT EL ALAMEIN

'OPERATION TORCH'—Montgomery's offensive at El Alamein—began on the night of October 23.

The secret of this massed, planned assault had been extraordinarily well kept. It came as a complete surprise, even though indications of an almost immediate offensive had been gathered and assessed by the German Staff during the twenty-four hours before the initial barrage opened.

The Eighth Army had been built up for a 'kill' since August 1; it had been reinforced by 41,000 troops, over 1000 tanks, and 9000 vehicles of various sorts.

The peaceful stars were shaken in their heavens when nearly a thousand guns flashed and roared simultaneously against us that night. Never had this age-old land known so shattering a drum-fire. The earth from the Qattara Depression to the Mediterranean quaked. Far back from the front line, men were jarred to their teeth.

Fifteen minutes of it, and then the firing let up for five minutes. That was just a lull before a renewed storm. Punctually at 10 P.M. the same vast number of guns, plus thousands of tank and infantry weapons, concentrated on our front lines. Australians principally, but also Englishmen, Scots, New Zealanders, and South Africans, attacked. Their main objective was the Miteiriyeh Ridge. It was occupied on the first night of the battle, but Montgomery did not consolidate his hold on it until after two days of desperate fighting.

The 15th Panzer Division in the north and the 21st in the south lay a short way behind the turmoil of the forward line. They had been split into battle groups in accordance with defensive plans that Rommel had drawn up before he left Africa for medical attention in Germany. In this we made a grave blunder. Rommel had intended that these battle groups should exist independently only during the period preceding an anticipated enemy offensive.

They were to be concentrated immediately an offensive became definite and its direction was perceived, since only a consolidated force of Panzers would prevail against the great tank strength which Montgomery had now built up. Rommel had never dreamed of allowing his Panzers to meet the enemy and be defeated in detail—as the enemy had in the past been defeated in detail by him.

Bayerlein, the Chief of Staff, was on leave. Rommel had to return, unavailingly, to the rescue. On the first day of Montgomery's offensive General Stumme had a heart attack when the unit he was with was attacked by enemy aircraft. Stumme's driver did not even see him fall out of his car on to the Desert. His corpse was found only later.

Central Intelligence in Berlin had told us that the British could not attack before the end of the month. . . .

Hitler telephoned Rommel in hospital in Germany at noon on the second day of the battle and asked him at once to fly back to Africa. The situation was desperate. Rommel had been under treatment for only three weeks and was still ill, but he did not think of saying No. He was airborne before daybreak the following morning, only stopping in Italy to find out what was going on, and particularly to learn whether his forces were getting enough petrol, whether more Panzers were on their way, and whether Kesselring had sent the supplies of *Nebelwerfers*—multiple-barrelled mortars—which Hitler had promised. He was at Panzer Gruppe Headquarters again a couple of hours after sunset that same night.

I think he knew then that El Alamein was lost: he had found out how short of petrol the Afrika Korps was. He told Bayerlein that we could not win, but he made desperate attempts to retrieve the situation. He was up almost all night planning a counter-attack against Kidney Ridge (Miteiriyeh) in the north. He strove desperately to assemble his Panzer forces in a cohesive whole, as they should have been earlier. The 15th Panzer Division had been practically destroyed, so he summoned the 21st and the Italian Ariete Divisions north, and moved the 90th Light and the Italian Trieste Divisions from their rear areas to protect the front near the sea.

The counter-attack, which Rommel directed in person, was smashed up by our old enemies, the medium bombers and the 25-

pounders. He tried again next day, but was beaten off once more. He lost Panzers he could ill afford—Panzers that would not now be replaced. The 9th Australian Division hammered him farther back.

Montgomery paused to regroup after three days of fighting. (The South Africans, apart from their ubiquitous armoured-car men, had now incidentally completed their main task in the El Alamein battle, and we were not to meet them again until Italy.) At Tel el Aqqaqir the fiercest tank engagement of the battle developed. Both sides suffered heavy losses, but we were the harder hit. Our Panzers were almost annihilated: only a few groups survived.

Montgomery's 'Operation Supercharge'—the new onslaught that followed 'Torch'—was the end at El Alamein. The 21st Panzers had put up their last effective struggle, and, although at one time they almost mastered their old enemies, the British 1st Armoured, they were beaten. Rommel decided to withdraw on the night of November 2–3.

He wirelessed his decision and his reasons to Hitler's headquarters that night. The report was passed to Hitler only the following day: the officer who was on duty when it came through had failed to wake him. (He was reduced in rank.) Hitler raved, and reviled Rommel.

Rommel's retreat was in progress when a wireless signal came from Hitler's H.Q.: 'The situation demands that the positions at El Alamein be held to the last man. A retreat is out of the question. Victory or death! Heil Hitler!' The message bore Hitler's personal signature. For some reason or other, although we were already withdrawing, the signal was circulated to Afrika Korps units.

The ridiculous signal could not improve our morale at that time. Nevertheless, having received it and being obliged to acknowledge it, Rommel could not treat it as non-existent.

Thus, when von Thoma, in command of the Afrika Korps, asked Rommel at the Panzer Gruppe Afrika H.Q. south of El Daba for permission to withdraw to Fuka, Rommel would not endorse the plan but merely gave him authority to act on his own judgment.

Next morning von Thoma gathered information that Tommy had already outflanked the southern wing of the Afrika Korps, and he passed the information up to Rommel. Rommel discredited the information, and said that the formation reported in the south must be a retreating Italian division. Von Thoma went out in a Panzer to check for himself. British tanks pounced upon him, set his Panzer alight, and captured him.

Bayerlein, the Chief of Staff, who went out in search of von Thoma, was also within an ace of capture when he approached to within a few hundred yards and, through his field-glasses, saw von Thoma being rounded up. He scurried back to safety, and succeeded to the command of what was left of the Afrika Korps.

CHAPTER THIRTY-FOUR

RETREAT

My battle began only when El Alamein had been lost. Until the retreat began, Special Group 288 was left out of battle. It was, indeed, the only unit that had taken no part in the fighting. Our consciences were uneasy through these days as we listened to the heavy battle going on a dozen miles to the east of us, while our weapons lay idle and there was nothing for us to do except swim or lounge in the sun.

When the last of the Panzers rolled westward, our task began. We were to be Rommel's rearguard. We pulled out last of all, and had retreated only a few miles along the coast road when we were engaged by armoured cars immediately south of the road. Our guns went into action, and we fought them off.

The Special Group moved back in leap-frog movements. One battalion was always halted in defensive positions to cover the retreat, and then it would 'up guns' and off. We reached Mersa Matruh on November 6.

I was ordered to take up temporary positions on Matruh's southern defence line and on both sides of the Siwa track. I sited anti-tank guns—each of my companies had five or six of these—at the most important tactical points. Our positions lay between the bunkers where the barbed-wire entanglements and minefields had been left intact as they had been in June when Auchinleck's men had thought to hold this line.

Late that afternoon I sighted British tanks on a rise south of Matruh. As darkness fell they opened fire on my positions along the oasis track. The pursuit was relentless. Under cover of darkness the surviving columns of our Panzer groups left the stronghold and resumed their westward march.

A few hours later a dispatch-rider brought me a written situation report. From it I learned that Montgomery's spearheads were already west of Matruh. I could expect orders at about midnight to abandon my present rearguard positions. I was to pull out on a given compass bearing, which alone would take me to the sole remaining passage through the minefield.

I remember regretting that I would not have a chance of locating and marking the entrance to the minefield gap in daylight; but at any rate it was a relief to know that during the night we should have a chance to evade the enemy, for it was a certainty that we should be trapped if we remained outside Matruh much longer.

My driver and dispatch-rider blacked out my truck with blankets. By the glow of a little bulb wired off a battery, we swallowed a meal from cans, and wrote letters home. Busy writing, I failed to note that midnight had come and long since gone. Then the '*Phutt! Phutt!*' of a motor-cycle. The machine stopped, and a voice called out, 'Is that Special Group 288?' A hoarse whisper: 'Shut up! Tommy can probably hear you!'

The dispatch-rider was led to me. A hand was thrust through the black-out blankets. A voice repeated the written order I read: 'Matruh evacuated. Rearguard to follow immediately!'

By now I had perfected the drill. Each detachment in the battalion had a messenger detailed to wait near my truck. Instructions took a moment or two, and then their vehicles were moving silently through the darkness to the gun positions. The guns were limbered up, ammunition loaded, and from all sides vehicles converged to form up near my vehicle in a slight wadi. But in spite of every care, the noise of running motors could not be muffled entirely, and I was both annoyed and concerned because several drivers had shouted while making contact with each other.

My column had just formed up when—'What was that?' Explosions, a crashing and a whizzing around us. Tank shells were plunging into the ground almost at our feet and whistling between trucks. Some vehicles were hit and burst into flame. At once we were lit by a lurid light—a lovely target for the British tanks, which must be hard upon our southern front.

I calculated that there were not many of them, but it was now too late—indeed, it would be futile—to dig in. We must pull out as ordered. But in case we had to halt and dig in, I thrust a short entrenching tool through my breast strap and diagonally across my shoulder. This action was almost to cause our undoing.

'At extended intervals—march!' I shouted the order and, standing in my truck, kept my eyes on the compass needle so as to navigate through the darkness to the minefield gap.

MAP 4

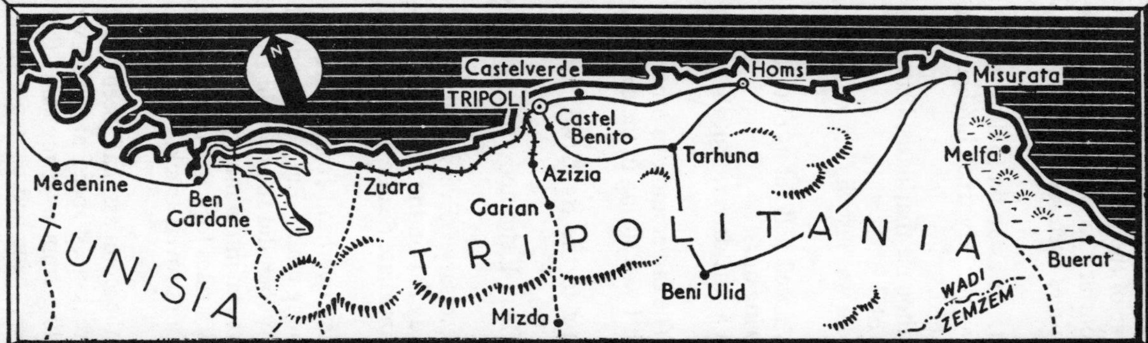

MAP 3

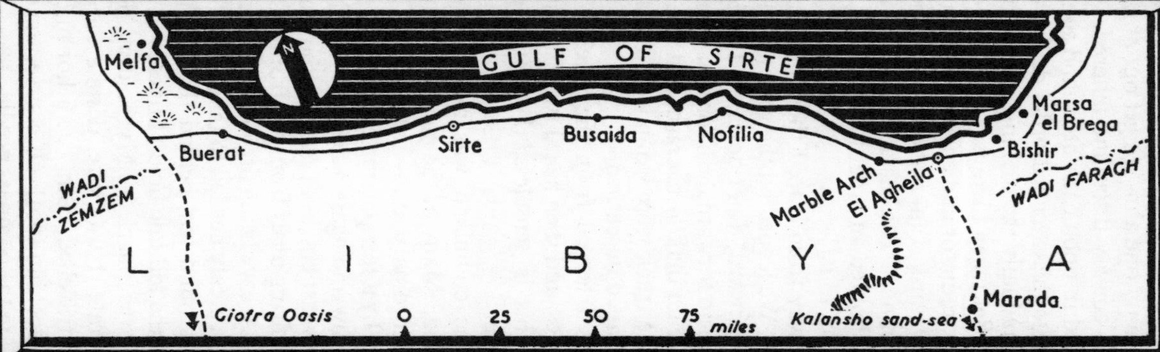

MAP 3: MARSA EL BREGA TO BUERAT

MAP 4: BUERAT TO MEDENINE

We drove through a minor storm of enemy shells. The drivers had only one aim—to get out of range of the pursuing tanks, and their convoy discipline faltered. Contrary to orders, the trucks closed in upon each other and sometimes even raced side by side, despite the extended-order drill.

Gradually the shelling petered out. I was about to draw a sigh of relief when there was a roar and a jolt. My truck lurched to a stop: radiator and engine were smashed.

'Damn! Tanks ahead!' was the thought that flashed through my mind. 'The bastards have cut us off.'

I shouted an order to my driver, who was just slightly wounded. 'Jump to it!'

Away from here, I thought. Only speed will get us out of this jam. We leaped on the vehicle following ours.

'Forward, don't deviate!' I yelled at the driver. But there was to be no forward dash for that truck.

Again that flash, crash, and jolt. The driver and two other men in the truck were wounded. Though I was sitting in the cab too, I escaped unscathed.

As I leaped from the truck I saw to the right two brilliant flashes, and then heard two explosions.

'This is senseless,' I thought. Then I shouted: 'Dismount! Dig in!'

The command was almost unnecessary. Every vehicle had halted. Many of the men were already flat on the ground. But—extraordinary, this—there was an immediate dead calm disturbed only by a few purring engines.

Now and again a desultory shell flew overhead from our rear—a few last cracks at us from the pursuing tanks. But who the devil was firing at us from the front? Only then did the thought strike me: Are we being fired on, or have we run into a minefield?

I scarcely needed to take those few strides forward and examine the ground just behind the nearest destroyed truck. Yes, there was the tell-tale hole. Mines!

I was puzzled. My reading of the compass had been dead accurate, I was sure, despite the break-neck speed at which we had travelled. But . . . a hot prickling crept over my skin: that entrenching tool! Of course, the steel spade had caused a variation in the compass needle.

The night was fairly dark. I held the compass close to my eyes and took a bearing on its palely luminous glimmer. Then I threw the entrenching tool away and took the bearing again. As I had expected, the needle pointed considerably farther to the left.

I had been foolish. Here we now were in the middle of a minefield, with enemy tanks hard behind us. It was up to me to retrieve the situation. I wrapped my mind in calmness, made my plan, and, with the men lying prone, stepped out to look for the edge of the minefield. A soldier who had robbed a comrade, and had in consequence been dishonoured when I called him a *Schweinehund* on a battalion parade a few days before, now insisted on accompanying me. He ran about regardless of danger, examining tracks and casting an eye round for mines.

Usually, we knew, the lighter and more easily detonated anti-personnel mines were sprinkled liberally round the heavier plate mines employed against Panzers and trucks. But it seemed that here the plate mines were smaller than the usual type, and there seemed to be no anti-personnel mines.

At length I discovered a rusty strand of barbed-wire, which indicated the edge of the minefield, and I soon located the gap. We had missed it by fifty yards. Only the leading vehicles and guns were actually within the minefield. With most of the men deployed in defensive array, I had the drivers of the rear vehicles head towards the gap. Other squads were detailed for the tricky and not entirely pleasant task of man-handling the endangered vehicles and guns backward over their original tracks to the edge of the minefield. One mine exploded, but fortunately it killed no one. The Desert all round us was dead quiet. Not a shot was heard.

It took two hours to get the column safely into formation again and moving through the passage. I had lost four valuable vehicles, but none of the men were killed. At the western perimeter a squad of anxious sappers were waiting for us. No sooner had we passed than they mined the gap. Half an hour later they overtook us and sped on.

We too scorched along the road to the west. Day was breaking, and Montgomery's tanks must be near—somewhere on our flanks, perhaps even ahead.

The first rays of the sun were on our backs and casting exaggerated shadows in front of us when a swarm of bombers roared low overhead. I extended my column swiftly, but the airmen ignored us. Had they mistaken us, I wondered, for the British vanguard? On the western horizon we saw them dive and drop their bombs. We now knew where the main body of the Afrika Korps was.

We moved through the Sidi Barrani region by night. The track was sandy and in places almost impassable. Several times we nearly capsized trucks and guns.

An hour or two before midnight the first parachute flares opened above us. I never saw them, but they struck me as emerging from the darkness with an almost idiotic exultancy. In a few minutes the heavens were filled with 'Christmas-trees,' the countryside was lit as though by limelight, and bombs thundered down from low-flying planes.

At times we raced madly amidst the thunder and the flashes. If we halted and went to ground the aircraft attacked even solitary soldiers whom they caught erect: their grotesque shadows danced revealingly across the ground as the flares flamed down to low levels. If we were not prone, we were visible.

We were hammered all through that night. Racing madly and stopping, we made slow average progress. We dared not let up, or else we should be cut off by tanks on the way up the escarpment before we reached the relative safety of Upper Sollum.

It was a grim night for the Afrika Korps. A count afterwards showed that it cost more men and Panzers than some armoured engagements had done.

I greeted daybreak with a moderated delight. Well I knew that the air attacks would continue, perhaps unabated; but at least it would be happier to see farther, and to be able to stand and put up some defence with one's own weapons.

Just as the sun rose my battalion column was overtaken by a posse of vehicles moving at speed. Overtaking in convoy was prohibited with us, as it was with the British, whenever there was danger of intensive air attack: jammed roads caused good targets. I was about to take steps to correct the behaviour of the furious drivers passing me when there was a brief interval. I ordered the driver to slow up, slewed round, and got ready to be peremptory.

Then I recognized the approaching vehicle. It was the old familiar Mammoth. It overhauled us. On top of it, shoulders back, was an even more familiar figure. I came smartly to the salute.

Rommel waved, and gave a shout which was carried away by the wind of our passage. But his face was set and serious.

CHAPTER THIRTY-FIVE

'THE HIGH-DOMED AMERICAN SHERMANS . . .'

WELL might Rommel have looked grim. The morning we evacuated Mersa Matruh, the first waves of Allied troops were landing on the beaches of French North Africa, two thousand miles farther west. Just ahead of Rommel lay the Libyan frontier, which he was now approaching for the last time—going the wrong way. He had a long way to fight back. Even then he foresaw that it would be his task to meet the new threat in Africa.

The pace of the pursuit was hot. The New Zealanders were briefly opposed in the Desert east of Sidi Barrani and on the line of the old British minefield at Buq Buq. By November 10 we were crossing, more peacefully than we had expected, the familiar coastal flats below Halfaya Pass. On the right stretched the beaches where Rommel and I had so often splashed round naked in the sea. We drove up the Serpentine towards Sollum.

The New Zealanders took Sollum, Bardia, and Capuzzo at our heels; the tanks of the 7th Armoured Division raced through the Desert along the edge of the escarpment and joined the New Zealanders.

Our first short halt was made near Sidi Azeiz, on the Trigh Capuzzo. As always now, we deployed our anti-tank guns instantly, as a precaution against aircraft as well as ground attack. Having dug in, we brewed tea to wash down our biscuits and bully—from among our dwindling hoard of spoils from Tobruk. Now we were scurrying back to Tobruk.

The water had scarcely begun to boil when we sighted those familiar little flags dancing on the horizon: the South African armoured cars were yapping after us. More and more of them showed up over the horizon. A good score of them came forward in a stout charge. Our gunners got into action quickly, for these guests were not welcome to tea. We opened fire at maximum range. The cars sheered off and disappeared behind a near-by crest.

We were without doubt the tail of the German-Italian Panzer

Army. And we were to remain the tail for many weary weeks. Our formation was the only one that had not been engaged at El Alamein, and as such had a good deal to make up.

I knew this country thoroughly, not only by reason of journeys with Rommel but also because of my rearguard experiences a year before. My unit had now developed into experts in the art of fighting rearguard actions. We could adopt our defensive positions within minutes, and abandon them as swiftly.

The exceptionally high morale of the Afrika Korps had hitherto been largely due to the faith of the men in the superiority of their Panzers and anti-tank guns (which protected the infantry so well against tank attacks) over enemy equipment. But now the balance of superiority had been changed. The high-domed American Shermans were becoming a nightmare to us.

We were badly shaken as we leap-frogged back along the Via Balbia. I had found a well-sited position from which to face the pursuers in the east, and was feeling pleased at the showing of some new reinforcements—sturdy parachutists from General Ramcke's formation who had gallantly fought their way out of encirclement at El Alamein. With an 88-mm. 'flak' gun ready, I felt prepared to take on anything.

American tanks hove up on the horizon. The ground was undulating, and they emerged into view, vanished, and then came into sight again. Let them come! My plan was to wait patiently in this well-camouflaged position and restrain my fire until the enemy tanks were near enough for our 50-mm. guns to fight with maximum effect. I emphasized this point to the senior gunner officer with me, but the new anti-tank men either lacked the training or the nerve of the old Afrika Korps gunners.

When two of the British tanks were still too far distant for the 50-mm. 'pak' guns, the 88-mm. gun opened fire. The two tanks at once dodged into dead ground. I kept the region scrutinized through my glasses. The tanks quickly had us under shell-fire, which was as effectively directed as though from regular artillery. Their fire concentrated on my 88 that had fired prematurely. And now the attacked gunners could not even see their opponents! I noticed movement not far from where the tanks had disappeared. That, then, was where the enemy was gaining his observation. But before we could deal with the O.P., the tanks had knocked out our 88.

Our motorized infantry did not like this. From experience they now knew that we must depend on the 50-mm. 'pak' guns; and it was clear that these could not measure up to the effective range of Montgomery's new tanks.

I appreciated more than ever the necessity for well-camouflaged positions and fire discipline if we were to secure the advantage of surprise and succeed in the long series of hit-and-run actions that had now become inevitable. The men were firmly drilled in these ideas, and we had an opportunity of putting them to the test when we turned to fight near Agedabia.

The British had entered Tobruk without opposition on November 13. Their main body had advanced 220 miles in six days and barely had supplies to continue the march; but they had got the ports of Mersa Matruh and Bardia working two days after they secured them, and so were able to keep at least light forces close behind us. They were in Derna by the 16th, and could thus use the aerodrome there, besides the Gambut landing-grounds farther back, to keep fighters in close support of the ground troops. Those fighters almost at once were able to give cover to a convoy from Alexandria which relieved Malta when the island was on the brink of starvation.

On the 18th the enemy armoured cars were beaten back by our rearguard at Sceleidima and Antelat on the main passes in the escarpment. We pulled out again in the night. We lost Benghazi. A couple of days of heavy rain gave us a brief respite at Agedabia before the enemy were up with us again.

Our formation, still about one regiment strong, formed a defensive line in sandy, hilly country. We were cheerful, I remember, because a near-by German supply dump had been abandoned, and we had gathered in an unaccustomed quantity of stores. The food from the field-kitchen was for the moment exceptionally good, and we had plenty of chocolate and cigarettes. I did not ration the men. Who knew what the morrow would bring?

We got our artillery and machine-guns well dug in, and the loose sand from the gun-pits was scattered. The mortars were set up in a wadi near the field-kitchen. Every position was camouflaged with camel-thorn.

Taking a leaf from Rommel's book, I inspected my positions from the front. They were difficult to locate. Only one Russian 76.2-mm. gun failed to satisfy me entirely, but before I could perfect its camouflage, my observer, who was keeping a look-out through a powerful telescope mounted on a tripod, sang out from his weapon-pit: 'Enemy tanks—north-east!'

I leaped into the hole beside him and had a look through the telescope even while I snapped the order: 'Prepare for action—tanks north-east!'

All visible movement in our line stopped instantly. Communications from then on was by field telephone only.

By now we could see tanks in other sectors as well. Two British reconnaissance planes flew overhead. They did not spot us. Immediately west of us light flak hammered at them, and both were shot down. Colonel Menton's headquarters telephoned me: one of the British pilots had saved his life by a parachute jump; he was a prisoner, and confirmed in some astonishment that he had had no idea he was over our positions.

A dramatic picture now unfolded before us. About thirty tanks gradually concentrated in a long, shallow wadi to our front. Our heavy artillery farther back at Agedabia was firing desultorily over our heads, but without much effect. Two batteries of guns plus infantry joined the tanks in the wadi. Ammunition 'quads' were limbered on to the guns. Through the telescope I could actually distinguish the movements of the gunners' hands manipulating their instruments as they laid down counter-battery fire in the direction of Agedabia. Their shells swooshed high over our heads.

Then I distinguished armoured command-vehicles. Several British officers, obviously 'brass-hats,' emerged from them. But our gunners had strict orders not to fire at anything that had not crossed a given line. All of them were behaving with exemplary calm and restraint.

Through the spy-glass now I saw a British officer, who was carrying a riding-crop, give a hand-signal: the Shermans began to roll towards us. Three of them approached along a track down which one of my guns was trained. The gunners were ex-Foreign Legionaries.

Steadily the three tanks neared the fire-task line. Other tanks now began to advance. The first tank reached the line and crossed it. In rat-tat-tat succession shells spat from the muzzles of our guns. The leading tank was struck—a direct hit on its dome-shaped turret. The shell ricocheted harmlessly into the air: the armour was incredibly good.

The tanks halted, and some of them, including the leading Sherman, turned about. As it swung, our next salvo took it in the flank. It went up in flames. We had found a vulnerable spot even in this formidable monster.

The duel between tank and 'pak' was now in full swing. It lasted two hours. Two of my gun positions were knocked out, but we had smashed up considerably more tanks, and the advance had been halted. With great skill and daring the British recovery men hauled their damaged tanks from the battlefield to safety while the fight still raged.

Our stand was unavailing. The vanguard of the 22nd Armoured Brigade, which had crossed 260 miles of Desert, arrived on our right and threatened to turn our flank. Once more we pulled out and drifted back to El Agheila.

Rommel had lost the whole of Cyrenaica.

CHAPTER THIRTY-SIX

TRIPOLITANIA LOST

At El Agheila I was summoned to Afrika Korps Headquarters. The Commander asked me for a brief report on the defensive possibilities of Marada oasis. Somebody on the staff must have remembered my mission early in 1941.

'Marada,' I said, 'can be defended easily if sufficient troops are based on it and if they can be ensured adequate supplies. It might be necessary to supply them by air. The land supply lines to the oasis can easily be cut by the enemy.' This sounds rather like a Child's Guide to War; there was a little more to the discussion than that. The General was in a friendly mood, and after dissecting my views for a while offered me a cup of coffee—the first good cup I had tasted for weeks.

I gathered the impression that the Marada idea had been dropped even before I arrived to report. No adequate El Agheila–Marada defensive system could be prepared in the brief time left before the enemy would be pressing hard upon us again.

Twice before El Agheila had been the high-water mark of British advances in Libya. It is the strongest defensive position in the country. First the attacker reaches an area of salt-marshes, then a gap between this and another salt-marsh to the south, a waste of soft sand and *seif* dunes—those sand-hills licked into crescent shapes by the Desert wind. Farther south lies an escarpment, more dunes, and yet more salt-marshes. El Agheila is 150 miles from Benghazi and 300 from Tobruk. Only a refreshed army, with its logistics guaranteed, could hope to break through here. But it was obvious at Headquarters that we could not hold out at El Agheila this time. Rommel, it is true, issued the pronouncement: 'El Agheila is the final front, where the advance of the Eighth Army must be brought to a halt.' But we could not be adequately reinforced for an effective defensive battle.

The air, of course, was thick with rumours. The troops gathered that heavy reinforcements had been landed in Tunisia.

Supply drivers who had arrived from Tunis spoke of giant 'Tiger' Panzers—the heavy tanks Hitler had promised Rommel before El Alamein—and also the legendary *Nebelwerfer*—smoke-throwers —which were to turn out to be multiple mortars from the Russian front. They spoke also of *Giganten*—massive transport gliders that could carry a light tank or 250 men.

Now at last, so the story went, the High Command in Berlin intended to do something for this Cinderella force in Africa. But at the front facing the Eighth Army we saw no real reinforcements; on the contrary, some specialized units were withdrawn from the Afrika Korps and hurried to Tunisia.

To the west, indeed, the Anglo-American invasion forces had got a tight grip on Morocco and Algeria, and at this very moment were within twenty-five miles of Tunis. Every ounce of reinforcement that could be spared for Africa went to Tunisia, not to Rommel in Libya. Counting every man we had picked up on the long retreat, we now had a force of only 25,000 Italians (by no means all of them effective fighting troops) and 10,000 Germans. We had fewer than 100 tanks.

Rommel's plan was not to hold El Agheila longer than he needed to force Montgomery to spread out and prepare an assault and then to nip back to Buerat to cover the port of Tripoli itself.

Early in December the enemy seems to have realized that we intended to withdraw farther. He probably perceived this because Rommel, realizing the danger of losing thousands of Italians for lack of transport as he had at El Alamein, moved them out first. He left the mobile German forces to hold the position until Montgomery struck in earnest.

We began to pull out on the night of December 12, for it was clear that the enemy was planning a frontal attack. Special Group 288 had to protect the rear of the Afrika Korps from south of the Marada road across the coastal road to the Mediterranean. The British were slow in working their way through our booby-traps, mines, and ditches, but by the 15th they ran up against us. We were hit hard on the Marada road by tanks of the 8th Armoured Brigade, and as a result lost almost a full company.

Though we held up the British tanks with a deep ditch across the main road, the New Zealanders were at the same time being employed on one of those 'left hooks' for which they became famous. They swung wide round the main position and threatened to cut us off at the Wadi Matratin, about sixty miles west of El Agheila. A considerable section of our rearguard, leap-frogging along the road, was still on the eastern side of the wadi, and the only easy way through it was along the main road. The New Zealanders got into position, but for once they were not at their best. They seemed to lose their way that night, though it was moonlight; and by breaking up into small groups, down to company strength, we managed to thrust through gaps among them. But we lost some tanks, guns, and men.

We blew up culverts and bridges at every wadi, and strewed mines along the route. The enemy had to push along cautiously. But still he was up with us at Nofilia on the night of the 16th. We skirmished with Montgomery's advance guard for a couple of days, and then drifted back towards Sirte.

By the 22nd only one division, the 15th Panzer, lay forward. The 21st Panzer and the 90th Light Divisions were back with the main body at Buerat preparing a fresh line. The enemy hesitated before he advanced beyond Nofilia, for he was now over 250 miles from his base at Benghazi. But he simply had to secure forward landing-grounds if he was going to fight us at Buerat, so he pushed his armoured cars forward to Sirte, another eighty miles. Light though the advance guard was, it threatened to outflank us, and once more Special Group 288 did some leap-frogging. The village was left to the enemy.

2

On Christmas Eve I found myself commanding the forward battalion of the rearguard on the Via Balbia, within eyeshot of Sirte. I could see Montgomery's troops entering the village that afternoon, and even see them clearing the landing-ground.

What a strange night to celebrate! We vamped up a Christmas-tree out of a wooden pole in which we had bored holes to carry camel-thorn branches. We decorated the tree with silver paper and we improvised candles of a sort. As Christmas fare each of my men received three cigarettes—we had been hoarding them for some time. The contents of a light mail-bag of letters from home were handed out. The letters were the best of Christmas presents.

We were busy lighting the candles on our Christmas-tree in the open air when we spied three men stalking us across the dark ground. I had them called in. They came forward hesitantly, and turned out to be a German patrol of one officer and two other ranks. The officer explained that his unit, farther west, had ordered him to find out who lay ahead of them.

'You needn't go any farther,' I said. 'Ahead of this there are only Tommies. You had better join us in this poor celebration.'

But he was super-conscientious and excused himself: he must continue his patrol. He disappeared eastward into the darkness. I heard what befell him when I met him accidentally in Italy long afterwards. He lost himself and after stumbling round for several hours found himself once again where we had erected our Christmas-tree. He concluded, rightly, that we should have mined the road when we pulled out. He stumbled on westward to locate the truck he had left when he started his patrol on foot. In it he followed us westward, but avoiding the track that he guessed would be mined. Even so, he struck a patch of mines, blew himself up, and was seriously wounded. His two companions, both slightly wounded, carried him until they came by luck upon a party of sappers still busy laying mines, and so they were brought back to safety.

This story has no particular moral, I suppose. Perhaps it only goes to show that one can be too conscientious on Christmas Eve.

3

Rommel made a show of standing again on the Wadi Zem Zem, just west of Buerat. The enemy at the time wondered why, and so did some of our officers. It seemed more logical for us not to defend this position, which was about twenty-five miles in length and could fairly easily be outflanked, but to stand on the naturally strong line between Homs and Tarhuna.

The truth is that the High Command had decided before the year ended to sacrifice the whole of Tripolitania and to concentrate on maintaining a bridgehead in Africa round Tunis. If we could hold out the Anglo-American forces there, we should still have a grip on the central Mediterranean, for we held Sicily, too. We should deny the enemy the free use of this sea. And, moreover, we should be holding him off the southern flank of Europe, which we knew he would dearly like to attack. Churchill had made that plain enough.

Early in January all the Italians were sent back west from Buerat. Our friends, the 21st Panzer Division, were detached from Rommel's German-Italian Panzer Army and sent to join General von Arnim. We were left at Zem Zem with the 15th Panzer Division and the 90th Light.

Montgomery could have pushed us out of the Buerat Line rapidly if he had known we did not intend to hold on. His problem was that if he won this battle, he must be ready at once to strike through to the port of Tripoli. Before he got there he would be 600 miles from his nearest sound supply port at Benghazi—a most vulnerable position.

He planned to strike at us up the main road with a couple of infantry divisions, and to send his armour and the New Zealanders on their usual outflanking job out to the left. Actually Benghazi harbour was so badly damaged by a storm that he had to immobilize one of the divisions he intended to employ in the frontal attack, and to use all its transport for rushing up supplies from farther back at Tobruk. He must have been a worried man.

But he need not have been over-concerned. We were not strong enough to put up a great resistance. The New Zealanders swiftly crept round our flank. On the front he got troops across the Wadi Zem Zem on the first day. Our old weary business of leapfrogging backward, laying mines, and blowing demolitions, went on again. By the night of January 17 we had given up Homs. The country was difficult and helped us against vastly superior numbers. We held up Montgomery stubbornly near Tarhuna, particularly with the Ramcke Parachutists and our now sadly dwindling Panzers.

The rearguard fought sharp actions west of Homs, but although the defences prepared here were sound, our numbers were small, and Rommel already had his eyes firmly on the back country in Tunisia. We scrapped a bit at Corradini and Castelverde, and then the 90th Light put up a last showing by night, a dozen miles outside Tripoli. And there was rearguard resistance at Castel Benito, Azizia, and Garian. Then we were finished, and leapfrogging away again.

Montgomery entered Tripoli on the 23rd, just three months after the battle of El Alamein had opened.

CHAPTER THIRTY-SEVEN

WE MEET OUR FIRST AMERICANS

BOTH we and the Allies now reorganized the whole set-up in North Africa.

Churchill, Roosevelt, and Eisenhower had met in Casablanca in mid-January and made plans. These provided that the Eighth Army would, when it entered Tunisia, come under the command of Eisenhower. But though Eisenhower was to be the Commander-in-Chief, Alexander was to be the principal fighting general, in command of what was called the Eighteenth Army Group—by combining the numerals of the Eight Army and the First Army, which, under General Anderson, had been responsible for the early fighting in Tunisia.

This British First Army at first did not include under its command the completely raw American Second Corps or the French Nineteenth Corps, which General Giraud refused to allow to be led by a British general. It was only after they had made rather a mess of things that Eisenhower had them removed from under his rather loose control and firmly placed in the hands of General Anderson.

Alexander took over the main command in a hurry on February 17, several days before he was due to do so, because Rommel had struck an unexpected and shrewd blow in the Kasserine area—of which more later. I had the good luck to be there.

Meanwhile Rommel had met von Arnim at Gabes and discussed the Axis plan. Von Arnim believed that, now that the two Axis armies had succeeded in linking hands, a strong bridgehead should be held from Bizerta to the Mareth Line, the 'African Maginot' which the French had constructed years before on the Tunisia-Tripolitania border. Rommel disagreed. He did not believe that such an extended front could be held for any length of time.

The Axis High Command now set up an Army Group H.Q. to fight the whole battle in Tunisia. Rommel, on February 23, was gazetted to supreme command of what was called the Heeresgruppe (Army Group) Afrika.[1] Von Arnim continued to lead our Fifth Army, which consisted of the original forces rushed into Tunisia to oppose the Anglo-Americans, and since heavily reinforced. When Rommel and most of his German staff set up their new H.Q., the German-Italian Panzer Army (the set-up Rommel had commanded since October 25, 1942) ceased to exist. Instead, the forces that the Eighth Army had pushed back from Egypt were now reorganized as the First Italian Army, under the command of General Messe, who had previously led an Italian Corps in Russia. The German Afrika Korps now came under his command. The Army also embraced the Italian 20th and 21st Corps.

The Tunisian forces were reinforced with divisions that would have enabled Rommel a year earlier to break through to the Suez Canal—provided he had been guaranteed supplies to keep them fed and moving. Von Arnim had got in the 10th Panzer Division veterans of France; the 334th Infantry Division; the Hermann Goering Panzer Division; the Barenthin Regiment and the Koch Storm Regiment, these two consisting of parachutists; Panzer Detachment 501, of battalion strength, equipped with the new Mark VI 'Tiger' tanks; the Manteuffel Division, which arrived earlier, and several Grenadier battalions of the 47th Regiment, consisting partly of men from Crete and partly of newly arrived replacements.

We now had three German Panzer divisions and another equipped with Italian tanks. All told, there were roughly fourteen divisions, of which half were German. Alexander had only about nine divisions when he took over, but his arrangements provided for an increase to about twenty divisions by May.

Meanwhile we were being reinforced probably faster than the enemy. Alexander calculated that we were getting in a thousand men a day. New formations were the best of all medicines for our sick Field-Marshal.

Without question his economical retreat with the remnants of the Afrika Korps from El Alamein (where the battle was lost before he arrived) to the Mareth Line was one of his greatest though probably least appreciated achievements as a tactical leader.

[1] He was officially Commander-in-Chief of this Army Group until May 13, the date on which all Axis resistance in Africa ended.—H.W.S.

I do not subscribe to the theory that Rommel was a superman. Close to him, I found him much more unimaginative and stolid than the romanticized pictures that have been drawn of him by both friend and foe. But as one of those who was almost constantly in touch with the enemy on the long haul back from El Alamein to Mareth, I hand it to him for the way he juggled us along, never losing more than he must, fighting for time while a formidable redoubt was built up for a trial of strength in Tunisia.

Typically, Rommel had barely linked up with von Arnim and withdrawn his harried Afrika Korps into the shelter of the Mareth Line, before he was planning to resume offensive tactics.

Meanwhile the danger was that the Anglo-American forces in Tunisia would launch an attack on the wide-open front in his rear. So he decided to strike first in a surprise attack with all his motorized forces in order to destroy as much of the enemy army as he could. Then he would turn again swiftly on Montgomery, to push him back to the east and so delay the offensive that the Eighth Army would otherwise mount.

I have no intention of writing a military study of the complex battle of Tunisia, fascinating though it is. If you are not a student of war you will not care why my unit was sent along the good road that leads from Gabes to Gafsa Oasis; if you are a student of war you will know that from the oasis run roads that cross the Western Dorsale range of Tunisia at Kasserine and Feriana, and the background of Rommel's plan will be obvious to you.

Rommel built up behind Faid an Army Group Reserve, the core of which was the 21st Panzer Division. The American 2nd Corps, made up of raw and still unblooded troops, was across the Faid plain, between Gafsa and Fondouk. The Kasserine Pass lay behind. The 1st American Armoured Division was dispersed round Sidi Bou Zid, on the Jebel Lessouda—an isolated peak north of the village—at Sbeitla, and on the Sbeitla–Pichon road.

On February 14 Rommel threw about a hundred Panzers and supporting troops at the Yanks, with Stukas for good measure to add to the discomfiture of the 'new boys.' The Americans' artillery was overrun. They lost thirty guns. Panzers knocked the American tanks about badly.

After an unsuccessful counter-attack next day the Yanks retreated towards Sbeitla, leaving their infantry on Jebel Lessouda cut off. Many were captured. Their tanks had been so gravely reduced—eighty-six were knocked out—that they could no longer hold the plain, and they retreated still farther to the Western Dorsale range.

My unit, Special Group 288, came into the picture on the second day of this offensive. We had been ordered to attack and occupy Gafsa Oasis, which we expected to find held by American parachutists and Free French. In actual fact the oasis had been held by American Rangers and the Derbyshire Yeomanry, who with our old Western Desert enemies, the 11th Hussars, were not long afterwards to have the honour of capturing Tunis. But they had pulled out to conform with the general American withdrawal to the Western Dorsale. The Free French, who had been on the Eastern Dorsale, also had to fall back to the other range.

Outside Gafsa, we were excited at the thought of meeting Americans on the battlefield for the first time. We did not then realize that the Americans at this stage knew nothing of the art of war and could not be compared with the redoubtable men of the British Empire against whom we had fought these past two years.

We lay east of the oasis, in the valley through which the Gabes road runs. While we prepared our weapons for action that afternoon, reconnaissance troops discovered that the oasis had been evacuated. We went in at sunset, feeling our way through minefields. The only fighting we had was a minor skirmish with a small group at the farther fringe of the oasis.

We hunted at once for cigarettes. Great was the joy of the men when we found several American trucks, one of them loaded with cigarettes. And, after our short commons on the great retreat, what a change it was to have lavish American rations fall into our hands!

At dawn my driver was planning a sumptuous breakfast of American food when I was summoned to speak to Captain Meyer, my new commanding officer. Hitherto I had commanded the 2nd Battalion of Special Group 288, but Meyer had just arrived from Germany and, as my senior, had superseded me. The Battalion had been cut down from three companies to two strong companies. I led one of these. Meyer and I were not particularly friendly; when I had handed over the Battalion he had shown not the slightest interest in anything I had to tell him about it.

Now Meyer discussed the strategical and tactical situation with me. I studied the map while he read out to me: 'Orders to the Battalion: Special Group 288 is to thrust forward along the road in the direction of Feriana immediately. Order of march for the Regiment will be: 2nd Battalion in the lead, followed by 1st Battalion and Regimental details.'

Meyer added: 'You will lead with your company. Heavy *Panzerjäger* [tank-hunters] will be attached to you.'

I got my company on the march at once, the *Panzerjäger* immediately behind my truck, then a detachment of sappers with mine-detectors. The road from Gafsa to the north was tarred and far better than I had expected.

Our move was not unmolested. Not far out of Gafsa we were shelled by artillery, whose observers must have been located on the high ground on our left. We returned the enemy's fire. The dive-bombers went for us. I lost two of my best vehicles. We re-grouped as the regimental order came up the line: 'Continue marching!'

A mile or two in the lead, my company sped on northward. Once more we were attacked by dive-bombers. But other low-flying aircraft left us alone.

We passed a dead American Negro lying in the road. He was naked—stripped, you could be certain, by Arabs.

I peered into the distance and sighted tanks moving northward. They must be Americans. My map suggested that we were nearing Feriana, and, indeed, when we had covered a mile or two more, the road dropped down into a valley and I could see houses at the bottom. We raced down the slope and reached the outskirts of the village as the tail of our column breasted the crest behind us. Guns in the village began to shell the tail of the column. Simultaneously, as we leaped from our trucks, we came under rifle-fire from the near-by houses. We replied by spraying the village with machine-gun fire for lack of positive individual targets.

The rest of the battalion detrucked swiftly and we went in, infantry-fashion, on a broad front. The sniping stopped. Out of the houses poured a number of Arabs—men, women, and children, waving and shouting in the false jubilation which these people always accorded any apparently victorious troops. Their sheikh recognized me as the officer in command and ran to me with outstretched arms. He gibbered words of greeting. But my right hand was on my automatic, just in case. He fumbled at me and tried to kiss my hands. When I pulled them back in disgust, he grovelled on his knees and kissed my boots.

The Arabs were at pains to prove themselves friendly, as no doubt they had been with the Americans not many minutes before. They pointed out minefields, warned us that American artillery had only just pulled out, and said that there were still a number of heavy tanks on the far side of the village.

The minefield was newly laid, and the fresh-turned soil betrayed the presence of each mine clearly. We picked our way through gingerly, with sappers at our heels marking the track for the guns behind.

Beyond the minefield the road began to climb again. I was rounding a sharp curve when I sighted and recognized a Sherman tank on the road ahead, within attacking range. I jerked the wheel in the driver's hand and the vehicle swerved sharply towards the left bank of the road. The detachment manning the gun immediately behind me were swift in taking their cue. In a matter of seconds they had jumped from their seats, unlimbered, swung round and fired their first shell, while the Americans still stood immobile, the muzzle of the tank gun pointing at a hillock half-right from us. Our first shell struck the tank at an angle in the flank. The tank burst into flames.

We probed ahead and soon ran into fire from tanks and machine-guns deployed on either side of the road. Sending a runner back to Meyer with word of the situation, I deployed my company under cover of our anti-tank guns to attack the rise on our right. We reached the crest with a few casualties. Meanwhile the other company, under Oberleutnant Buchholz, moved up on to the heights on the left and continued to advance.

Steady fighting went on for an hour. Then thick columns of black smoke rose ahead, followed by explosions, obviously in an ammunition dump. The enemy tanks ceased firing. We continued to advance, accelerating our pace now, and saw moving off tanks that were obviously the tail-end of the enemy's holding force.

There was no time to spare for loot or leisure in Feriana. A detachment was detailed to save what was possible from the burning fuel, ammunition, and supply depots. We moved on at speed towards the near-by aerodrome at Thelepe, where we began to appreciate the results of the new offensive. The enemy had left sixty unserviceable aircraft here; many of them, plus stores, had been destroyed by the enemy before he retreated.

We spent the night in defensive positions north of the aerodrome. Before daybreak we received orders to thrust on northward. We met with no resistance at all until we encountered individual tanks (of the American 1st Armoured Division) on the plain west of the mountain range that overhung us on the right. A situation report from Higher Command explained why: 'The 1st American Tank Division, after heavy losses, is withdrawing to Tebessa. Special Group 288 has reached area Jebel Lessouda.'

At midnight that night (February 16–17) the Panzers attacked Sbeitla again, and after stern fighting broke into the town during the morning. The American Armoured Division withdrew westward and was pulled into reserve south-east of Tebessa to re-form. Anderson, the British general, was so concerned at the American failure that he halted a British armoured brigade that was on its way to the rear to exchange its aged, outdated Crusader tanks for modern Shermans. With their old tanks and some Shermans manned by scratch British crews, he sent them to stiffen up the Yanks.

On the 18th Rommel halted his mobile force, now fully concentrated, to regroup and refuel. He had forced a deep salient into the Anglo-American line and could turn the enemy flank still farther by advancing along three different roads—through Kasserine, through Sbeitla and Sbiba, and through Feriana towards Tebessa.

As we learned later, the enemy was at sixes and sevens. General Alexander flew from Tripoli to Algiers on the 15th, intending to take over command five days later. Instead he had to rush to the front and take over in person at once. He found the position even more critical than he expected, as he wrote later. In the confusion of the retreat American, French, and British troops were inextricably mingled. There was no co-ordinated plan of defence, and there was definite uncertainty as to command. At the first mountain pass he visited—the Dernaia Pass above Feriana on the Tebessa road—he had to nominate on the spot the senior American officer as the responsible commander of that sector, and to tell the American that he must hold the ground to the last.

Yes, Rommel had created havoc in his own old way.

As I drove on everywhere I came on detached groups of American infantry who had hidden in the rocks and bush of the mountain slopes. Their transport was tucked away in the valleys. A considerable number of jeeps and trucks fell into our hands—all new, and, to us, astonishingly well equipped.

I tried to converse with some of the Americans we captured. To my surprise I discovered they were Poles—sons of immigrants who had gone from Europe to the United States.

I had sent a scout, an elderly Austrian, into one deep valley to report whether it held any isolated groups of Americans. He came tearing back at speed: 'Herr Oberleutnant, there are enemy tanks in the valley!' We penetrated the valley cautiously with anti-tank guns. Yes, indeed, there on the rise where the bush began we saw some tank-like vehicles trying to reach the protective undergrowth of a gully. They were not tanks, however, but armoured half-trucked troop-carriers mounting small-calibre guns. We opened fire, and at once the drivers left their vehicles for the bush. We raced on and took all six vehicles. One driver also fell into our hands. These six vehicles were a welcome reinforcement for my company, for I had lost six of my own through enemy action. Now we were quits.

CHAPTER THIRTY-EIGHT

KASSERINE PASS

THE road dropped steadily and swung left. Ahead it topped a notable feature. This was the Kasserine Pass.

I had just reached the bend when a regimental order arrived: 'Attack Kasserine Pass—1st Battalion left of road, 2nd Battalion right of road. Make fullest use of motorization. Regimental H.Q.—first house north of bend in road.' That was all.

Buchholz had already got the order. His company was deploying towards the high ground on the right. My company was formed up in a few minutes. At mad speed we roared through a meadow, through gullies and over rocks, towards the hill dominating the pass on the right.

Enemy artillery, well directed, flung shells at us. But we charged through the shell-bursts, our trucks widely spaced. Only one truck was hit. The rest raced to the foot of a slope. A deep wadi across our course forced us to detruck. The men leaped out with their weapons, and the trucks turned to roar back to cover.

We worked our way up rugged cliffs, using every rock and fold in the ground for protection against the American artillery and infantry weapons. Soon we had scrambled to a height level with Buchholz's company, whom we could see on the mountain to our left across the road. I remember reflecting vaguely that my right flank was in the air. Bathed in sweat, we worked our way higher and higher towards the mountain crest.

The crest itself was a steep ridge of rock. I grasped an outcrop and pulled myself up. As my head topped the crest a machine-gun burst drummed past my ears. I dropped. The Yanks had a machine-gun position just ahead of us—thirty yards away at the most.

Under an overhanging rock I paused for a moment with a few of my men to take stock and a swig of water from a water-bottle. My wireless section had come up on my heels. Swiftly I reported back to Regimental H.Q.

To my left Leutnant Becker, a troop-leader, had also reached the crest. He was admirably sited to lay down flanking fire. He forced the enemy machine-gun crew to abandon their position ahead of me. From the bush on my open right flank came sporadic fire. But we had virtually attained our first objective—the heights.

From Becker's post we could keep the whole valley behind the Kasserine Pass under observation. The main road led through the valley up to the Pass on our left. American vehicles rumbled up and down in a steady stream. Those that came up were presumably carrying munitions or reinforcements. And there we were above them, looking down on the whole hinterland of the American front as though we were spectators at the manœuvres of a midget army. How small the men and trucks and guns seemed there below, and how innocuous!

'Our Panzers are going to attack the Pass.' The report came through to our wireless section. We waited anxiously for more news. The grumble and then the thunder of battle rolled up the mountain towards us. The Americans were laying down heavy defensive fire against our assault force.

'Attack failed.' God! I got more details. For some reason I was not so concerned at this major news as at the subsidiary report that Meyer had gone into the attack, in support of the Panzers, with my six captured American half-trucks and had lost all but one of them.

While I was receiving this news, bit by bit, Becker was studying the road far below through his glasses. Suddenly he nudged me. He was a young officer who had joined us in Africa only at the end of our long Desert battle and retreat, but I knew already that he was able and enterprising.

'Herr Oberleutnant!' he nudged me. 'D'you see that small bridge away down there on the road? If we could reach that, if we could only get there, we'd cut the American communications in the rear.'

I studied the ground. 'A daring plan, Becker,' I concluded, 'daring, but possible. Let's go.'

CHAPTER THIRTY-NINE

THE BRIDGE AND THE MAN FROM BROOKLYN

SWIFTLY I mustered an assault platoon of three officers and twenty-one men armed with automatic weapons. With as much ammunition as we could carry we crawled through the cover of the undergrowth towards the nearest gully.

The undergrowth ended. With the others at my heels, I jumped into a dry gully that ran down the slope. We scrambled along in the shelter of this for several hundred yards. Then the gully levelled out, and I feared to find that we should emerge in open ground, but luckily twenty yards farther on we sighted another dip. The gap of twenty yards, though, was a danger-point. It was bare of even a bush. If an eye were on the ground we should be seen.

'Cross singly,' I ordered. Leutnant Ebenbichler with an automatic weapon made the dash first. One by one we slipped across. Strangely, we seemed to have run the gauntlet unnoticed, for not a shot was fired. Had we, I wondered, been mistaken at a little distance for Allied troops? The enemy might not have expected us to be on this side of the mountain barrier.

Now the sun was sinking. We must act soon, I thought, if we were to succceed in our plan. That bridge must be ours.

Our luck held. The gully we were in now ran right into the wadi which the bridge crossed. It was not much of a bridge, a mere culvert, twin-arched, a little above six feet high and perhaps twelve feet long.

We got there, and we breathed again.

I had two machine-guns positioned on either side of the approach to the wadi and the bridge, facing in the direction of the enemy's rear.

Darkness dropped suddenly on the valley. And then, within minutes, a vehicle approached from the hinterland of the enemy region. As it rolled towards the bridge we tried to hold it up. The truck slowed down, but the men in it recognized us as

Germans. One of them fired at us from the standing position. The truck accelerated and thrashed its way across the bridge before we could recover from our surprise.

That was a lesson. We were wiser when the next vehicle was heard rumbling towards us and loomed up in vague shape in the thickening darkness. The truck came on fast. Close by, both my machine-guns let rip at it from either side of the road. The truck swerved off the road and capsized. One of my men leaped up and made prisoners of the men in it—four men, two of them wounded. One was badly hit. We wrapped him in blankets and took him, with the other three prisoners, into the darkness and safety of the wadi below the bridge.

Our machine-gun fire betrayed our presence. American infantrymen somewhere down the wadi opened up loose rifle-fire in the general direction of the road. I sent three men with an N.C.O. to reconnoitre.

One of the patrol came panting back, silent though swift: 'A group of American soldiers approaching—quite close!'

A few minutes later six American riflemen were crossing the bridge. They were almost in the middle of it when they were taken with a gasp: my men pounced on them from both sides and had them pinned before they had time to feel fully bewildered.

Within seconds we heard the sound of another truck approaching. We leaped for cover and as the truck approached the bridge we turned the machine-guns on to it. This time our prisoners included three officers.

We held the captured officers under one arch of the bridge, where my little group of reserves lay. The American other ranks were kept under guard below the second arch.

With the two shot-up trucks, I had my men rapidly improvize a road-block on the bridge. Several more American trucks ran up to the road-block, slowed down, stopped—and we took the men in them without firing a shot.

I had a patrol out ahead still. One of the men came back breathless, alive with the curious exhilaration of escape. He gasped: 'Herr Oberleutnant—the others have fallen. . . . We were rounding a bend down the wadi when we found ourselves face to face with the Americans. They must have seen us coming. Before we could do a thing they were shooting at us with Sten guns. . . . I was slightly behind the others . . . I got away. . . .'

I sent another machine-gun crew down the wadi to the bend to protect our flank.

2

One of the captured American officers began to talk. My English was scanty, and I could barely understand him. I gathered that he was asking whether I was the officer in charge, and he led me to two badly wounded men below the bridge. He thought they should have more attention. But the ambulance man with us had already done all he could, and there was nothing more one could do for one of them. He had been hit in the head. He groaned. How harrowing to hear the groans of that unconscious man under that bridge in the darkness of Tunisia. An insignificant concrete culvert—that was all.. And yet men in the African night were dying because of it, taxing their courage to absurd limits, having their skulls smashed by deadly little bits of metal.

I moved back quietly in the darkness. Another captured American officer spoke to me. He introduced himself as Captain Smith. As good a name as any other in the circumstances, I thought.

'My truck is close behind the smashed-up trucks in your road-block—in the ditch at the side of the road,' he said tentatively. 'I haven't a razor or a toothbrush with me. Allow me to fetch them, please.'

His truck could not have been more than twenty paces away, but it was a dark night, the American infantry were close at hand, and I suspected that Smith was seeking a chance of escape. Once away, he would lead back reinforcements to fall on us.

'Do not worry, Captain Smith,' I said gently. 'I have a new razor in my kit-bag, and I can even give you a new toothbrush.'

I do not know whether he smiled disbelief in the darkness, but it was quite true. In the captured jeep I had been using these two days past I had found a complete new toilet outfit—a present no doubt from some now-anxious woman in the United States. Did she ever imagine when she gave it to her man that some day I, the enemy, would be using it?

Another of the prisoners was a lieutenant. He was a more breezy character than Smith. We chatted away in a strangely cheerful way under that Kasserine bridge about our private affairs. He came from Brooklyn, he confided. He lived there with his wife and two children.

'A magnificent city,' I managed in my broken English. 'I should like to see it some day.'

'That,' he said half mockingly, 'can probably soon be arranged.'

I got his meaning, and side-stepped: 'I think it's going to take us some time to win the war. . . .'

We both laughed.

Where did I come from? he asked. Was I married? I told him. I remember our discussing the futility of war. One or other of us said it was a terrible and unnecessary arrangement.

I told him I had been born in Natal, and that my sister had been born in New Jersey, U.S.A. He said he was familiar with New Jersey.

Our conversation was interrupted by the buzzer of the portable wireless set. Regimental H.Q. wanted word of my exact position. I let them have it as accurately as I could from my map. Not long afterwards H.Q. demanded the information again, stressing that the references given could not be correct. I repeated my previous figures.

Despite signals from me, they had not clearly grasped that we had cut the road behind Kasserine.

Half an hour had passed since the last truck had run into our road-block. Now I heard a droning in the distance to the north. The ground began to tremble slightly. Suspicious, I climbed from the wadi to the top of the bank. In the open air the sound of motors purred clearly from where we knew the Americans lay. Enemy tanks, undoubtedly.

'If tanks advance on the bridge,' I ordered the nearest machine-gunner, 'do not shoot—let them cross.'

'*Jawohl, Herr Oberleutnant*!'

The drone of the engines and the clank of the caterpillars grew louder. A tank loomed up on the road, appearing colossal against the background of the starry heavens as I stared up from the rim of the wadi.

The hatch was open, and the commander was standing exposed and looking around. The tank pulled up. 'Why this barricade?' a voice rang out. The tank commander got no reply. My men had pistols in the ribs of the prisoners below the bridge. The tank commander spoke swiftly to his driver. The tank thrust on, heaving the wrecked trucks to one side.

And then one of our machine-guns let rip directly at the tank turret. Damn! I had forgotten to ensure that my order reached the machine-gun on the far side of the wadi. And here was the gunner firing as though a Sherman were cat's meat for a machine-gun! Like a rabbit at a bolt-hole, the commander dropped down into his turret. The tank sprayed out fire wildly. At the first shot we dropped down the bank and scrambled below the bridge where he certainly would not get us. Thundering, the heavy tank rolled over the bridge above our heads. It had crossed; but the droning went on, and then the rumbling thunder again, the squeak and rattle of tracks, the firing of cannon and machine-guns, with the earth trembling. Another tank passed over the bridge, another and another, one more then, the fifth and last.

They swept on towards the Pass, then swung right in roughly the direction where I reckoned the American infantry were lying. Now, I feared, they might be able to enfilade us under the bridge. Both we and our prisoners would be helpless. But we lay unmolested, and the droning died down. Had the tanks gone on towards their threatened front? Or had they stopped in the neighbourhood because they had learned from their infantry that both enemy and captured Americans were sheltering under the bridge? Again I thought what an odd and absurd business this war game is.

I imagined that I could still distinguish the shapes of individual tanks in the distance and the darkness. If we left the bridge now, we should swiftly be slaughtered by the tanks' formidable weapons. No, the only thing to do was to remain under the bridge until the tanks moved clean away. . . . But they must recross the bridge. Wouldn't they come back with infantry to deal with us? Or they might drop sticks of grenades from their turrets on both sides of the bridge into our ditch. . . . And there I was, with none of my familiar anti-tank guns, no bombs for detonating the tanks' tracks, no demolition charges to destroy the bridge. And, of course, that bridge might be vital to us intact. . . .

The next hour was tense. The American lieutenant from Brooklyn offered me some chewing-gum and a cigarette. I seldom smoked, but I felt that a cigarette might do me good. The possibility that I might see Brooklyn, or at least some part of

America, even before the end of hostilities no longer seemed so remote. I reflected: all I really wanted to do when I qualified was to go farming in East Africa. It is true I should like to see America some day. But not this way; not this way. Oh, dammit, why couldn't the world have let me just finish my studies and go farming in Africa!

I could feel the American captain and the lieutenant watching me intently. I put on my calmest face and inhaled deeply, pretending to enjoy it like a regular smoker. . . . I'll send out a small patrol, I thought, and if the tanks have definitely pulled off I must get back the way I came and take these prisoners with me.

'Well, what's happening, bud?' The American lieutenant had moved closer. I shrugged my shoulders indifferently and replied shortly. 'Wait!' Desultorily, we dropped into our rather aimless personal conversation again. It was an odd situation. Neither American nor German knew who would be the prisoner next morning. So on both sides we were affable and (we hoped) confident.

Then again the droning of tanks. This time from Kasserine way. We stared at each other in silence. Hands grasped Tommy-guns. My machine-gunners dropped down into the cover of the wadi. Some distance away the returning tanks opened fire on the bridge. Their cannon shells whammed past and into the bank. Again the shaking of the earth below our feet, the clank and grumble of the tracks, the thunder overhead.

One. Two. Three. Four. Five.

The tanks went over and on. My machine-gunners scrambled back to their positions. The drone of the tank engines faded in the distance, like tuneless bagpipes.

The Americans and I looked at each other again. The lieutenant from Brooklyn grinned. 'Have some gum, bud,' he said.'

3

I reckoned that as soon as the tanks reported to higher command, action would be taken against us. We should be winkled out from under that bridge fast.

I wrapped out orders: 'Leutnant Ebenbichler with a few men will take the lead. Leutnant Becker will form a small rearguard.'

The men got ready. But first we had to make the wounded as comfortable as we could. I turned to the small group of officers, and in my indifferent English tried to say: 'Gentlemen, one of you, together with an ambulance man, may remain with the wounded. He will have to give his word of honour not to take immediate action against us or to follow us for an hour after we leave. Agreed?'

They listened intently, and nodded silent agreement.

I left it to them to decide which of them was to stay behind. They did it swiftly, spinning a coin, heads or tails, eliminating. The final spin lay between Captain Smith and the lieutenant from Brooklyn. Now I was interested too. The coin spun in the darkness again, and dropped on the earth. A glimmer of a light. Heads!

The lieutenant from Brooklyn had called heads. He was to stop. He was not to be my prisoner, and I was glad of it.

The captain, looking a trifle downcast, said: 'So I'm coming. What about my razor and toothbrush in that truck?'

'Don't worry,' I said. 'I'll fix your needs when we are back in our lines.'

Ebenbichler and his men had gone ahead silently. I followed with my men. As we left the archway the lieutenant from Brooklyn called out in a laughing whisper: 'Goo'-bye, bud—see ya in Berlin!'

His gay mockery was not unpleasant. I called back softly: 'Auf Wiedersehen—in Brooklyn, when the war is over.'

A wave, and I was scrambling up the bank with my men and the prisoners.

We climbed cautiously to the crest of the mountain overlooking Kasserine, and then scrambled down the long descent. I got back to Battalion H.Q. and handed over the Americans. Then I gladly stretched myself on the ground with my men and slept.

When I woke a trace of dawn was in the sky. The prisoners had already been hurried back towards their interrogation and our make-shift P.O.W. cages. I had not been able to offer Captain Smith a razor and a toothbrush.

Day was breaking. And with day came a new order to attack.

CHAPTER FORTY

AMERICANS IN THE MIST

LET me skip a lengthy description of strategic developments and leave General Alexander to tell the story in the brevity of his dispatches:

On February 19 'the enemy carried out exploratory attacks,' he says,

> against all three roads, attempting to find out which would prove the easiest for an attack. His main weight was on the right, against Sbiba; the attack on the pass above Kasserine was made by about a battalion of infantry, and the force probing the Dernaia Pass above Feriana, on the Tebessa road, was only of the nature of a small reconnaissance. South of Sbiba, the 1st Guards Brigade held firm and repulsed the enemy, but the attack in the Kasserine Pass was more successful and the enemy began to infiltrate through the American positions. Accordingly on the next day, the 20th, this thrust was strongly reinforced and the other two abandoned; the Pass was cleared and the 21st Panzer Division, with the infantry and some of the armour of the detachment from the German Afrika Korps, pressed on into the basin beyond. Here Rommel found himself faced with two alternatives, for the road after traversing the Pass, diverges to west and north. The former direction would take him to Tebessa, our main southern base and airfield centre.

2

Rommel himself watched us go into the new attack, standing on a high point near the Kasserine Pass.

Though the road through the Pass had been taken, American infantry and tanks tenaciously resisted the German advance on to the plain beyond. Special Group 288 was ordered to clear the way for the main thrust along the road. We were deployed on both sides of the road. The two companies of my own battalion which had taken the heights above the Pass were positioned to the right of the road. The heights on which we had fought were above us, on our right. Some American infantry had infiltrated back up the slopes and had set up a couple of machine-gun nests that were a thorn in our side.

I swept the road in the distance with my binoculars, in search of the bridge that had been the scene of our nocturnal adventure behind the American lines, but I decided it was probably hidden by a dip in the country. Once I sighted a Sherman advancing towards the road from the enemy rear areas. It showed a white flag, so we took no action. It picked up casualties and turned back. I reckoned that the bridge must be somewhere near its turning-point.

We did not go forward until the afternoon. The operation orders were complex and provided for a combined effort by various arms. The infantry—that was us—were to break the resistance ahead, but we were promised Panzer, artillery, and aircraft support.

Earlier experience in attack had taught me not to rely overmuch on promised support, but this time the whole operation was neatly dovetailed. A Panzer group led by Captain Sloten advanced as planned behind us. When they came abreast of us, the newly landed *Nebelwerfer* were let loose with their howling, eightfold muzzles spitting fire in an effective barrage that crept just ahead of us. Then Stukas swept over and lent additional weight to the bombardment.

We surged forward. The thin line of American infantrymen found the fury ahead of them too much. They withdrew hurriedly to the steep, broken slope, covered with thick bush, behind them. American tanks simultaneously broke out of a gully and made to escape before they were cut off. Two tanks got stuck in a wadi just as we plunged into it; their crews abandoned them and fled.

Darkness fell on our advance, but the way ahead had been opened up as Rommel wanted. His small initial attack had developed just as he planned, and with this readiness to exploit initial success, he decided to thrust on as heavily as he could.

3

Special Group 288, relatively small though it was, was now given a big task. We were to smash along through the night towards the American positions at Tebessa and penetrate them if we could. What we lacked in *matériel*, said Rommel, we were to make up for through our battle experience. We were to take our chance in the confusion he expected would arise.

That night's march was made through darkness and difficulties. We ran into many obstacles, and we of the 2nd lost contact with the 1st Battalion.

As day was nearing we came to the foot of a gradual rise. We left our trucks and went ahead on foot. Dawn broke as we cat-footed it up a grass-covered slope, but thick mist hid us.

Leutnant Becker, alongside me, grabbed my arm. A break had swirled open in the mist, and we could see other figures clambering up the hillside near us.

'Americans, I think,' said Becker.

I thought he was mistaken: they must be some of our own company. But a minute or two later Becker jerked my arm again. He stammered excitedly: 'But definitely—Americans!' He pointed to other figures that had momentarily loomed up through the mist. Still I did not believe him, though he insisted he had recognized the shape of their helmets.

A few seconds later I was convinced: only a few yards ahead of me two bent figures were trudging up the hill, and without doubt they were Americans.

We dared not shoot. Before the sun dispersed the mist and we were left naked in the daylight, we must be firmly ensconced on the crest.

But the Americans, too, had eyes, and they did not hold their fire. Becker and some of his men stumbled across more of the enemy. A few fierce shots rang out before the mist closed in again, and Unteroffizier Wagner, one of our best men, dropped—mortally wounded.

It was full daylight when we reached the crest. There I discovered that it was merely a false crest: the ground levelled out for only a short distance before rising again to another crest. There was nothing else for it now but to dig in where we were, for obviously we were thrusting our faces up against the enemy.

Commanding on the right flank, I found a useful H.Q. in the dry, rocky bed of a little stream. From here there was a good field of view over the flat ground on our flank.

Yank guns began to hammer us as the light grew. The day, in fact, opened unpleasantly. I crawled forward from my position in the stream-bed to the top of alittle ridge. From here I could see, not far below, artillery positions and a number of tanks. We had landed close to the core of the 1st Armoured American Division.

The day grew wilder. Shells seemed to rain on us from all directions. Away to the left I watched the 1st Battalion, under Captain Moll, being attacked and virtually encircled by tanks. So serious was their plight that only precipitate withdrawal saved them. With our force halved, I felt that my unit was more isolated than ever.

Behind us and to the right, in the battle for Thala, heavy fighting blazed up between our Panzers and Anglo-American tanks.

Alexander, rightly judging that Rommel would thrust north, had ordered the British commander, General Anderson, to concentrate his armour in defence of Thala. The British rushed to the area a composite force mostly of the 26th Armoured Brigade Group, reinforced by two battalions of British infantry and two American field artillery battalions.

The fighting that followed in open country was as Alexander reported afterwards, 'extremely fierce and the fortunes of war were changeable. At one moment a few German Panzers succeeded in forcing their way over the low pass south of Thala village, but they were shot to pieces by field guns at close range. The situation was exceedingly grave and was only stabilized after periods of extreme danger by the energy and initiative of the handful of gallant troops on the spot.' At all events, the comparatively fresh 10th Panzer Division, whom Rommel had passed through the 21st for this attack, were held. And on the Kasserine–Tebessa road, the 1st American Armoured Division held us at Jebel Hamra. . . .

Our battalion's position became untenable. An order to withdraw reached us in the afternoon, but was impossible to carry out in daylight. When the protective darkness fell we hurriedly but systematically evacuated our line. We retreated all through that night.

Rommel gave up all the ground he had gained during the preceding days. He extricated all but nine of the tanks with which he had attacked. Mines and demolitions discouraged the enemy in his pursuit. But by the 25th the Anglo-Americans were back at Kasserine Pass. And Montgomery was beginning to threaten us, too, at Mareth.

CHAPTER FORTY-ONE

GOOD-BYE TO THE DESERT FOX

FOR the moment the Mareth Line was again our concern. The situation in Africa seemed to be regarded optimistically by the High Command in Berlin, and continuous reinforcements up to company strength were arriving steadily now. Colonel Menton found himself in a position again to form a third battalion in Special Group 288.

I was entrusted with its formation, and took over command at Sfax. That led to several welcome days of rest from battle.

2

At the crisis in the Kasserine battle, on February 21, Alexander had ordered Montgomery to create as powerful a threat as possible on our southern flank. Montgomery could not achieve a great deal, because he was not yet ready to strike, but he moved up fairly powerful forces forward of Medenine, though not yet in contact with us. After we had begun to fall back at Kasserine, Alexander told Montgomery not to prejudice their future plans by taking undue risks in launching an attack.

Rommel's plight was not graver than it had been. It is true that Alexander says 'as in his advance to El Alamein, Rommel had considerably over-exploited a considerable early success to leave himself in a worse position than before.' But you cannot blame him for boldly attempting to snatch a victory, and he nearly succeeded both times. When he saw himself resolutely opposed and halted after his first disruption of the Americans he did not run further risks. It is absurd to say that the results of the Kasserine adventure were 'disastrous.'

Rommel knew full well that at best, if the long chance of a notable victory failed, he could only hope to stave off Montgomery for a time. His best hope now lay in hitting Montgomery before

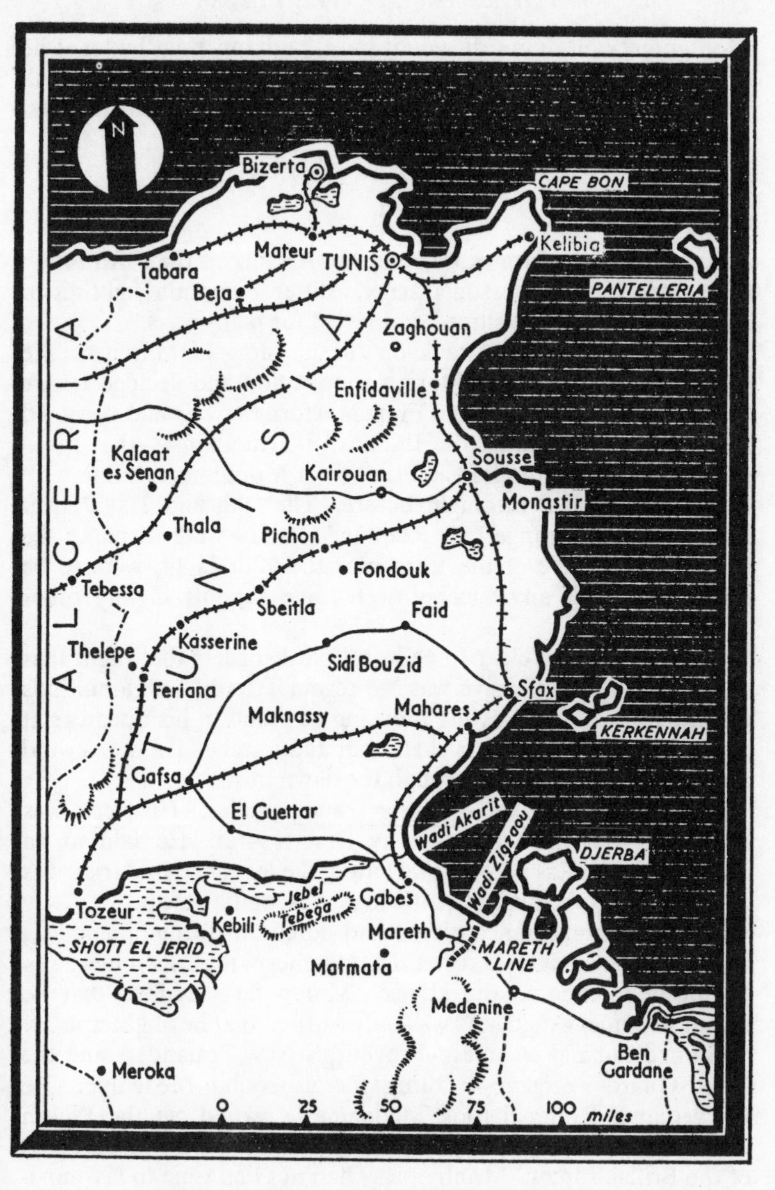

MAP 5: BEN GARDANE TO TABARA

Montgomery hit him. It would have, perhaps, been better if he could have hit Montgomery just a little earlier; but you will remember that he had weighed up the dangers lying in the First Army behind him.

3

As we withdrew from Kasserine, von Arnim, on the Fifth Army front, struck at Anderson's army. Bitter mountain fighting in miserable weather developed and lasted for many days.

Rommel decided to attack on the morning of March 6. He massed his troops in the Mareth Line region and decided to use the plan of attack which the French before the war had designed for possible use against the Italians in Tripolitania—that is, to sweep out of the mountains on the left of Montgomery's line.

We were briefed the night before. The 10th and 21st Panzer Divisions—the strongest in Rommel's hand—were to make the initial assault. We of the 15th, plus the 90th Light, were to be ready to exploit any success or to give support in any other development.

Rommel made it clear to us in his battle orders that night that the object of the offensive was 'to regain Tripoli'—an ambitious undertaking. The following morning he stood in his open car at the top of the Pass at Ksar el Hallouf and watched the tanks wind down the road to attack through the dawn mists.

He was a sick man, suffering from jaundice. His neck was bandaged—he was tormented by Desert sores. He said to an intimate that unless he won this battle, the last hope in Africa was gone. It was to be his last battle in Africa, and a defeat.

Enemy reconnaissance planes had noted our formations massing. Alexander had warned Montgomery that Rommel was obviously moving to the attack. Montgomery replied that he hoped Rommel would, and was only worried that he might not. . . .

He had our old enemies—Freyburg's New Zealanders and the 201st Guards Brigade—waiting for us round Medenine. He knew that if Rommel took Medenine he would cut the Eighth Army's communications with Tripoli and encircle the greater part of the British forces. Montgomery had not had time to lay minefields, but he had masses of anti-tank guns dug in, with a short field of fire planned to enfilade attacking Panzers.

Rommel did not know how strong the enemy position was going to prove. We made four attacks that day and lost over fifty tanks—a number we could ill afford. As at Alam el Halfa, Montgomery did not commit his tanks—indeed, he used only one squadron—and we spent our strength against rows of anti-tank guns. At nightfall Rommel broke off the hopeless battle.

That evening he realized that there was only one chance left for his forces in Africa—to get them, if possible, safely to Italy to fight again. The only thing he could do was to bring his personal influence to bear with Hitler and get permission for an evacuation.

On March 9, 1943, two years after his arrival in Africa, Rommel left this theatre of operations, on his own initiative. Alexander suggests that although his going was genuinely due to sickness, the German High Command also did not want to risk having so famous a leader captured by the enemy.

Rommel's mission to Hitler was futile. He was held for command in Europe and forbidden to return to Africa. Von Arnim took over the Army Group, and von Vaerst, my old commander when I was with the 115th Regiment in the 15th Panzer Division, became commander of the Fifth Army. Berlin signalled in code to the Higher Command in Africa: 'The removal of General Feldmarschall Rommel is to be kept a secret in all circumstances.'

It was a grievous blow to the Afrika Korps.

4

I was to see the Field-Marshal only once more. This was in northern Italy, at a staff conference by Lake Garda. As before, he recognized me among the group and surprised a mass of my seniors by pausing for a personal chat in the midst of the preliminaries for the important discussions that had been arranged.

But this Rommel was no longer my old chief—the 'Desert Fox,' dusty, with a scarf round his neck, his 'recognition flags,' the dust goggles on his high-peaked cap, and just one or two of his personal aides accompanying him. Now he was surrounded by an entourage of glittering staff officers; his cap was new and strange to me; and he carried a Field-Marshal's baton in his hand.

'Are you happy, Schmidt?' he asked. 'Ah, I think those were better days when we were in Africa, matching our wits with the Eighth Army. . . .'

CHAPTER FORTY-TWO

HELL IN THE MARETH LINE

MARETH was the next of our big battles. But first, on the day after Rommel had left Africa, there was the brief and bloody encounter of March 10.

On Rommel's instructions an effort was made to win some slight success to bolster morale after the Medenine fiasco, and by continued activity to keep the enemy from settling down to his preparations for a decisive battle. Reconnaissance units from the 21st and the 15th Panzer Divisions, with Stukas, attacked the Free French force—veterans of the long advance through the African oases from Lake Chad under General Leclerc (de Hautecloque)—at Ksar Rhilane, an outpost in the Desert west of the Matmata mountains. Montgomery undoubtedly planned soon to pass an outflanking force through here if he could.

Our attack failed, largely because the French fought back like they did under Koenig at Bir Hacheim, and because of the powerful intervention of the R.A.F. and the S.A.A.F.

2

The Mareth Line itself was about twenty-two miles long and ran from the sea to the Matmata mountains. At the coastal end the line lay behind the Wadi Zigzaou, a natural anti-tank ditch which the French had artificially strengthened. The defences were a system of inter-connected strong-points, strengthened with concrete and partly underground. Wire and mines filled the gaps. The French when they built it in pre-war days reckoned that it could not be outflanked in the Desert west of the Matmatas. Montgomery's Long Range Desert Group had proved otherwise, but still Alexander considered our line here almost as strong as at El Alamein.

Montgomery's plan for the reduction of the Mareth Line

included a frontal attack on the Wadi Zigzaou near the coast. His troops after breaking into the line were to roll it up from the right. He also planned that the New Zealanders, with the Free French and a brigade of tanks, would deliver a 'left hook' round the mountains and cut the Gabes-Mareth road so as to pen us in.

Alexander arranged also for the Americans under General Patton (who replaced Fredendall) to exert pressure against our right rear. They were to take Gafsa and then the El Guettar defile. They started advancing on March 16. A German reconnaissance unit kept in touch with them but put up no opposition at Gafsa, falling back to the pass east of El Guettar village.

Meanwhile activity increased on the Mareth front itself, and the New Zealand force with 27,000 men set out to sweep round our right flank. Montgomery's main attack was timed for the night of March 20. Our old enemies of the 30th Corps, now composed of the 50th and 51st Divisions, the 4th Indian Division, and the 201st Guards Brigade, were to smash at the Wadi Zigzaou and the bunker line. If and when they got through, the 10th Corps, with two armoured divisions, was to strike on towards Gabes and Sfax.

3

My unit, Special Group 288, had lain for three weeks close to the Gabes oasis, behind the front line, engaged in training. My task was to integrate my own new battalion for the inevitable battle.

I was just about to settle down to write a long letter to my fiancée on the morning of the 20th when there was an urgent call from Regimental H.Q., and my battalion was ordered to prepare for action immediately. We were to place ourselves at the disposal of the staff of the 90th Light Division within four hours.

The Italian 20th Corps held the coastal sector of the Wadi Zigzaou, with, under command, the 90th Light plus two Italian divisions—the Young Fascists and the Trieste. Three other divisions held the Matmata mountains end of the line, with the 15th Panzer Division in immediate reserve behind them. The 21st Panzers were held farther back, ready if need be to defend the gap between Jebel Tebaga and Jebel Melab, against which the New Zealanders were marching this very day.

I reported with a few officers of my battalion to the 90th Light Division H.Q. at the time prescribed. Only a few minutes earlier an American bomber formation had carpeted the area with explosives. Wounded men were still being carried away.

We were at once given a brief situation picture. With the first few words I realized that we were in not for a mobile task but for a period of bitter static fighting.

There was no denying the gravity of the G.S.O.'s words: 'Gentlemen, I am pleased that you have arrived so quickly. Every minute that will give you a chance of inspecting your front-line positions is precious. We have received reliable reports from agents that the Eighth Army intends to launch an attack on this sector to-night.'

He directed us to study the large situation map, and we made rapid notes of boundaries and neighbouring troops on the talc of our own map-boards. And the G.S.O. went on: 'As you see, the Young Fascists occupy this sector. Their fighting value is very low. This fact indeed may have induced the Eighth Army Command to concentrate the attack at this point. It is absolutely essential that these troops be relieved immediately. Before nightfall you must have prepared your sectors and be ready to throw back the most determined enemy assaults.'

The whole conference lasted less than ten minutes. By the end of it I had divided my sector and allotted areas to the companies.

More rapidly than I had expected, and without interruption, we carried out the relief of the line. A considerable section of the Italian troops had indeed been pulled out before we arrived.

I was delighted with the French-built bunkers on the edge of the Wadi Zigzaou. Some of them had been armoured with steel and were practically shell- and bomb-proof. But among them were bunkers that had been constructed with an eye for cover rather than for field of fire. Others had no loopholes. Then, too, most of them had been planned to house French 25- and 47-mm. anti-tank guns and were too small for our 50- and 75-mm. guns, which we had to leave behind the bunker line. There were a number of machine-gun and mortar positions ready in the centre of the trench system—constructed in the sandstone ground.

The Wadi Zigzaou in front of our bunker line was partly flooded. A few hundred yards ahead of it stood a steep knoll which interrupted our field of vision, but likewise limited the distance from which the enemy could observe our positions. An isolated trench system on the knoll had been prepared as an advanced post. Hesitantly, and only because of a direct order, I detailed a detachment about a company strong to man the knoll. And then in the few hours before sunset I hastened to acquaint myself with the sector, site my weapons systematically, and detail responsible men to command the support points.

Scarcely an hour before sunset additional reinforcements arrived in the shape of German troops who had been landed in Africa by aircraft only a few hours before. No time was wasted in ascertaining details about the new troops: they were parcelled out in haste among the front-line sectors.

Feldwebel Ammon, the sergeant-major I had sent to command my extreme left-hand bunker, was subject to strong artillery fire during the last hour of the day. He reported back that he could see enemy troop movements. He also reported that the obviously essential communications with the Italian troops who were his left-hand neighbours were non-existent. There was a wide gap between his post and them. I reported back to my Regiment and was promised help.

At ten o'clock that night I climbed on to the roof of the bunker which was my battle H.Q. It was a mild and starry spring night.

The night was so quiet that I began to wonder whether our agents had misled us—as they often had before. Perhaps the Eighth Army would not strike that night. A lone aircraft droned overhead. Judging by the sound of its engine, it was a Messerschmitt night-fighter. Away on the enemy horizon parachute flares were dropping slowly in the darkness. So our own bombers were busy.

Suddenly the whole horizon before me was lit as though by a flash of lightning. 'What terrific "flak" the enemy is putting up!' I exclaimed to my dispatch-runner. The lightning was limitless: as far and as wide as the eye could see, flash followed flash. Then suddenly I knew that it was no lightning but Montgomery's barrage.

Seconds later there was a howling, whizzing, screeching, and then the bang-blast of explosions all round us. In one leap I jumped from the bunker roof into the deep trench below. Not a moment too soon: the British high explosive plastered the ground all round.

All reflections were whirled away in that terrific barrage. 'Fight—fight for your life!' I felt myself murmuring. I reckoned that soon we should have to reckon on an infantry or tank attack, perhaps both, with the artillery pulverizing us first. An intolerable drum-fire continued and continued.

I ran through the trench system and tried to check that every man was standing ready to fire and that every sector had pushed forward an observer to give adequate warning of the enemy's advance. Already the shape of my trenches had altered considerably. Despite the hard sandstone, the sides of many had collapsed. I was constantly scrambling over shattered masonry or heaps of rock, even leaping over dud enemy shells.

In some shelters dead and wounded men lay alongside their weapons. Immense courage was demanded of those who occupied the less-protected forward observation posts for even half an hour.

I reached one of the lower bunkers in the centre of the sector on the lip of the Wadi Zigzaou. A number of the detachment there lay dead round their gun. In front of the bunker entrance and a little to one side, in a trench, I came across two soldiers who had been lightly wounded.

'Tanks on the rise immediately ahead of us!' one shouted to me. I did not know him—he must have been one of the replacements.

'The tanks have destroyed our bunker armour with direct hits,' he shouted again. 'It is suicide to remain in the bunker.'

'Heavens, man,' I roared in exasperation, 'British infantry is likely to break in at any minute. Occupy that machine-gun position next to the bunker immediately.'

Wounded or not wounded, we were involved in a matter of life or death. I scrambled into the wrecked bunker and dragged out the machine-gun. I turned and saw the two men still lying in the trench where I had left them. They did not move. Within those few seconds an exploding shell had killed them.

I hurried back towards my own bunker. The journey was harder than even the outward one. Fresh bursts forced me to ground every few seconds. The trenches were crumbling and caving in more and more.

When at last I got to the bunker, I detailed three men to man the machine-gun post. Among them was my best runner, a small man full of fun. Within a few minutes he was back, panting,

'Herr Oberleutnant, Tommies are attacking—they are already lying right in front of our trench.'

Now the game was on. Men raced about the trenches giving the immediate alert: 'Infantry attacking—weapons in position!' In a few seconds the machine-guns that the enemy artillery had not blotted out were blazing away criss-cross over the front. Our fire, both frontal and enfilade, against the wadi, was terrific. Belt after belt whipped through the guns.

The company holding the advanced post out in front had been overrun. A quarter of an hour before we had acknowledged their signal: 'Tanks attacking.' Now there was no news of them. And fierce tank fire was coming at us from where they had been.

I sent a runner out to Ammon's flank position. The runner had to cross open country and did not get through. I was not surprised. He had stumbled upon British infantry and been bombarded with Mills bombs. It was clear that some of the British had scaled the wadi bank with fascines. Theirs had been a most courageous and spirited undertaking. The British artillery fire was as intense as ever. They had come forward over open ground which was still under their own barrage.

A group was detailed to clear our left-flank forward trenches of any invaders who had pressed in there. The bunker at the end of this trench system was retaken with three prisoners. But some of the attackers held out determinedly in isolated spots and greeted us with a hail of grenades. We could not get at them, and had to be content to bar the way to our main trenches

Ammon's support post wirelessed back to me: 'English infantry thrusting past us right and left. Support post still being held.'

When day broke I saw some British Valentine tanks on the hillock where my advanced-post company had been lying the evening before. We were unable to bring them under fire: our heavy anti-tank guns were still lying behind the bunker line, as there had been no time the evening before to prepare suitable positions for them. But with concentrated fire from machine-guns and mortars we were able to clear the knoll by the afternoon. The infiltrating infantry were also mopped up as their ammunition became expended. During the day I regained all the trench positions in my sector except for the extreme left flank.

We took prisoner a number of the 50th Division Englishmen.

They were chagrined that the flooded Wadi Zigzaou which they had crossed on foot had been impassable for wheels. Only a few of the heavy tanks had churned their way across. They could not be reinforced.

Our doctor bandaged a young English lieutenant who had been wounded. 'What are you still fighting for?' the Englishman demanded. 'We have an overwhelming superiority of men and materials. It is only a question of days or weeks and the war will be over for you anyhow.'

We refused to believe this and laughed at his optimism.

'Do you like Goebbels?' the Englishman demanded of the doctor, a sensitive young Viennese surgeon. 'What should my reply be?' he asked me. I shrugged and said nothing.

Away to our left the Eighth Army men had broken more deeply into the Mareth Line. Far in rear of the bunker line directly behind our backs, I sighted a small group of Englishmen running over a rise.

We were entirely out of touch with our own people in rear. Had they already written us off? I sent back a wireless message of inquiry. A few hours later the reply came back: 'Hold position at all costs. Reinforced Regiment will counter-attack.'

Ammon's support position lay like a small island on my left flank. He wirelessed to me: 'Enemy is trying to move tanks over ground ahead.' We ourselves were being subjected to more well-aimed fire from tanks standing immediately behind the knoll ahead. It was almost impossible to lift one's head above cover.

The second night fell. We expected more enemy artillery activity, but surprisingly it did not develop. Nor was it followed, as I thought it would be, by another infantry attack. As a precaution I had the wadi swept spasmodically with mortar-bombs and machine-gun fire. A few British assault troops tried again to advance from the trenches they had taken the night before, away to our left. They worked forward with grenades and tommy-guns, disregarding their losses. Again we lost the bunker on my left.

Now I began to feel my own losses. With every important position manned by two gunners, I had no more reserves to lay on local counter-attacks. Again I had to bar the end of the trench system and depend on keeping the enemy out with a screen of mortar-fire. There was no sign of the promised Regimental counter-attack. I began to wonder whether the wireless signal was merely a cheap consolation in what might be our extremity.

But no, in the early afternoon we received another signal: 'Rifle Regiment 115 is attacking. Take precautions not to fire on own troops.'

Soon afterwards I saw German infantry far behind us advancing in leap-frogging movements. They continued relentlessly, obviously regaining lost ground. We kept a closer eye on the action in rear than we did on our own front. But we had no need to worry about further local attacks. I felt some pride in and gratefulness to my old Regiment. They were truly coming to our rescue.

Our own artillery started to shell the trenches held by the enemy on our left, and also the hillock to the front. Despite its initial terrific bombardment, the British artillery was now quiescent. Was it that the Eighth Army did not know the location of their own forward troops, or had the guns been shifted to another part of the front?

Filled with new courage, we advanced from our bunker line in short rushes. I left only a few important support weapons manned. The bulk of the men thrust out to the left and into the Wadi Zigzaou itself. We discovered British infantry unexpectedly close, some of them crouching only a few yards in front of our positions. The enemy tried to withdraw. Many succeeded. Others fell into our hands. We turned over about a platoon of prisoners when Grenadiers coming up to reinforce us arrived.

Soon we held the entire bunker line again. I established direct touch again with Ammon, who for two days had shared his outpost trench with the British invaders. Fresh German infantry filled up the gap on his left, and I felt secure again.

Under cover of artillery fire the British bridgehead troops across the wadi were pulled back on Montgomery's orders. The frontal attack against the Mareth Line had failed.

CHAPTER FORTY-THREE

THIN LINE AGAINST THE YANKS

ABANDONING his original plan, Montgomery called off his frontal attack and reinforced the outflanking attack. At dusk that evening he sent another division of tanks[1] to back up Freyberg's powerful column, which had now begun to batter at the Jebel Melab area. Our 21st Panzers and 164th Division, from the western end of the Mareth Line, had been rushed there to hold off the New Zealanders and the 200 tanks with them. With the fresh armoured divisions Montgomery had now moving up, he expected to be able to attack us in the rear with 300 tanks.

Meanwhile, Alexander ordered Patton, with his Americans, to push a division of infantry down the Gafsa–Gabes road and a division of tanks down the Gafsa–Maknassy road.

There was nothing else for our High Command but to give up the strongest defence line in Tunis, this 'Maginot' of French North Africa at Mareth.

We were pulled out that night and once more retreated.

With the 15th Panzers also flung into the fray now, the 21st and the 164th Divisions held off the New Zealanders from El Hamma while the Mareth troops were withdrawn through the corridor behind them to the next defensive position at the Wadi Akarit, north of Gabes. Ferocious fighting went on for days before Freyberg entered Gabes at midday on March 29th. By this time our German–Italian army had lost 7000 prisoners, mostly Italians, plus many guns and Panzers.

Meanwhile my battalion was involved in a fresh fight against the Americans at El Guettar.

2

Messe, the Italian general commanding the remnants of our Alamein army, had ordered the evacuation of the small Gafsa

[1] The 1st Armoured Division.

oasis garrison much earlier and had improvized a new defence line five miles east of Maknassy with a German and an Italian reconnaissance unit. This line was reinforced by the 10th Panzer Division, three German infantry battalions, and some Italian tanks, and they held the pass against the American 1st Armoured Division. The American infantry attack down the Gafsa-Gabes road was stopped until March 25 by a succession of counter-attacks by the 10th Panzers.

So often had Special Group 288, with its anti-tank guns, been used as a 'fire-break' that I was not in the least surprised, when we were pulled out of the Mareth Line, to find that we were to be thrown into the valley at El Guettar. We were greeted, as though by old friends, by the guns of Patton's American Corps.

A tracked armoured troop-carrier swept towards me carrying the 10th Panzer's Divisional Commander. We were under heavy shell-fire, and he stopped only a few moments to put me in the picture. Friendly and obviously fearless, he shouted to make himself heard above the din of the shelling: 'Advance as soon as possible with every available man. In the valley in front—there, behind the rise you see next to the road—there should be an Italian defended position. But it's possible the Italians have already been overrun. We've observed a large number of Italian prisoners behind the American front. Your task is to take up a suitable position as far forward as possible and, together with any remaining troops there, build up a new defence line.'

'*Jawohl, Herr General,*' I acknowledged.

'Any further advance by the Americans must be stopped at all costs,' added the Panzer general. 'If this line is broken, it will be the end of all Rommel's forces. Do your best!'

I broke in with a command while the General still spoke: 'Unload weapons and ammunition! Vehicles retire!'

The General knew as well as I that we were in a state of emergency. He did not choke me off for interrupting. 'Do your best, then,' he repeated calmly, and drove off.

Under the prompting of shells the detachments carried out their orders swiftly. The high trucks that acted as magnets to the enemy artillery sped off. The shells followed them. We had a short respite. My men lay to the south of the road, their weapons alongside them. In the breathing spell the officers were able to orientate themselves.

My orders were brief: 'Form infantry line and advance on a wide front! Remainder, follow!'

Our best chance was to advance as rapidly as possible. I ran forward to take the lead. The battalion went forward swiftly on the right of the Gafsa road, snatching every chance of cover that offered. Within a few minutes we reached a wide, shallow depression. It lacked cover. In it the Americans would see each man individually. All hell, I thought, might be let loose at any minute.

Across as quickly as possible!

I ran as if possessed or chased by all the devils in creation. Hesitation meant destruction. The men tore along behind me. We were truly in the heart of an inferno. Here and there a soldier went down. 'Ambulance!' The cry went up again and again. Comrades ran to assist the fallen. Others ran on and on behind me.

Half an hour later the barrage still hung like a curtain behind us. Scarcely two platoons had got through with me. The rest tried and tried again, but were forced to ground with heavy losses.

We, who had survived the cauldron, worked our way steadily forward. Sometimes we had a moment's breathing space behind cover. Shells still exploded among us and near by, but the fire was a bagatelle after what we had come through.

We had crossed the hillock the General had pointed out to me, but we could see nothing—neither Americans nor Italians. Now the ground afforded more cover.

Against a rise I spotted a cave entrance. In front of it stood an Italian soldier. We move towards him. I demanded information —and water. '*Aqua? Niente aqua*,' he replied. '*Vino, buono vino rosso!*' Obligingly he handed me his flask. I took a deep swig. New energy seemed to course through my tired body. A long row of Italian flasks was brought out of the dark cave. Every one of my men had a swig.

My eyes became accustomed to the darkness of the entrance. I peered into the cave. It held about sixty Italians.

'*Dove est vostro posizione?*' I asked. 'Where are your positions?'

'*Niente posizione, soltanto Americani*,' answered an Italian officer indifferently. 'No positions, only Americans.'

The Italians began to worry at our massing in front of their cave: we might betray their hiding-place.

I deployed my men swiftly. Then we ran into a fresh artillery barrage. Ahead of us now I saw a slope pitted with holes and slits. There was not a single soldier to be seen, but I was certain these were the Italians' positions. I had grown familiar with their customary defensive set-up: they dug in, well covered, behind a crest, with only a few advanced posts commanding any real field of fire.

Swiftly, with a sense of relief, I dispersed my men among the abandoned Italian slit-trenches. I spread the men over a wide area, with a lieutenant commanding the sector on either flank on both sides of the road. I stayed on the southern side of the road.

While I was seeing to the posting of a group to the left of the slope, I discovered a dug-out containing three German self-propelled assault-guns. And I found the officers in charge of them in a deep Italian bunker, strongly protected with layers of stone and earth, which must surely have been built expressly for a senior Italian officer.

Commanding the assault-gun detachment was an Oberleutnant who was overjoyed to learn that German infantry support had arrived. Except for his men the sector was deserted. During the night Americans had attacked and hauled out all the Italians except for those who fled to the rear.

'Immediately ahead of us over the slope, only forty paces away, there is a nest of Americans,' he said.

While he spoke he kept a look-out through the slits in the bunker. He seemed keen and courageous. And how disappointed he was when he learned that I had no anti-tank guns forward with me! It would be impossible, in the face of the American shelling, to have these pushed forward until nightfall.

Suddenly the Oberleutnant exclaimed: 'Tanks are attacking!'

About a dozen of the colossal Shermans were rolling towards us. They disappeared into a dip, with some individual turrets just visible. And now I saw them being backed up by American infantry—two companies strong, as far as I could judge.

The officer next me became uneasy. I reassured him: 'The tanks themselves are not likely to attack—they'll probably just give supporting fire to the infantry.'

He thought differently. 'I can't match my assault-guns against these American tanks. And infantry without anti-tank guns can't protect my guns against those tanks.'

He might be right. Nevertheless I said: 'I am the responsible commander in this sector. Remain covered in this dip with your guns, but support us with fire against the infantry.'

It was high time I alerted my men. I had only a few heavy machine-guns and five mortars forward, and only limited ammunition for these. In a few minutes the report came back to me from all weapon positions: 'Ready to fire.'

My order, 'Free fire,' to the mortars, was to be taken as a general signal for all weapons.

Simultaneously my whole line opened up. After firing half a belt, each machine-gun crew dived into cover again. The whole thing was splendidly done—more slickly than I had ever seen it in training or on manœuvres.

The result was what I wanted: the attacking American infantry kept their heads down.

When the first wave advanced again, our weapons were slipped out of cover and positioned. I took a couple of steps away from the heavy machine-gun near the hole that served as my command-post. A shrieking shell dropped on the spot. The gun's detachment of three men was blotted out.

The American tanks now began to concentrate their fire on our positions on the rise. And a few minutes later the three German assault-guns broke cover and sped past us. As if to excuse his flight the officer in charge of them shouted to me as he passed: 'Tank attack! We must get back!'

No, I said to myself. This would never have happened in Rommel's old Afrika Korps. We are facing defeat in Africa.

But, as I expected, the American tanks did not come on. We were alone at the front, not two platoons of us, and heaven knew what enemy strength was glowering at us.

I decided that the Italian choice of defensive positions was not, after all, so unreasonable. . . . We were happy to withdraw from the crest, leaving only an observation post behind a heap of stones, and to retire to the reverse slope. From cover we kept up a defensive mortar-fire and held off the attack—but not before we had fired almost our last round.

We had only one ambulance man with us, a Catholic priest in civilian life who had, before the war, studied in Switzerland through the assistance of American charity. I sent him out to tend the wounded and collect the identity discs from the fallen. Relying on the Red Cross brassard on his arm, he climbed to the crest when the firing stopped and moved about in full view of the Americans. Tank muzzles pointed menacingly at him, but the enemy commander had recognized his badge through binoculars, and he was left unmolested. I respected the Americans for their chivalry in all our encounters.

After dark, troops who had earlier failed to get through the barrage joined us, and I was able to extend my front north of the road, where Captain Moll and the survivors of his battalion lay. In the darkness we moved our anti-tank guns forward and I sited them along the road flanking our infantry positions in the valley.

I detailed a strong group to occupy a sugar-loaf observation point ahead, under an N.C.O.—a prospective officer, who answered to the distinguished name of Rommel but was no relation of the Field-Marshal. Rommel and his men took possession of the hillock and dug in during the night.

Soon after midnight we heard the sound of mortars ahead of us. A patrol crawled forward and reported that the Americans were receiving munitions and supplies. They were so close ahead that my patrol could distinguish the glow of their cigarettes.

We, too, received rations and, more important still, ammunition. The enemy artillery graciously left us alone. But in the morning a reconnaissance plane flew overhead, and soon we were subjected to continuous artillery fire, though because we were lying behind the crest most of the shells whistled harmlessly overhead.

Night fell again. Between one and two in the morning we heard another American supply-column coming up. Leutnant Becker with six mortars and four heavy machine-guns blazed away for exactly one minute. I regretted this hostility, for at once the Americans, as if resentful at the breaking of some tacit agreement, began a sporadic fire that went on all night. While previously we had been able to stretch our legs by strolling outside our foxholes, now irregular salvoes of up to a dozen shells made this a dangerous recreation.

When daybreak came we were at long last reinforced by seven Panzers, which took up positions immediately behind us in the wadi. When Patton's tanks and infantry advanced later we felt decidedly more confident.

A number of American infantry disappeared into a wadi on the slope south of the road. Some of them emerged unexpectedly behind our backs in our own wadi. Their attack was repulsed with the help of our Panzers. We took some prisoners. The fighting was bitter, but by now we scarcely distinguished one hour of tension and action from another.

In the evening came a signal from Field-Marshal Kesselring: 'I thank you for your brave defence. Hold positions at all costs.'

Moll and I held a conference, and decided to send a reply direct to the Field-Marshal. We drafted it and we sent it. It read: 'We will hold positions. Where is the alcohol?'

That was a brash message from two junior officers, but to our surprise it worked and brought no reprimand. During the evening a truck came forward with 'Jerrycans' of Muscatel wine. For the first time since I had come to Africa, barring perhaps my flight out of Asmara, I drank a good deal of wine. It was surprising how well it seemed to agree with all of us. It made our task seem distinctly lighter. Where *were* those Americans?

3

For two nights we had been unable to establish contact with Rommel's observation post on the sugar-loaf. Now our forward patrols came under strong fire from that very point. . . . Two men came back at dawn and reported that they were the sole survivors of young Rommel's party. American infantry lying at the foot of the hill had cleaned them up with mortars. Rommel, they said, had fallen.

A year later I met him during a short visit to Germany. He had not been killed, but, badly wounded, had crawled throughout a terrible day and a night to the cover of a wadi on the southern slope, where he was later discovered by German parachute troops, who moved him to a field-hospital. When he told me his story he was freshly discharged from the hospital where he had convalesced.

The following day—it must, I think, have been April 6—brought the heaviest American infantry attack upon us. The enemy reached our positions, but were thrown back before they could break in.

The next day, or even the next attack, would, I reckoned, be the end. The Panzers had been withdrawn. We were again alone. But once more the order to withdraw saved us. We got out at daybreak. Guns and vehicles away, Becker and I were the last to leave. As the early daylight brightened, we looked back to see the first American patrols reach the fox-holes where we had fought so long and, it seemed, so pointlessly.

CHAPTER FORTY-FOUR

LAST BATTLE

PLEASE do not think that I am trying to convey that my battation alone was now fighting in Africa. In actual fact, the most complicated mass conflict had been initiated.

In the north the enemy's First Army had reorganized after Rommel's unpleasant surprise at Kasserine, and had now returned to the offensive in an involved set of operations against von Arnim. On March 27, by Alexander's direction, American infantry had entered Fondouk and threatened to press through the Eastern Dorsale range towards Kairouan, thus threatening the rear of General Messe's German-Italian line on the Wadi Akarit.

And Montgomery prepared to attack the Wadi Akarit frontally with the three divisions[1] of the 30th Corps. He broke through the Wadi Akarit on April 6, in a single day's battle which he thought as bloody and savage as any he had been through since El Alamein. Attack and counter-attack clashed in the hills, and Alexander afterwards said that both Germans and Italians 'showed a quite reckless determination and unimpaired morale.' But there was no standing up to three hardened British and Indian divisions, plus 450 guns.

The 15th Panzer and 90th Light Divisions fought perhaps the best battle of their distinguished careers (again I quote Alexander), but the writing was on the wall. Our retreating army lost a further 6000 men as prisoners. And the following afternoon, on the day we left the El Guettar line, the Americans from Algiers and the Englishmen from Cairo linked hands for the first time. That was why our 'hard but irrelevant' battle at El Guettar was broken off.

Under orders, I retreated across country with my battalion from the scene of the last fight, skirting Maknassy and Sidi Bou Zid on the Tunisian plain, giving a wide berth to Fondouk, until I reached the holy city of Kairouan on April 10. We halted for a few minutes.

[1] The 50th Tyne and Tees, 51st Highland, and 4th Indian Divisions.

I spent them in the dim religious peace of the theological high school there. Those few minutes were a benison on my taut nerves. All the way from El Guettar we had been harried and hammered and bombed and machine-gunned by Allied aircraft. Apart from this airborne horror, we had been fighting for months. Would it never end? Would there never be peace and a time for reflection again?

But time pressed. We pulled out of Kairouan, and as I skirted the city walls at the tail of our column, I saw the first British armoured cars rolling in. The holy city had exchanged guests within minutes. Would they, too, pause for a moment's spiritual refreshment?

General Messe had no hope of making a stand south of the mountain line at Enfidaville. With understandable solicitude he whistled his Italians back to his next possible line of defence between Zaghouan and the sea, leaving the Germans to fight the rearguard actions as usual.

At Zaghouan the mountain peaks jutted up abruptly from the wide southern Tunisian plain. Giant crags and deep gullies in rocky wadis offered excellent protection against artillery and bombing. Here the pursuing tank masses could not swiftly over-run us. Here, I thought, we may be able to hold out until re-inforcements are sent from Europe.

My comrades differed sharply about the future. Some thought we should be whirled back to Cape Bon and shipped over to Sicily for a renewed battle. Others believed that Hitler would not give up North Africa, that 'Tiger' Panzers in great numbers and new types of Luftwaffe aircraft would be hurled into action to equalize the numerical and material superiority of the Allies. The supply problem would be solved with *Siebelfahren* ferries (which could carry two tanks and were armed with 88-mm. flak guns), fighters, and towed gliders called *Giganten*. Spain would play a big rôle. . . .

2

Quiet days followed. We built up defences and sited weapons behind rocky shelters. By night enemy artillery fired at just one prominent feature, a height to the east near the coast. I did not envy those who held the mountain, and thought: 'This time we have been lucky.' But that very afternoon we were ordered to move to the shelled heights and make a counter-attack from there.

Well, we went into the attack that night, in pouring rain. Enemy sharp-shooters lay ahead of us, firing with deadly accuracy. Shells and mortar-bombs rained down on us.

We were a sorry lot. The hardships and nerve-strain of the past months had sapped our vitality. Indifference and exhaustion gripped my men. They could not fight an overwhelming desire for sleep when they dropped for shelter into the churned-up mud of shell-holes. Death began to loom up as a brother, and it seemed absurd that one should fear him. He would be kind. . . .

I was suddenly awakened. My arm was being shaken energetically. A mud-splattered soldier dropped down beside me in my shell-hole. He was panting breathlessly after hours of scrambling about the vague battlefield and leaping from one scrap of cover to another.

'I have been looking for you for hours, Herr Oberleutnant,' he gasped. He handed me a muddy note.

'Probably,' I thought, 'another stupid order to press home the attack.'

In the glow of the blacked-out torch of the runner lying next me I read it: 'Oberleutnant Schmidt, Special Group 288. Oberleutnant Schmidt is to report immediately to Army Headquarters.'

Underneath this, Regimental H.Q. had scribbled in pencil: 'Hand over battalion at once to Oberleutnant Ebenbichler.'

What did this mean? Trouble? It was not for a soldier to question orders. I handed over command within the hour and, by early dawn, exhausted and caked with mud, had trudged dangerously back from the line to my car.

CHAPTER FORTY-FIVE

A CHUCKLE AMONG THE CHESTNUTS

I REACHED Army Headquarters at midday. I missed the old busy activity. It seemed that there was now only a remnant of Rommel's staff left, though the H.Q. flaunted the proud title of 'Army Command of the German-Italian Panzer Army.' A few almost empty German command-vehicles gave the impression that they housed merely a small liaison staff attending the Italian commander, General Messe.

I reported, wondering what bad news awaited me.

A captain of the II a Section reflected, sorted out his papers, and said:

'Over a year ago you applied for permission to get married. Here it is. You are granted fourteen days' immediate special leave. On your return, please report to Army Command for further instructions.'

Within hours I had reached Tunis and was driving in a jeep to the aerodrome. It was Easter Day—April 25.

My driver stopped for a moment and, with the shrewdness of the old soldier, scrounged a bottle of liqueur from somewhere—a banana liqueur. We drank it together.

'Would you like to go to Germany on leave too?' I asked him.

'Would I not, Herr Oberleutnant!' he smiled.

In my pocket I had a sheaf of standard forms authorizing home leave for men of my battalion. My quota had not been exhausted. I could easily give the driver authority to come with me.

Indeed, I fixed it with a Luftwaffe pilot that he should have a place in a plane. But my driver said: 'First, Herr Oberleutnant, I must pay a visit to the hospital. . . .' He went off on his brief personal errand, saying, 'I shall be back soon. . . .' He did not come back. I never saw him again.

Through the dark night I huddled in an overcrowded transport plane. It droned across the Mediterranean and landed at dawn at Catania, in Sicily. On I was whirled to Italy, and on to Germany.

2

Herta and I were married on May 5. Two days later Tunis fell to the British and Bizerta to the Americans. Organized resistance crumbled. The end came swiftly in the wild peninsula of Cape Bon.

We were honeymooning at Baden-Baden among the blossoming chestnut-trees of the Black Forest on May 13. The wireless was discoursing a gentle symphony. The music ended with a blunt news bulletin: 'After an heroic fight the German-Italian Panzer Army in Tunisia has suspended the struggle against terrific odds. With this, the battle in Africa has ended.'

A quarter of a million men laid down their arms. Six hundred and sixty-three escaped.

There was no Special Group 288 for me to rejoin, no Army H.Q. at which I should be expected to report. I had got out of Africa with the same unplanned good fortune that had taken me out of Asmara in the last plane and landed me on the staff of Rommel.

The ponderous army machine had rumbled along in its routine fashion. The domestic affairs of an obscure junior battalion commander had been duly considered and disposed of. As a famous part of the great machine was grinding itself into wreckage in Africa, a message had come through, amid a welter of Top Secret and Operations Priority signals, to say that the little officer who wanted to get married now had permission to do so. The message reached him in the hand of a dispatch-runner who risked his life with it; and it jerked the young officer out of his last battle in Africa, from among hundreds of thousands.

Somewhere among the quiet chestnut-trees of the Black Forest a bride and her bridegroom heard Mars chuckle. Once more he had made ironic sport of men.